THE POLITICS
OF REGRET

The Politics of Regret is a work that every scholar interested in the intersection of memory and politics will need to own. In a series of linked essays, Olick makes a compelling case that society is simultaneously constituted by organization and narrative. Focusing on the case of postwar Germany, Olick demonstrates how regret and the attempt to escape and erase that regret allow for the existence and legitimacy of the modern nation state. Olick understands, following Nietzsche, that sometimes we confront too much history, yet the insights of this volume suggest that we never can have too much wisdom. This is the work of a first-rate mind and a groundbreaking sociologist.

—Gary Alan Fine, John Evans Professor of
Sociology, Northwestern University

This is an extremely interesting and sophisticated set of essays from one of the leading theorists and analysts of memory. The essays provide a clear and persuasive case for the author's approach to studying "social memory," and the essays are written with verve and elegance. Essential for anyone interested in problems of memory and society.

—John Torpey, Professor of Sociology,
CUNY Graduate Center

JEFFREY K. OLICK

THE POLITICS OF REGRET

On Collective Memory and Historical Responsibility

Routledge
Taylor & Francis Group
New York   London

Routledge
Taylor & Francis Group
270 Madison Avenue
New York, NY 10016

Routledge
Taylor & Francis Group
2 Park Square
Milton Park, Abingdon
Oxon OX14 4RN

© 2007 by Taylor & Francis Group, LLC
Routledge is an imprint of Taylor & Francis Group, an Informa business

Printed in the United States of America on acid-free paper
10 9 8 7 6 5 4 3 2 1

International Standard Book Number-13: 978-0-415-95683-3 (Softcover) 978-0-415-95682-6 (Hardcover)

Library of Congress Cataloging-in-Publication Data

Olick, Jeffrey K., 1964-
The politics of regret : collective memory in the age of atrocity / Jeffrey K. Olick.
p. cm.
Includes bibliographical references and index.
ISBN 978-0-415-95682-6 (hardback) -- ISBN 978-0-415-95683-3 (pbk.)
1. Collective memory. 2. Regret. 3. Political atrocities. I. Title.

HM1033.O29 2008
303.601--dc22   2006038498

Visit the Taylor & Francis Web site at
http://www.taylorandfrancis.com

and the Routledge Web site at
http://www.routledge.com

Contents

Preface

Beyond quelling the clamor of adoring hordes, the only justification for a collection of essays such as this is that the whole adds up to more than the sum of its parts and as such provides substantive value to the reader. As I thought about the collection and subsequently reworked the essays that compose it, I was not only reminded of my own intellectual trajectory (a subject of admittedly narrow interest); more so, it struck me—even more than when I first wrote these papers—how much I have over the last ten years been teasing connected themes and developing a consistent line of argument, whether in reflections on postwar Germany, on sociological methodology, or on the rise of what I here call the *politics of regret*. Many of the essays in the pages that follow thus begin in similar places — with the rise and spread of the term *collective memory* in scholarly and public discourses, for example. And several formulations, perspectives, and programs appear repeatedly throughout — the dangers of reifying collective memory, for instance, or the connections between a particular form of temporality in modernity and the rise of retrospective politics, for another. Though I have eliminated some of the redundancy inevitable to papers addressing connected themes in different contexts, I have left some such passages as they originally appeared. Indeed, as I composed the introduction and reworked the papers, I was comforted to see the apparent repetitions because, it seemed to me, therein lies the value added, beyond the convenience of satisfying the aforementioned hordes with an easily transportable compendium of my dispersed papers: the consistencies in concern, method, and approach despite the varied occasions for the individual papers. The themes I address in the following pages may indeed lead to — which is a gentle way of saying may require — a more monographic statement at some point in the future. But my hope is that the solutions these papers offer from a variety of angles but repeatedly with the same accents are nevertheless clear enough to guide future research and suggest the outlines of the larger theory these papers have started to limn.

Written over the course of ten years and in a wide variety of contexts, these papers have benefited from the advice and reading of many friends and colleagues. Because of the papers' independent provenances, I have left the title acknowledgments as they originally appeared at the beginning of each. The personal and intellectual debts I accrued in working on each remain much in my thoughts. Beyond being grateful to the many people over the last ten years who have helped me in one way or another, a number of friends and colleagues have in various ways contributed in particular to this book as a whole, either by reading and commenting on the introduction or otherwise discussing it with me or in various other capacities harder to specify as I was working on it. To begin, I heartily thank Joan Snapp and Eric Taubel for their generous and valiant help creating the manuscript in the first place. I thank David McBride for his sponsorship of the project before his departure from Routledge, as well as for substantive advice on the introduction and overall format. I am grateful to Stephen Rutter, Anne Horowitz, and Sylvia Wood at Routledge for stepping in and taking good care of the manuscript through the production process. I thank Daniel Levy, Brenda Coughlin, and Chares Demetriou, co-authors on earlier versions of three of the papers, for permission to revise and include here their work. And I thank the following people, many of whom I am grateful by this point to think of as "the usual suspects" for their advice of various kinds about this book, whole or parts: Duncan Bell, Alon Confino, Sarah Corse, Chares Demetriou, Gary Fine, Krishan Kumar, Daniel Levy, Doug Mitchell, Tanya Omeltchenko, Barry Schwartz, John Torpey, Vered Vinitsky-Seroussi, and Robin Wagner-Pacifici. I am lucky enough that this list, limited to those who had some direct connection to the project of making this book, does not begin to exhaust the number of people who have helped, advised, or accompanied me in various ways over the last few years.

Last but not least, indeed most, as always, this book is for Bettina, Hannah, and Benjamin.

PART I

CHAPTER 1

Introduction

From Collective Memory to the Politics of Regret

The Society of Narratives

In the mid to late 1980s, when I began graduate school, *organizations* was the watchword for many sociologists in training, particularly at Yale, which was a real center for organization theory. This made a lot of sense. Corporations seemed to be dominating more and more aspects of life, and multinational and nongovernmental organizations were becoming ever more important political forces in the "globalizing" world. Max Weber was clearly the theorist of record, and students were mobilized by Chick Perrow's (1991) mantra that we now lived in a "society of organizations."

By the same token, literary theory and philosophy in the prior decades had also been taking a number of dramatic turns — mainly to language and culture. This too made much sense, given the increasing power and complexity of mass media in contemporary life alongside the persistence of sacred rituals — both political and religious — in the midst of the seemingly secularized economy and polity.

For me, the two trends came together in a seminar on symbolic politics taught by David Apter, in which many students were writing papers on activist social movements of various kinds. What struck me as most interesting in that context was that all the movements we were discussing — as well as the more official kinds of political "representation" — were concerned, even seemed obsessed, with stories. Whether the movements were small, local, and haphazard or large, national, and professionalized, movement participants, leaders, and the organizations themselves were investing tremendous time and resources in telling stories about their origins, trajectories, and purposes. These stories usually sought to answer the following sorts of questions: How did the movements come about? What historical events were central reference points? What lessons were learned through these turning points? And what would the future look like? Given the resources they were investing in such stories, even in difficult circumstances or at the cost of other projects, agents of organizations clearly thought such narrative work was exceptionally important.

As much as we live in a society of organizations, then, it seemed to me that it is as true, or even more so, that we live in a society of narratives.[1]

The German Case

In my own intellectual narrative, the key turning point through which I emerged from this primordial theoretical soup came when I read a review of a book by the historian Charles Maier (1988) on the so-called German historians' dispute of 1985–86. Following the return of the Christian Democratic Party to power in West Germany in 1982, a number of neoconservative commentators had become more public with their belief that the centrality of National Socialism in German historical narrative had exceeded its natural life. It was time, they argued, that this particular past pass away (Nolte 1987). If Germany was to be a healthy nation, one prominent historian argued, its natural sympathies would turn not to the victims of the "final solution," but to the suffering of the German army on the Eastern front (Hillgruber 1986), and German history, Chancellor Helmut Kohl repeatedly intoned, included many highs as well as lows and could not be reduced to those few terrible years of Nazi rule. In contrast, the critical theorist Jürgen Habermas (1987) charged the critics — and the conservative Kohl government, which was also pursuing a number of controversial museum projects at the time — with a sort of conspiracy to rework the foundations of West German political culture. For Habermas, the centrality of Nazi crimes in German historical and political narrative was not only not a barrier to a healthy German national identity, but was its *sine qua non*. The attempted changes in the national narrative therefore had to be pushed back.

Though this historians' dispute — and Maier's (1988) trenchant intellectual history of it — interested me substantively in many regards, what was most important in this first exposure was that this case seemed to provide an especially perspicuous window on what I was trying to understand about narrative and identity. Though writers ranging from David Carr (1991) and Alisdair MacIntyre (1984) to Robert Bellah (1985) and

Immanuel Wallerstein (Wallerstein and Balibar 1992) or even the psychologist Robert Coles (1990) were providing me with general statements about the importance of stories to life, here, it seemed, was a place and a way to study the process as a sociologist — not just to make theoretical pronouncements, merely gather examples, or make functionalist assertions but to specify the changing roles of stories in political legitimation and identities. How so?

If narrative is constitutive of identity, an instrument of politics (i.e., rhetoric) and an expression of culture (i.e., representation), what happens when an organization — small or large, family, social movement, or nation-state — cannot tell such stories in an unproblematic fashion? Germany, it seemed to me, was a great case for building sociological theory because the past posed unique problems there. If states and their spokespersons usually tell heroic stories about their collective pasts to underwrite identity and legitimate contemporary programs, what happens when a state does not have recourse to an unproblematic past? All nations, of course, have aspects of their pasts they would prefer not to acknowledge. But the problem seemed much more significant in Germany; given the extent of public discourse about the relationship between the Nazi past and the German present — not least in the historians' dispute but in virtually every other context of German commentary — this conclusion seemed fairly obvious.

What I found as I began my empirical work on Germany, however, produced a much more complex picture than any of my theoretical apparatus — again, comprised mostly of general assertions about the importance of narrative for identity — had led me to expect or had enabled me to handle. Speakers said an enormous variety of things in different times and places; that variety changed in remarkable ways over time, and rarely was it what a naive observer might have expected such speakers to say, given the verdicts of popular historical consciousness about German guilt. It was at this point that, on the advice of Juan Linz, I first read Maurice Halbwachs (1966, 1992) on collective memory.

Halbwachs' Legacies

Halbwachs is widely considered the founding father of contemporary collective memory research — and rightly so, even if he often serves as a more totemic than substantive referent in contemporary discussions. Reading Halbwachs provided me not just with a label for what I was interested in — *collective memory* — but with the conviction that what I was noticing about organizational and national storytelling was indeed a topic for sociology proper, not merely the application of a social metaphor for a fundamentally psychological or individual phenomenon nor something epiphenomenal to real sociological processes. For though Halbwachs did argue that memory is carried largely by individuals, he showed that even the most primally individual memories are socially framed and that, thus, at the limit, the very distinction between individual and social memory is problematic and that memory is no mere byproduct of group existence but is its very lifeblood.

Though the "social frameworks" of memory took up the lion's share of Halbwachs's attention, Halbwachs was also unmistakably his teacher's student: The very term *mémoire collective* was stamped with the memory of Emile Durkheim's master concept of *conscience collective*. As such, Halbwachs's work on collective memory also drew our attention not only to the social frameworks of individual memory or even to social memory (i.e., the memory of groups) per se but also to collective memories as *representations collective*, publicly available symbols and meanings about the past — what Jan Assmann (1992) many decades later called cultural, in addition to social and individual, memory. Memory, the Durkheimian Halbwachs implied, is not just individual, nor is it just a binding activity for groups; it is their cultural inheritance, whether actively or passively maintained.

In this way, my reading of Halbwachs also seemed to fit well with what I was finding in the growing and changing literature on political culture, the other obvious place for someone interested in political symbolism, representation, and meaning to turn. In its classical period in the 1950s and 1960s, political scientists largely understood political culture as the aggregate of subjective orientations toward political outcomes.[2] In other words, different political institutions rested on different attitudes in the population, attitudes about those specific institutions and about wider issues of authority and obligation. The principle agenda of the most important work in this tradition — Almond and Verba's (1963) *The Civic Culture* — was to understand what set of orientations supported democratic regimes and what set was more likely associated with authoritarian ones. Political psychology was thus the culture — as a Petri dish to bacteria (i.e., cell culture) — in which political institutions grow.

Nevertheless, in the decade or two before I began thinking about collective memory, political culture theory had undergone something of a revolution. Under the influence of French structuralism and Geertzian anthropology, theorists now questioned whether culture was properly conceptualized as norms, values, and attitudes — in other words, as subjective meanings — rather than as intersubjective or objective symbols. If political culture could be reduced to political psychology, critics asked, what was the point of having a concept of political culture at all (Dittmer 1977; Elkins and Simeon 1979)? As with culture more generally, analysts were now reconceptualizing political culture as meaning systems in which significant symbols were to be understood not as subjective orientations but as parts of objective systems that give meaning to political outcomes without primary reference to whether they appear in any particular proportion of individuals' minds. The tools of this new political culture analysis thus turned away from survey research and toward structuralist, hermeneutic, and semiotic approaches, in which political culture theory no longer involved measuring the distribution of norms and attitudes but interrogating symbols and the ways their meanings are related to each other (Hunt 1989; Ortner 1999).

This turn in political culture theory fit well, I found, with the more Durkheimian moments in Halbwachs, in which collective memory — the property of groups and a sometimes embodied, sometimes disembodied, cultural inheritance — had an ontological status sui generis. Collective memory, I argue below, is not identical to the memories of a certain percentage of the population but constitutes a social fact in and of itself — though, as I also argue below, we need to be very careful about the transcendentalism implied by this formulation. These theories also helped me think about political memory in Germany, focusing my attention not on what speakers there meant to say with their symbols and words but on what symbols and words were available to them in which times and places and hence with how those cultural frameworks are prior to, and thus shape, their intentions. In other words, contrary to any instrumentalist take on political language, in which words and symbols are tools politicians use to get things done — albeit often things not so obvious from the words themselves[3] — I approached German political discourse as a structure of possibilities that shaped, as much as were shaped by, the intentions of its participants. Combining insights from the linguistic philosopher J. L. Austin and from Karl Marx, I was motivated by the analytical principle that people do things with words, but not in circumstances of their own choosing (I first presented this formula in the paper that appears below as chapter 3).

The Dynamics of Collective Remembering

This effort to understand the complex dynamics of political speech about the past in postwar Germany, I should note, also fit very well into an emerging sociological research program, shaped most significantly in the United States by Barry Schwartz. In his seminal work on the sociology of collective memory, which he began publishing in the 1980s, Schwartz showed that sociological studies of collective memory were caught between two equally unsatisfying theoretical options (Schwartz 1982, 1991, 1996; Schwartz, Zerubavel, and Barnett 1986). On the one hand, essentialism assumed that memory and images of the past are to be understood as expressions of historical reality-become-social structure. Here, a potent model is Karl Mannheim's (1952) theory of generations, in which a shared set of significant experiences by members of a birth cohort shape their generational identity and future memory, thus coloring their future experiences and perceptions distinctly from members of other cohorts who did not experience the same events at the same formative moment in their biographies. On the other hand, presentism assumes that memory and images of the past are produced in the present for present purposes and hence are indices not of anything that happened in the past and its effect on the present but of the structure of interests and needs of the present. This view is often attributed to Halbwachs, who distinguished collective memory from history in terms of its relevance to the present; another key figure here is Eric Hobsbawm (1983a), whose concept of invented traditions encourages a debunking posture on the part of historians and social scientists, whose job it apparently is to unmask false traditions and decode instrumental motives. As the work of Schwartz and others makes abundantly clear, however, neither of these theoretical positions (granted, drawn here and in the literature as strawmen) provides an adequate depiction of the statics and dynamics of memory, either individual or collective. The challenge, then, has been to come up with theoretical models as well as explanatory strategies and modes of analytical presentation that transcend this sterile dichotomy.

A crucial first stage in this effort, I believed, was to understand the ways in which, and reasons for which, images of the past change or remain the same rather than to define memory a priori as inherently durable or malleable. In my own effort to sum up the work that had been done on collective memory across numerous fields by the mid 1990s — a literature review of what I had come to think of as *social memory studies* — I identified three distinct kinds of both statics and dynamics of memory: instrumental, cultural, and inertial (Olick and Robbins 1998). Often, social actors engage in concerted action to either maintain or transform images of the past — the former represents orthodoxy and the latter progressivism. This instrumentalism, however, though capturing so much of the sociological attention, is not the only process at work. Images of the past change or remain the same also to the degree that they fit into a changing or stable culture, a process that calls our attention away from cynical manipulations to an analysis of culture sui generis.[4] Images of the past also often change or remain the same (these are always degrees, not polar opposites) to the extent that their media and institutions continue to support them. I called these dynamics inertial because they refer to processes relatively beyond culture and action, for example, the burning of a library or the "sands of time." This typology serves, I believe, both as a useful summary of various strands in the scholarly literature and as a guide to sociological theory and analysis, which calls for us to specify the processes and practices that characterize what we designate with the label *collective memory.*

Collective Memory and Historical Sociology

Though Halbwachs stands rightly at the beginning of any discussion of the sociology of collective memory, however, as an historical and theoretical sociologist more generally I have found most of my inspiration and models elsewhere, particularly in the writings of Norbert Elias, Mikhail Bakhtin, and Pierre Bourdieu. There are, obviously, many important differences among these three. But the similarities are intriguing. All three, for instance, have focused significant attention on the writings of Immanuel Kant and have expended great effort to articulate their rejection of him — Elias (1924) in his doctoral dissertation, in which he attacks Kant's first critique (the epistemology), Bakhtin (1986) in his book on the philosophy of the act (likely first drafted in the 1920s) on Kant's second critique (the moral philosophy), and Bourdieu (1984) in his contemporary — though in part influenced by Elias and Bakhtin — postscript to *Distinction* on Kant's third critique (the aesthetics).[5] But though each has his own distinctive accent, what they share seems even more important, namely an effort to overcome dichotomous thinking — what they all saw in their own ways as the legacy of Kant — in which form stands outside of history (Bakhtin), structure stands above action (Bourdieu), and society stands against the individual (Elias). As Elias (1991, p. 15) put it, and the others would presumably agree, transcendentalism — of which all three of these dichotomies are varieties — was "the worm in the apple of modernity."

The central lesson I take from this theoretical troika — though they are by no means the only inspirations available — is an approach to historical sociology that seeks to be genuinely historical, that is, one that avoids wherever possible transcendentalism. As Philip Abrams (1982) argued in his Elias-inspired manifesto, not all sociology that focuses on the past is historical, at least not in any more than a truistic sense. Rather, for sociology to be genuinely historical — that is, nontranscendental — it must appreciate that social life takes place in time without relegating that temporality to a residual category, like longitudinal analysis or comparative time points. Historical sociology — and, by implication, the rest of sociology, too — must avoid what Elias called *process-reduction:* the treatment of ongoing processes as if they were things. Indeed, for Elias, this meant going so far as to replace the label *sociology* with *historical social psychology,* by which he sought to avoid the dichotomy between individual and society and the transcendentalism he believed the resultant concept of society implied.

These insights apply especially well to the study of collective memory, for what more egregious process-reduction do we have in our colloquial and scholarly languages than memory; what more transcendental idea do we have than a disembodied collective memory that stands disconnected from the neurologically and experientially grounded memories of individuals? One of Elias's favorite demonstrations of process-reduction in everyday discourse is the example of wind, which we take as a noun, which in turn engages in a specific activity: blowing. But what on Earth could wind mean except blowing (Elias 1978, pp. 111-12)? The same could be said of memory. So much of our colloquial and scholarly discourse indeed treats memory as a thing: the memory. But what is memory except the variety of practices that comprise remembering? The problem is even worse in Durkheim-inspired collectivistic approaches, which go even further and treat not just collective memory as a thing, but THE collective memory of a society as ONE thing. As I discuss in chapter five, this is but one of what I call, following Charles Tilly (1984), several "pernicious postulates" of the field.

The challenge for the field of collective memory scholarship as I see it, then, is to find a way to talk about the process of social remembering in time and the varieties of retrospective practices in such a way that does not oppose individual and collective memory to each other. And here is where both Bourdieu and Bakhtin are so helpful. From Bourdieu, as I make clear in several of the following chapters, I have taken a fluid and flexible concept of *practices,* adapted here as *mnemonic practices.* In the first place, practices are always multiple. And clearly, *collective memory* — or *remembering* — conflates a variety of distinct practices (e.g., recollection, recall, commemoration, modeling), each shaped by distinct constellations of forces, intentions, fantasies, and resources. In the second place, *mnemonic practices* avoids reifying THE memory as an entity. As chapter two demonstrates, this fits well with the contemporary understanding of memory in even the most physiological psychology, which has shown that memory is not an agency of storage but an active process of construction and reconstruction in time (as chapter three mentions, the philosopher Henri Bergson can also be associated with this more active account of remembering).

As far afield as Elias and Bourdieu are from the contemporary sociology of collective memory, Bakhtin seems an even odder source. And yet his conceptual and methodological legacies have been perhaps the most tangible for me of the three, while also the most general. Beyond precluding a reflexive solipsism — which I have always been surprised to find so common in sociology — Bakhtin's emphasis on dialogue, on the fact that no utterance (or, by extension, mnemonic practice) can be understood outside of an ongoing discourse, provides a useful methodological guide for untangling the complexities of any mnemonic gesture in its temporal and relational surround. More than that, however, Bakhtin's emphasis on historicity great and small provides a model and language for a historical sociology — and historical sociology of retrospection as part of that — that is genuinely historical. For central to Bakhtin's understanding of dialogue — indeed, his dialogical approach to language and action — is the recognition that dialogue is always simultaneously deeply conditioned by its past as well as "unfinalizable" in the present.[6] This principle, it seems to me as both a sociologist of retrospection and as a historical sociologist more generally, provides exactly the resources for avoiding both process-reduction as well as transcendentialism in sociological analysis, emphasizing both the relational and processual constitution (and constituting) of all culture. By the same token — and this is at the heart of its radical implication for social sciences — it calls into question any easy specification of cause and effect, dependent and independent variable, durability and malleability of the past, essentialism or presentism. Difficult as these are to live without, this seems to me the way out of the analytical exhaustion in the field. And memory seems to be a crucial site for thinking this through, as memory is neither a thing nor merely a tool but mediation itself (chapter five elaborates on this at length).

The Sociology of Retrospection

Elias, Bourdieu, and Bakhtin, as well as Durkheim, Halbwachs, Mannheim, and Schwartz, are figures running throughout the four papers comprising part one of this collection, in which I present various versions of my approach to collective remembering and efforts to untangle different dimensions of it as a process (or, more appropriately, variety of processes). I begin with "Collective Memory: The Two Cultures," because it assays the definitional resources available for grounding one's analysis philosophically, interrogating the concept of collective memory and its relation to more individualistic conceptualizations. In this chapter, it may seem as if I argue rather hard against a purely individualistic approach. My real point, however, is to present the conditions for a negotiated peace between individualists and collectivists and to argue for an inclusive approach: Collective memory may be a social fact sui generis, but brains and minds and individuals need very much to be a part of the story. They are just not the whole story. By the same token, we need as always to be wary of the transcendentalist temptations that inhere in collectivism taken too literally.

Chapters three and four take a rather different form: detailed empirical analyses of the German case. Nevertheless, though the German case is indeed intriguing in its own right — and provides an essential background for the essays in part two — my main point in the chapters comprising the book's first section is to develop transposable insights into the operation of collective remembering in its complex contexts. In "Collective Memory and Cultural Constraint," originally written with Daniel Levy, I begin the search for specific cultural frameworks shaping the statics and dynamics of images of the past. In particular, we found that consistency and transformation in images of the Nazi past in Germany depended on the moral status of those images — that is, whether their import was seen as mythic or rational. Mnemonic practices — in this case official representations by the government — the paper argued were figured by the deep matrix of the politically sacred and profane, operating alternatively as duties or taboos, prohibitions, or requirements. Collective remembering, by implication, is tied into the deepest dimensions of moral order, though as always this is to be understood as an order in time rather than as a transcendental structure.

In "Genre Memories and Memory Genres," I continued the search for mechanisms of mnemonic dynamics and found something I consider remarkable: what I call the *memory of memory*.[7] Where extant models emphasize either the relationship between commemoration and the original event or between the commemoration and contemporary needs, examining the trajectory of a single commemorative occasion over time makes clear the fundamentally temporal nature of commemoration. Commemoration is not just a relationship between past and present, nor are repeated commemorations just one such relation after another. Instead, commemoration — and by extension all mnemonic practices — are continuing processes of utterance and response, just as Bakhtin's theory described. Even more interesting, later commemorations do not need to make explicit reference to earlier ones to manifest this relationship, nor do subsequent commemorators need even to be aware of the earlier ones. This is, as I make clear, the sociological magic of genre as a central motor of cultural history.

Following these two more fine-grained empirical analyses, I turn again more explicitly to programmatic ambitions, in this case to provide a general methodological statement for the field as a whole: a rather grandiose aim, to be sure. But even more than it might at first appear, for the framework I advance in chapter five — "Figurations of Memory" — I argue, applies to empirical historical sociology in general as well. This chapter is an effort to concretize the methodological implications of the Bakhtinian–Eliasian–Bourdieuean perspective for political culture analysis. In short, the argument is that we need to develop a genuinely processual and relational vocabulary for analysis; I offer specific methodological and conceptual proposals for how to do this, developing not only the genre concept articulated in the prior paper but also a Bourdieuan concept of mnemonic fields, as well as a typology of media and a description of political cultural profiles as irreducible wholes. My hope is that this chapter provides a useful model for future work in diverse contexts.

The Politics of Regret

There is obviously much work left to do on the statics and dynamics of collective memory and on German political culture and to elaborate the Bakhtin–Elias–Bourdieu paradigm for historical sociology. But my interest in both Germany and in Bakhtin in particular have led me beyond the German case to issues that leave the sociology of retrospection defined narrowly to what I and others have called the *history of memory* more broadly. For Bakhtin's concept of dialogue not only points out the mundane, interactive, and referential qualities of all utterances; it also calls attention to what he called *great time:* the centuries-long history of basic concepts as they develop and are articulated in continuous use, rather than as formal types or definitions.[8] Such concerns arise clearly out of the German crucible as well, for it is obvious to ask both how the postwar accounting with National Socialism fit within longer-term trajectories of collective remembering as well as how it has contributed to them.

In my opinion, for instance, we all too easily overestimate the epochal significance of the "Nuremberg principles" as well as the unusualness of the West German culture of memory. To be sure, Nuremberg represented a new stage in political accountability and has served as a powerful referent for subsequent moments of transitional justice.[9] And a kind of political guilt or public culture of collective remorse has also taken unique and historically important forms in the Federal Republic of Germany. But the post-Nazi sensibilities are no more developments outside of history than was National Socialism itself. Interestingly, celebratory histories of Nuremberg and the subsequent Universal Declaration of Human Rights oscillate unproblematically between unsociological assertions about the universality of human rights (echoes of transcendentalism abound) and historical claims about the contingencies and departures of 1945–48. Nevertheless, as a sociologist I take as axiomatic that the conditions for thinking universalistically are not themselves universal and hence that we must specify exactly what those conditions are. Additionally, as an historian of postwar Germany I see the many ways in which the West German discourse draws on longer-standing resources, develops over time, as well as is not nearly as complete or successful as glib references to "the German model" of transitional justice assert. Here, the recent efforts of the Bush administration to use Germany as a model for U.S. policy in Iraq stand out in particular, in which it was first argued that since we were so successful in Germany we could expect equal success in Iraq and then, three years later, that we had to remember that the occupation of Germany was no easy success either.

For me, then, the obvious questions emerging from my close reading of the German discourses of memory as well as from my efforts to understand the statics and dynamics of historical imagery in narrow contexts have been those of the longer-term trajectories of memory. As already mentioned, one line of inquiry emerging within the Halbwachsian universe as well as elsewhere has been the effort to delineate the longer-term history of memory itself.[10] For what we mean by *memory* and the forms it takes have clearly changed over time. Part of this story is obviously technological, including the rise of writing in antiquity, through church-based record keeping, the rise of mass literacy, and now the age of computing, with its implied nearly infinite storage capacity. If, as I argue in chapter two, there are technologies of remembering other than the brain, the broader story of media is certainly part of the history of memory, itself the medium in which we work out and elaborate our historicity.

Beyond the history of technologies of memory, however, there are questions about the moral and political implications of the transformations in our modes of apprehending and processing our temporality. And it is such questions as these that I take up in the four chapters composing part two of this collection. There I address the rise of what I see as a new framework for confronting past misdeeds: what I call the *politics of regret*. It is not that regret is an entirely new emotion, though I do argue that the dominance of a particular form of temporality underlies regret's prevalence in contemporary discourses. What is new is both its ubiquity and elevation to a general principle. It may be, I explore, that regret is the emblem of our times. The question that motivates me here, however, is what kind of a world expresses such an emblem — in other words, what kind of world makes *collective memory* as such a prevalent scholarly problematic as well as endows the strange or new postures toward it that we are currently witnessing in so many different contexts. Here I follow Hannah Arendt (1991), who shows in her account of the French Revolution that misery was always part of the human condition and that every culture has the capacity for compassion; however, it is only in a certain context, she argues, that pity is elevated to the level of a political principle — that is, becomes a central part of legitimation.[11] I pursue this theme in all four chapters of part two, exploring in each elements for a theory of modernity that places the forms of temporality and their relations to each other at the heart of the account: an approach that, in my opinion, contemporary sociological theory has neglected at its peril.

In chapter six, I identify and describe the *politics of regret* as a new principle of political legitimation, point out what I see as the inadequacies of the two dominant approaches to it in the literature (i.e., the discourse of universal human rights and scholarship on transitional justice), review a number of theoretical resources for alternative accounts, and highlight the value of a long-term, developmental account that sees contemporary forms of accountability as arising at a particular conjuncture in history rather than as an abstract choice outside of it.

In chapter seven, I take a somewhat less analytical and more normative tone, motivated by the space between Friedrich Nietzsche and Max Weber. Throughout his work, and particularly in his *Untimely Meditations* (1997), Nietzsche argues that "too much history" could be "the gravedigger of the present." By the same token, Max Weber (1946a), who was more profoundly influenced by Nietzsche than we sociological legatees usually remember, argues vociferously in his most famous essay, "Politics as a Vocation," that the modern politician had to be motivated by an "ethic of responsibility" rather than by an "ethic of conviction." So the obvious question, it seemed to me, was whether all forms of the politics of regret — with their moralistic overtones — are matters of conviction or whether there can indeed be a responsible politics of regret. If not, how are we to evaluate the current discourses about trauma, reparations, therapy, and compensation? In chapter seven, I argue, on the examples of Germany and South Africa, that efforts aimed at theologically inspired images of reconciliation between victors and perpetrators are indeed matters of conviction, whereas efforts aimed at truth and the conditions for understanding not between victim and perpetrator but among their children can be considered responsible in Weber's framework.[12] The operative distinction, I argue, is between quiescence, which is cheap and temporary, and peace, which is expensive but durable.

I again take up the Nietzschean challenge in chapter eight — "From Theodicy to *Ressentiment*" — in which I connect my concerns with regret to the concepts of trauma, *ressentiment*, and, ultimately, theodicy (i.e., the explanation of evil and suffering). Indeed, I argue that theodicy gets us to the very heart of the matter and lays the groundwork for a more sociological account of these issues, although theodicy is not usually understood sociologically, despite the efforts of Weber and Max Scheler. But sociological it is, as I attempt to show, because the forms of compensation — sacred or secular — depend very much on our understanding of the sources of suffering — whether retributive, fateful, predictable, or meaningless — which are very much socially conditioned by deeper temporal structures of perception and social organization. Here, I take recourse in the theories of Reinhardt Koselleck (1985) — who is not usually identified as a social theorist — though also in Durkheim and Elias. A discussion of these temporal structures, already alluded to in chapters six and seven of this section, form the core of chapter nine, in which I sketch a broad outline of what a sociological account of modernity that tackles the aforementioned issues more directly might look like. Clearly, this sketch — as all the others in the second half of the book — is intended as suggestive, limning the contours of a new line of inquiry rather than providing its definitive statement.

Conclusion

"Political legitimation," I argue at the beginning of chapter six, "depends just as much as it ever has on collective memory, but this collective memory is now often one disgusted with itself, a matter of 'learning the lessons of history' more than of fulfilling its promise or remaining faithful to its legacy." Understanding this, however, requires the full resources of both *sociological poetics* (Bakhtin's term for the analysis of dialogue in specific moments) and a sociological account of modernity that highlights the centrality of history and its associated forms of compensation — which, I believe, is implied in Bakhtin's concept of *great time.* In this way, the sociology of collective memory and the history of the politics of regret form two sides of the same coin because we live in a society of both narratives and organizations.

CHAPTER 2

Collective Memory

The Two Cultures[1]

Collective memory, one might plausibly argue, often plays an important role in politics and society. Such claims are by now commonplace in scholarly as well as political discourses: Images of the Vietnam War limit support for American military activities; memories of the Nazi period constrain German foreign and domestic policy; recollections of dictatorship shape the activities of transitional and posttransition regimes from Eastern Europe to Latin America; and Watergate has become the perennial reference point for all subsequent scandals in Washington, to name just a few possible such hypotheses. Indeed, the term *collective memory* has become a powerful symbol of the many political and social transitions currently under way, though there is also something broadly epochal about our seemingly pervasive interest in memory. New regimes seek ways to settle the residues of their predecessors, while established systems face a rise in historical consciousness and increasingly pursue a *politics of regret*.[2]

Whatever its sources, the flurry of recent interest in and use of the term *collective memory* raises an important challenge to scholars interested in the diverse phenomena it apparently indicates. Before, or at very least as part of, offering the kinds of hypotheses just mentioned, we need to be clear about what exactly the term means. I do not mean that we need to operationalize collective memory postivistically to generate empirically verifiable covering laws. Rather, I mean that we need to inquire into the value added by the term, to specify what phenomena the term sensitizes us to as well as what kind of a sensitivity this is.[3]

Some critics have charged that *collective memory* is a poor substitute for older terms like *political tradition* or *myth*. Gedi and Elam (1996, p. 30), for instance, call its use "an act of intrusion ... forcing itself like a molten rock into an earlier formation ... unavoidably obliterating fine distinctions." Others worry about the leap implied in adapting a term that refers to an individual-level phenomenon — memory — to the collective level. Fentress and Wickham (1992, p. 1), for instance, are wary of "a concept of collective consciousness curiously disconnected from actual thought processes of any particular person," a concern not entirely unfounded given the term's origins in the Durkheimian tradition. On the other hand, Burke (1989, p. 98) argues that "if we refuse to use such terms, we are in danger of failing to notice the different ways in which the ideas of individuals are influenced by the groups to which they belong."

The real concern, of course, is not with the term itself but with the ways in which such a label structures — that is, both enables and constrains — our conceptual and empirical work. What are the advantages and disadvantages of *collective memory* in comparison to other terms like *commemoration, tradition,* or *myth*? What does it mean to say that the memories of individuals are influenced by the groups to which they belong? Are ideas ultimately individual-level or collective-level phenomena or some combination of the two? Or does the study of social memory demonstrate the uselessness of that sort of distinction?

Origins

Contemporary usages of the term *collective memory* are largely traceable to Emile Durkheim (1961), who wrote extensively in *The Elementary Forms of Religious Life* about commemorative rituals, and to his student, Maurice Halbwachs, who published a landmark study on *The Social Frameworks of Memory* in 1925 (Coser 1992).[4] Durkheim and his students, of course, have often been criticized for an organicism that neglects difference and conflict. Indeed, Durkheim did write *Society* with a capital S, and collective representations in his work do take on something of a life of their own. Halbwachs was somewhat more careful, employing *groups* in place of Durkheim's *Society,* and characterized *collective memory* as plural, showing how shared memories can be effective markers of social differentiation (Coser 1992; Wood 1994).

Nevertheless, there is, in my reading, an unresolved tension between individualist and collectivist strains running through Halbwachs's work on collective memory, one that depends largely on the different arguments to which he responds. For Halbwachs, who accepts Durkheim's critique of philosophy, studying memory is not a matter of reflecting on properties of the subjective mind, as Bergson (1990) emphasizes; rather, memory is a matter of how minds work together in society, how their operations are structured by social arrangements: "It is in society that people normally acquire their memories. It is also in society that they recall, recognize, and localize their memories" (Halbwachs 1992, p. 38). Halbwachs argues that it is impossible for individuals to remember in any coherent and persistent fashion outside of their group contexts. His favorite examples include the impossibility of certainty regarding particular childhood memories: It is very difficult, at the limit, to say whether what we remember is somehow individual and independent or the result of cues and suggestions given to us by our families.

However, Halbwachs (1992) offers these arguments as an analysis of the social frameworks of memory, rather than of social memory per se, and elsewhere (Halbwachs 1966) talks about the distinctions between individual and collective memory. Halbwachs reminds that it is only individuals who remember, even if they do much of this remembering together. Group memberships provide the materials for memory and prod the individual into recalling particular events and into forgetting others. Groups can even produce memories in individuals of events that they never experienced in any direct sense. Halbwachs therefore resists the more extreme internalist subjectivism of Bergson, as well as the commonsense view of remembering as a purely — perhaps even paradigmatically — individual affair. At the same time, however, he does seem to have preserved the notion of an individual memory, however shaped that memory is by social frameworks and identities.

On the other hand, there is a more radically collectivist moment in Halbwachs as well, largely in his reaction to Freud and in the attempt to distinguish collective memory from history. Freud, providing one of the most important theories of memory in Halbwachs's intellectual universe, argues that the individual's unconscious acts as a repository for all past experiences. Forgetting, rather than remembering, is what takes work in the form of repression and the substitution of "screen" memories that block access to more disturbing ones. In contrast, Halbwachs argues that memory is in no way a repository of all past experiences. Over time, memories become generalized "imagos," and such imagos require a social context for their preservation. Memories, in this sense, are as much the products of the symbols and narratives available publicly — and of the social means for storing and transmitting them — as they are the possessions of individuals. As such, "there is thus no point in seeking where … [memories] are preserved in my brain or in some nook of my mind to which I alone have access: for they are recalled by me externally, and the groups of which

I am a part at any given time give me the means to reconstruct them" (Halbwachs 1992, p. 38).[5]

This is the more authentically Durkheimian moment in Halbwachs's theory of social memory, in which imagos are collective representations sui generis. In contrast to his discussion of *The Social Frameworks of Memory* — in which what individuals remember is determined by their group memberships but still takes place in their own minds — in works like *The Legendary Topography of the Holy Land* and elsewhere Halbwachs (1992) focuses on publicly available commemorative symbols, rituals, and technologies.[6] This more Durkheimian discussion undergirds Halbwachs's contrast between *history* and *collective memory* not as one between public and private but as one based on the relevance of the past to the present: Both history and collective memory are publicly available social facts. Halbwachs thus alternately refers to *autobiographical memory, historical memory, history,* and *collective memory.* Autobiographical memory is memory of those events that we ourselves experience (though those experiences are shaped by group memberships), whereas historical memory is memory that reaches us only through historical records.[7] History is the remembered past to which we no longer have an "organic" relation — the past that is no longer an important part of our lives —whereas collective memory is the active past that forms our identities.

Collective memory in Halbwachs thus indicates at least two distinct, and not obviously complementary, sorts of phenomena: socially framed individual memories and collective commemorative representations and mnemonic traces. The problem is that Halbwachs does not present us with an integrated paradigm that identifies the unique structures involved in each of these and shows how they are related — though he does provide some useful suggestions on all of these matters. Halbwachs is in this sense still a "nineteenth-century" theorist, one who sees individual- and collective-level problems as problems of different orders. In such a dichotomous worldview, the options are to emphasize one or the other, to present a grand theory of aggregation and translation between the levels, or to produce a sometimes productive hodgepodge of insights about a particular range of problems. This last, it seems to me, is the road Halbwachs took in his seminal work on collective memory, and it is a solution that, in my reading, has predominated the field since then, though not always in quite such a felicitous manner.

Two Cultures

The problem is that these two sorts of phenomena to which the term *collective memory* can refer — in Halbwachs and in general — seem to be of radically distinct ontological orders and to require different epistemological and methodological strategies. Yet precisely this kind of clarity has been missing from the rather indiscriminate (in the true sense of the word) usage of *collective memory*.[8] *Collective memory* has been used to refer to aggregated individual recollections, to official commemorations, to collective representations, and to disembodied constitutive features of share identities; it is said to be located in dreamy reminiscence, personal testimony, oral history, tradition, myth, style, language, art, popular culture, and the built world. What is to be gained, and what is to be lost, by calling all of these *collective memory*? Pierre Nora (1992) — one of the most prominent practitioners in the field of social memory studies (Olick and Robbins 1998) — for instance, attempts to identify all of what he calls *lieux de mémoire* (realms of memory) in French society; the result runs to seven volumes, including entries on "Vichy," "Right and Left," "Divisions of Time and Space," "The Land," "Street Names," "Gastronomy," "Bastille Day," "Joan of Arc," and "The French Language," raising the question of what is not a *lieu de mémoire*. The same may be said of collective memory: Since social action and social production take place with capacities and materials handed down from the past, collective memory becomes synonymous with pattern-maintenance per se.

Nevertheless, even if we restrict the term *collective memory* to explicitly commemorative activities and productions — a popular analytical strategy — the problem remains, and remains unarticulated, of choosing between individualistic or collectivistic procedures. This is because two radically different concepts of culture are involved here: one that sees culture as a subjective category of meanings contained in people's minds versus one that sees culture as patterns of publicly available symbols objectified in society. Each of these culture concepts entails different methodological strategies and produces different kinds of knowledge. To be as clear as possible about the sensitivities of the term *collective memory,* we need to understand exactly how these two culture concepts play out. What the hypotheses about the role of memory in politics I began with mean, for instance, depends fundamentally on how we conceptualize the phenomenon, on what kind of a process or thing we think this collective memory is.

In this effort, we have an advantage because just such a discussion has already taken place in debate over the meaning of the term *political culture.* Indeed, scholarly work on collective memory can be seen as part of the field of political culture research insofar as it is concerned with the cultural constitution of political identities and activities. The term *political culture* is perhaps most widely known from a line of work on political development begun in the 1950s and 1960s by political scientists Gabriel Almond, Lucien Pye, and Sidney Verba, among others. There the term was used to refer to aggregate patterns of psychological orientations toward political outcomes (Almond and Verba 1963, 1980). In perhaps the most famous work in this tradition, Almond and Verba (1963) hypothesize that a distinct set of subjective orientations — what they call the *civic culture* — is essential for generating and maintaining democratic political institutions.

Political culture theorists in this tradition thus refer to culture in the sense of a nurturant environment rather than in the sense of publicly available ideas and symbols. They therefore develop and employ methods — primarily survey research — to discover and aggregate the hidden sources of social patterns in people's heads. Political culture analysis in this view is a kind of collective political psychology: Individualistic in both its politics and in its ontology, it identifies the black box of human minds as the source of institutional outcomes. Political culture and other phenomena like public opinion are nothing more than the attitudes and opinions of individuals added up into general pictures. To be sure, macrosocial and "objective" variables influence those dispositions, but they are by no means to be seen as sui generis. Though it poses its behavioral (i.e., purely observational) methods as a scientific response to political philosophy, there is thus a great deal of ontology implied in interpreting survey data either as an indicator of cultural structures or indeed as the cultural structure itself.

In recent years, interpretive social scientists, many of them coming out of the Durkheimian tradition, have reinvented the concept of political culture (Baker 1990; Berezin 1994; Brint 1994; Hunt 1984; Olick and Levy 1997; Somers 1995). In contrast both to the political culture work just discussed as well as to various instrumentalist strategies that dismissed cultural dimensions of politics, new political culture analysis defines culture not narrowly as subjective values or attitudes but broadly as the symbolic dimension of all social situations. Culture here is regarded as intersubjective — or even as objective — and as embodied in symbolism and patterns of meaning. Rejecting the association of political culture with collective political psychology, new political culture theory highlights the discursive dimensions of politics, seeing political language, symbolism, and claim-making as constitutive of interests and identities. Political culture, as newly conceived, is thus the symbolic structuring of political discourse, and the analysis of political culture is the attempts to understand the patterns and logics of that discourse. Political culture can therefore be measured only crudely by survey analysis; instead, it must be excavated, observed, and interpreted on its own terms as culture (Olick and Levy 1997). At the very least, there is an ontological hiatus between survey data and political culture, between aggregated opinions and public opinion.[9]

Collected versus Collective Memory

This debate over the concept of *political culture* — and over the appropriate strategies for studying it — is directly germane to the present question of collective memory: The same two conflicting culture concepts underlie the varieties of work on collective memory as well, though the practitioners of different kinds of work on collective memory have not joined the fray in this manner. Social memory studies form a nonparadigmatic, transdisciplinary, centerless enterprise, and work in different historical, geographical, and disciplinary contexts proceeds largely independently of work in other such contexts (Olick and Robbins 1998). There has to date been very little in the way of conceptual and methodological discourse on collective memory; although some very useful insights have been developed within the different contexts, this work has — from a systematic, scientific point of view — been a rather unproductive hodgepodge. The remainder of this chapter, therefore, distinguishes between two basic concepts of *collective memory* at this fundamental level, neither to argue for one over the other nor to deny their real differences, but as a productive prolegomenon to understanding their relations.

Collected Memory

The first kind of collective memory is that based on individualistic principles: the aggregated individual memories of members of a group.[10] Surely, work of this sort does not preclude that some transformations may occur when individual memories are aggregated, through the activities either of the people involved or of the social scientists collecting or measuring their memories. But the fundamental presumption here is that individuals are central: Only individuals remember, though they may do so alone or together, and any publicly available commemorative symbols are interpretable only to the degree to which they elicit a reaction in some group of individuals. This ontology of memory does not exclude the possibility that different rememberers are valued differently in the group — that the memories of some command more attention than those of others — but some of the research strategies here function either technically democratically (e.g., surveys that assign the same value to every respondent) or even redistributively (e.g., oral history projects, which often aim at recovering the lost or neglected memories of those who have been disenfranchised).[11]

From the point of view of what I call this "collected" memory approach, notions of collective memory as objective symbols or deep structures that transcend the individual risk slipping into a metaphysics of group mind. There is no doubt, from this perspective, that social frameworks shape what individuals remember, but ultimately it is only individuals who do the remembering. And shared symbols and deep structures are only real insofar as individuals — albeit sometimes organized as members of groups — treat them as such or instantiate them in practice. It does not make sense from an individualist's point of view to treat commemorative objects, symbols, or structures as having a life of their own: Only people have lives.

One advantage of the collected memory approach is that it can avoid many of the potential reifications and political biases of approaches that begin with collectivities and their characteristics. First, as already mentioned, accounts of the collective memory of any group or society are usually accounts of the memories of some subset of the group, particularly of those with access to the means of cultural production or whose opinions are more highly valued. One way around this is to resist the temptation to speak of one collective memory in favor of many different kinds of collective memory produced in different places in the society. Scholars have, in this way, proliferated distinctions such as between *official* and *vernacular* memory, *public* and *private* memory, *historical* and *folk* memory, among others (e.g., Bodnar 1992; Schudson 1992). Nevertheless, merely substituting finer-grained collective categories for the collective memory does not necessarily eliminate the tendency to reify the new categories, as has often been the case, for instance, in oral history research, which has counterposed the "authenticity" of vernacular memory to the "truth" of historical memory or to the sterility and monochromaticism of official memory. And although this approach may avoid macrolevel reifications, moreover, it does so by reifying the individual. (I discuss this in greater detail later in this chapter, having already noted the presuppositional democracy of survey methods.)

Second, collected memory approaches often assume a posture of behaviorist neutrality that makes the object of study hypothetical rather than categorical. In other words, collected memory approaches do not necessarily begin by assuming the existence of a collectivity which has a collective memory — though they often do begin in this way — but instead use the inquiry to establish whether or not the colloquial collective designation is or is not salient. A good example of this occurred in the 1970s in West Germany (Schweigler 1975). The central motivation of West German foreign policy at that time was to protect the fate of the German nation as an identity under the condition of division. But instead of taking German national identity as a given, as the ineluctable force of nature hypothesized by Romantic nationalist ideology — particularly that of the German tradition, which saw the nation as an organic entity based on the ties of blood and soil — Chancellor Willy Brandt's government commissioned a survey to inquire into the subjective sentiment of national identity: Did a significant portion of the population have a strong subjective commitment to the idea of the German nation? Instead of seeing German nationality as a taken-for-granted and permanent characteristic, this approach saw it as the product of a collective — or, more accurately, collected — will. Such a conceptualization marked a decisive shift in the basis of German identity, at least in some quarters.

Treating collective memory, as well as collective identity, in this way thus resists the witting or unwitting adoption of certain ideological categories, particularly those that make demands on the individual (e.g., nationalism). A similar effort, deriving from the Mannheimian tradition in the sociology of knowledge, has redefined generations not as objective periods but as subjectively defined cohorts: A generation exists if and only if a number of birth cohorts share a historical experience that creates a community of perception. In this tradition, Howard Schuman and colleagues (Schuman and Corning 2000; Schuman and Rieger 1992; Schuman and Scott 1989; Schuman, Belli, and Bischoping 1997) have undertaken numerous surveys in different national contexts to measure cohort differences in the perception of particular historical events. How do individuals born in different periods remember and evaluate earlier moments? A great deal of the answer depends on whether they experienced the event in question, as well as how old they were when they did so; historical events are more memorable to people still in their formative years. The salience and evaluation of historical memories, Schuman's work demonstrates, is thus powerfully shaped by generational effects understood in this way: Generations and memories are mutually constitutive, not because of some objective features of social or cultural structure but because of experiential commonalities and resultant similarities in individual memories of historical events. However objectified generational structure may be, individual experience remains its central medium.

Because it locates shared memories in individual minds and sees collective outcomes as aggregated individual processes, moreover, the collected memory approach is formally open to the investigation of psychological or even neurological factors in social memory outcomes, though its behaviorist approach — manifest in survey methodology or in the oral historian's interest in merely giving play to neglected voices — tends to treat the human mind as something of a black box. In substantive but not formal contrast, cognitive, behavioral, and even physical psychologists have highlighted the roles of both mind and brain in individual and, by extension, social memory processes. Perhaps the greatest advantage of the collected memory approach, then, is that it leaves open the possibility of dialogue among the physical, behavioral, and social sciences. With this formal opening, we have the opportunity to move beyond the apparent mutual irrelevance of neurological and psychological studies of memory on the one hand and sociological and cultural approaches on the other.

Indeed, even the briefest survey of the physical and cognitive psychology of memory — enormous and growing fields in their own rights — demonstrates some provocative points of potential contact. First, even within the most physicalist research paradigms — those investigating the biochemical, cellular, and neurological foundations of remembering — there are obvious points of relevance for sociological and political work on memory. Laboratory studies have shown, for instance, that the ability to recall is cue dependent (i.e., provide the word before or after the word in question on a test of a memorized list of words, and subjects can produce the test word more accurately) as well as state dependent (i.e., recreate the circumstances of original exposure more closely and the subject is able to recall the item more easily and more accurately). "Explicit remembering," Daniel Schachter (1996, p. 61) reports, "always depends on the similarity or affinity between encoding and retrieval processes." Neurophysiologists have hypothesized that this has to do with sympathetic firing of neural networks in areas of the brain where pieces of memory are stored.

Neurological studies, moreover, have demonstrated conclusively that memories are not unitary entities, stored away as coherent units to be called up wholesale at a later date. Neural networks channel bits and pieces called *engrams* to different places in the brain and store them there in different ways. The process of remembering, therefore, does not involve the reappearance or reproduction of an experience in its original form but the cobbling together of a new memory. People do not perceive every aspect of a situation, do not store every aspect they perceive, and do not recall every aspect they store. "A neural network," Schachter (ibid., p. 71) writes, "combines information in the present environment with patterns that have been stored in the past, and the resulting mixture of the two is what the network remembers ... When we remember, we complete a pattern with the best match available in memory; we do not shine a spotlight on the stored picture."[12]

Cognitive psychologists, moreover, have drawn important lessons from these physiological brain studies in their efforts to understand the mind. Because the ability to recall is highly cue and state dependent, remembering is obviously highly dependent on a number of contextual factors, factors that are always in flux. Cognitive psychologists, as a result, have opened up their investigations to social variables, though they have not usually brought sociological concepts to bear here. Along these lines, the cognitive psychologist Ulrich Neisser (1982) criticizes laboratory studies of memory for neglecting both formal and substantive impacts of natural settings on remembering. Work in this tradition has thus studied the impact of various social variables like race and class on how particular historical events are remembered by individuals: When people evaluate particular events as more or less consequential, they are more or less likely to recall them as decisive moments; when they have created these so-called "flashbulb" memories, they tend to remember more of the details surrounding the experience. Many people, for instance, recall — though not always accurately — a great number of specific details about their surroundings when they heard that U.S. president John F. Kennedy had been assassinated. Social factors like race and class influence the likelihood that any individual will code and store in the associated ways an experience as a flashbulb memory (see also Pillemer 1998).

An individualist approach to memory thus has a great deal of potential for producing insights about social memory outcomes. One problem with much of the psychological work that has been done, however, is that it works within a very strict independent–dependent variable format, in which the ability to recall is the dependent variable. Social contexts thus remain undertheorized. Aggregate outcomes, moreover, are largely irrelevant to the physical or cognitive psychologist, whose job it is to explain individual behavior. Yet the ways in which individual brains and minds work clearly have an effect on aggregate outcomes. Race and class may affect flashbulb memories, but it is also possible that flashbulb and other kinds of memories shape the salient group identities, as Schuman's work with his graduate students on generations implies. And not only do the psychological processes of powerful individuals — such as political leaders — affect their broadly consequential acts; common psychological dispositions can also shape the way large groups of people react to shared experiences. Documented tendencies toward cognitive consistency, for instance, perhaps in part based on neurological and cognitive organization, might constrain certain collective courses of action or the appeal of particular political programs — though we clearly have vast capacities, some psychological and others cultural, for bypassing such constraints — whereas psychologically based analogical reasoning and typification clearly play a great role in how groups of people interpret new situations in common.

Collective Memory

Nevertheless, the collective — as opposed to collected — memory tradition offers a number of powerful arguments that demonstrate the inadequacy of a purely psychological (individual or aggregated) approach. Three major varieties of argument are relevant here. First, certain patterns of sociation not reducible to individual psychological processes are relevant for those processes, as Neisser's (1982) "natural setting" approach implicitly allows. This is a version of Halbwachs's (1992, originally 1925) social frameworks approach: Groups provide the definitions, as well as the divisions, by which particular events are subjectively defined as consequential; these definitions trigger different cognitive and neurological processes of storage. Moreover, as many political historians of memory have demonstrated, contemporary circumstances provide the cues for certain images of the past. Quite consistent with the neuropsychological image of remembering as an active and constructive process rather than as reproduction, sociologists have demonstrated the ways the past is remade in the present for present purposes (see Olick and Robbins 1998). These more sociological observations are thus quite assimilable to the individualist perspective, though their focus is somewhat different. Other arguments, however, depend on a more radical ontological break between individualist and collectivist perspectives.

A great deal of work, for instance, has argued that symbols and their systems of relations have a degree of autonomy from the subjective perceptions of individuals.[13] Of course, the nature and degree of that autonomy vary greatly depending on the approach. Whether built on a Saussurean distinction between *langue* and *parole*, on Durkheimian notions of *collective conscience*, on hermeneutical approaches to the history of ideas, or on vernacular ideas about national character and heritage, however, it is fairly common to assert that collectivities have memories, just like they have identities, and that ideas, styles, genres, and discourses, among other things, are more than the aggregation of individual subjectivities. Though discourses are instantiated in individual utterances, such a perspective views it as a trivial truism to say that there are no ideas without thinking individuals. More extreme versions of this approach have certainly produced extravagant metaphors that have often been misunderstood — and sometimes even foolishly intended — such as that texts write authors. But clearly there is something to the argument that ideas and institutions are subject to pressures and take on patterns that cannot be explained by the interests, capacities, or activities of individuals except in the most trivial sense.

It is on the basis of such arguments, mostly implicit, that many scholars and commentators have employed the concept of *collective memory*.[14] From this perspective, the collected memory approach to memory misses a great deal of what is going on. Indeed, in this way, one might argue that survey research on social memory excludes much of what is genuinely social about memory. In the first place, there are well-documented aggregation effects that cannot be predicted from individual responses: Groups, for instance, tend to act more extremely than individuals. Additionally, there are clearly demonstrable long-term structures to what societies remember or commemorate that are stubbornly impervious to the efforts of individuals to escape them. Powerful institutions value some histories more than others, provide narrative patterns and exemplars of how individuals can and should remember and stimulate memory in ways and for reasons that have nothing to do with the individual or aggregate neurological records. Without such a collective perspective, we are both unable to provide good explanations of mythology, tradition, heritage, and the like either as forms or in particular as well as risk reifying the individual. In regard to the latter, collectivist approaches to memory challenge the very idea of an individual memory. It is not just that we remember as members of groups but that we also constitute those groups and their members simultaneously in the act, thus "re-member-ing." Robert Bellah and colleagues (1985, p. 153) therefore refer to "genuine communities as communities of memory" and highlight the role of "constitutive narratives." Individual and collective identity, in this view, are two sides of a coin rather than different phenomena.

There is an additional argument for collective as opposed to collected memory that does not necessarily abut such metaphysical and ontological matters, which I call the *technologies of memory* argument. Quite simply, there are mnemonic technologies other than the brain. Historians of memory, for instance, have demonstrated the importance of various forms of recording for our mnemonic capacities (e.g., Le Goff 1992). These affect both individual rememberers as well as societies. For individuals, being able to write a note or record a message or take a photograph vastly extends the capacity to "remember," not simply by providing storage space outside of the brain but also by stimulating our neurological storage processes in particular ways; in this manner, we have become genuine cyborgs with what several authors have called "prosthetic" memories (e.g., Landsberg 2004). And this implies no particular attachment to modern computer technology: Medieval orators are legendary for their mnemonic capacities, which depended on conceptual devices collectively known as *ars memoriae*, the arts of memory (Yates 1966).

Perhaps the clearest demonstration of the genuinely collective nature of remembering is the degree to which it takes place in and through language, narrative, and dialogue. Language, for instance, is commonly used as the quintessential example of a supra-individual phenomenon (see note 13). And it is not merely that individuals remember in language, coding their experiences as language and recalling them in it. Language itself can be viewed as a memory system. This is the approach taken by the literary critic Mikhail Bakhtin (1963, 1986) when he emphasizes that language is inherently dialogical. By this he means not only that language takes place in exchange between real people rather than in the minds of isolated individuals, nor only that words thereby respond to their contemporary situation, but also that, in his inimitable words, "Each individual utterance is a link in a chain of speech communion. Any utterance, in addition to its own theme, always responds (in the broad sense of the word) in one form or another to others' utterances that precede it" (1986, pp. 93–4). Utterances, according to Bakhtin, thus contain "memory traces" of earlier usages, meaning not that any utterance can be decoded to reveal earlier usages but that the specificity of every term is the product of a long historical development. This development, Bakhtin (1963, p. 121) argues, takes place through genres, each of which "lives in the present, but always remembers its past, its beginning. Genre is a representative of creative memory in the process of literary development."

At the societal level, moreover, different forms of social organization have clearly depended on different technologies of memory. There is the famous sociological argument about the importance of double-entry bookkeeping for the development of commercial society. Particular forms of record keeping are obviously associated with the possibility of an administrative state (Carruthers and Espeland 1991). Nineteenth-century European states increased their power and legitimacy vastly by developing new mnemonic forms like the museum, the archive, and indeed professional historiography itself. Returning to the kind of hypotheses with which this chapter began, moreover, there is a powerful argument about the role of the mass media in the development of international norms of justice: Aryeh Neier (1998), for instance, argues that a decisive moment in the development of principles of political regret was the emergence of war correspondents in the mid nineteenth century, who were able to present the horrors of modern warfare to their readers at home. Our current concern with memory in political contexts is thus in direct ways a result of technologies of memory outside of the brain.

An Example: Individual and Collective Dimensions of Trauma

The importance of both individualistic and collectivistic culture concepts for our understanding of social memory — both collective and collected — may be clearer if we consider very briefly a central concern in recent public discourse: the problem of trauma. One reason calls for memory have been so morally charged in recent years is the palpable responsibility we feel for — and indeed as — the victims of trauma. Yet there are numerous ways to understand this vague term. What can we mean when we speak of *trauma,* and what different implications can it have?

In its earliest usages, of course, *trauma* referred — and continues to refer — to a physical injury, as in "blunt-force trauma." When we use it to refer to psychological matters — to say nothing of social applications — we are thus already operating at a figurative level. In the psychological context, trauma takes on specific implications directly relevant here, namely of a psychic injury caused by emotional shock the memory of which is repressed and remains unhealed. Psychology has taken this understanding in at least two directions. First, psychologists have hypothesized that there are emotional events of such disruptive magnitude that they create neurological alterations in the brain: Much like an electric shock, an emotional shock disrupts normal brain functions. And second, focusing on the mind's need to tell a coherent narrative, psychoanalysts have understood trauma as a stumbling block in our abilities to do so, leading to a neurotic condition so long as it remains repressed. In both accounts, the residue of "psychic traumata," as William James (1890) put it, creates "thorns in the spirit."

Whether inscribed physically on the brain or cognitively on the mind, of course, such thorns in the spirit have profound implications at the personal and aggregate levels. We worry rightly about the so-called "walking dead" in our midst, those who have suffered the blunt traumas of dislocation, dictatorship, torture, and war. On the one hand, we know that these victims are particularly fragile, and we often feel we owe them both protection from easily provoked and easily understood fear as well as every help toward healing. In some cases, this involves material and symbolic restitution, compensation, apology, and the like; in others it means merely lending a willing ear, helping them give voice to their experiences and promising not to forget. On the other hand, we know well the dangers that can arise out of unconfronted horror and unreconciled experience: personal violence, revenge, perpetuation of hostilities, blood feuds, and sympathy for extreme political solutions. There is currently much debate about which measures are likely to soothe the psychic wounds of history best. Although some call for forgiveness and forgetting, others point out the oxymoronic qualities of that pair: Forgiveness requires some kind of acknowledgment of the wrongdoing (Shriver 1995). Of course, there are many different kinds of acknowledgment, ranging from personal and collective exculpation to the genuine "memory work" that many critics drawing on psychoanalytic and ethical models advocate.

The burdens of trauma, of course, do not reside purely at the personal level. As already indicated, suffering individuals can take out their aggressions on those around them, in forms ranging from cynicism to terrorism. A number of psychoanalytically oriented critics, including figures like Alexander and Margaret Mitscherlich (1967) and Theodor Adorno (1986), point out the risks of collective — in my terminology more appropriately collected — syndromes from unworked-through pasts. Adorno worries about the persistence, for instance, not of fascist tendencies against democracy but within democracy, which he believes resulted from a failure of Germans to work through their past. Earlier, Adorno and colleagues (Adorno et al. 1950) accounted for the rise of an "authoritarian personality" partly on the basis of unresolved childhood traumas exacerbated by the structure of the Prussian family. In their famous argument, the Mitscherlichs diagnosed a collective — again, in my terminology collected, though the line is blurred in their work — neurosis deriving from German people's inability to mourn the loss of their all-powerful leader. That inability to mourn prevented an honest and therapeutic confrontation with the legacies of their devotion.

Many observers, of course, move easily from such collected diagnoses to genuinely collective diagnoses. In sometimes worrying forms, such efforts operate in terms of facile concepts of national character or of anthropomorphized collectivities in which the collectivity itself has singular desires, needs, and will. But there are better versions of such collective diagnoses, particularly those articulated in terms of collective narratives. If genuine communities are communities of memory that constantly tell and retell their constitutive narratives, as the earlier cited Bellah et al. (1985) quote asserts, there can be genuinely collective traumas insofar as historical events cannot easily be integrated into coherent and constructive narratives.

Surely this is what we mean when we speak, for instance, of the U.S. civil war as a trauma for American society or of the memory of Vietnam as an ongoing problem. In the case of the former, there were indeed multitudinous individual and, as a result, powerful collected traumas. But the last individuals who personally experienced the event have been gone for quite a while now. Though we might speak of the residue of individual traumas, insofar as parents or grandparents imparted to their offspring stories of their experiences, psychological traumas cannot be passed down through the generations like bad genes. In the first place, the fact that the memory of such personally traumatic experiences is externalized and objectified as narrative means it is no longer a purely individual psychological matter. And in the second place, discussing the ongoing nature of the trauma in terms of such transmitted personal narratives does not capture what we really mean — that is, an unassimilable breach in the collective narrative. In regard to Vietnam, then, there certainly are many traumatized individuals walking our streets, suffering from a wide range of neurotic disorders, of which posttraumatic stress is only the best known. But Vietnam was traumatic not just for American individuals — to say nothing of Vietnamese individuals — but also for the legitimating narrative that we as individuals produce for us as a collectivity. In this way, for instance, the trauma of Auschwitz will not disappear with the death of the last survivor; nor is it carried only through those — mainly their children — who suffered its personal ripple effects: Auschwitz remains a trauma for the narratives of modernity and morality, among others (Bauman 1989). It clearly makes both ethical and conceptual sense to speak of that trauma as irreducible to individual and aggregated psychology.

Conclusions

What, then, can we conclude about the value of *collective memory* as a designator and about the work done employing it? There are, it seems to me, three possible answers. First, following the advice of Gedi and Elam (1996) quoted at the beginning of the chapter, we can abandon the term altogether as a poor replacement for a variety of more specific terms like *myth, tradition,* or *commemoration.* The advantage of such an approach is that it avoids an overly unifying framework that washes over genuine distinctions of kind. But this is its disadvantage as well. For surely there is something — or perhaps many things — that make it compelling to see the diverse forms of historical reference and mnemonic activity as related. Historically, for instance, it is clear that changes in the different forms of mnemonic activity at individual, collected, and collective levels are epochally related, a theme I take up at length in subsequent chapters. Major alterations in the forms of sociation in the nineteenth century, for instance, included a proliferation of monuments, the invention of new traditions, the spread of popular genealogy, and the development of psychoanalysis and other so-called "sciences of memory" (Hacking 1995). The German word for *modernity* is, literally, *new time* (*Neuzeit*), and its development undergirded alterations in collective as well as individual forms of perception and expression (Koselleck 1985). There are numerous other historical examples of such relations (Olick and Robbins 1998). Conceptually, moreover, it follows directly from virtually all of the approaches discussed here that different mnemonic forms, be they political or cognitive, are highly interrelated.

A second possibility would be to use the term to refer only to what I have called genuinely collective memory, that is, to public discourses about the past as wholes or to narratives and images of the past that speak in the name of collectivities. The advantage here is that doing so provides needed conceptual clarity and resists the temptations of the predominant methodological individualism in the social sciences. In some versions of physical and cognitive psychology, that temptation has produced a full-blown sociobiological reductionism, one which implies that sociology — with the possible exception of rational choice approaches — is largely superfluous. Of course, the reason to resist this is not to defend sociology at all costs but that the position relegates most of history to a residual category: Holding grand evolutionary considerations constant, the neurological processes of memory do not change over time. The disadvantage of reserving collective memory only for social memory seen collectivistically, however, is that doing so answers one reductionism with another. For surely the capacity of human minds is a relevant "variable" in or at least parameter of human history.

The third possible solution, the one I advocate here, is to use *collective memory* as a sensitizing term for a wide variety of mnemonic processes, practices, and outcomes, neurological, cognitive, personal, aggregated, and collective. A better term for such an approach would be *social memory studies*. Unlike collective memory studies, *social memory studies* does not raise confusions about its objects of reference. And unlike another candidate — *social studies of memory,* which sounds as if the social component is outside of memory, that is, in the study of it — it remains presuppositionally open to a variety of phenomena while pointing out that all remembering is in some sense social, whether it occurs in dreams or in pageants, in reminiscences, or in textbooks.

Of course, to try to change an established designation is to waste time tilting at semantic windmills. The real point is to open our thinking about the variety of mnemonic processes, practices, and outcomes and about their interrelations. This is not a call, then, for a grab bag of disconnected concepts and research activities, all equally legitimate. For it is clear that reductionistic strategies, though perhaps useful in the short run, cannot be the last word. We need an enterprise not that allows neurological, cognitive, attitudinal, and cultural work to go on side by side but that brings these enterprises into dialogue with one another.

In our theoretical work, this means beginning to inquire into the ways in which each of these kinds of mnemonic structures (indeed, that is what they are — ways of organizing remembering) shapes and is shaped by the others and developing theories about their interactions. This is more difficult than it sounds, for one of the lessons of social memory studies is that these are never completely separate processes, even analytically. There is no individual memory without social experience, nor is there any collective memory without individuals participating in communal life. Thinking about remembering in this way demands that we overcome our inculcated tendency — as both social scientists and modern social actors — to see individual and society, in the words of Norbert Elias (1978), as separate things, "like pots and pans" (p. 53).

In our empirical work, particularly on questions like that of the role of memory in politics, it means being open to the variety of different forms and meanings of the question. It means remembering both that memory occurs in public and in private, at the tops of societies and at the bottoms, as reminiscence and as commemoration, as personal testimonial and as national narrative, and that each of these forms is important; it also means remembering that these differing forms of remembering are not always equally important for each other (e.g., the personal experience of leaders, under some conditions, is more important than those of "ordinary" people, but not always), though it also means that they are always relevant to some degree; there is, as we have seen, no personal memory outside of group experience and that does not take some stand on "official" and "unofficial" collective versions. We can no more speak of the collective memory than we can speak of a presocial individual memory, even if we include both side by side; an infinity of social and neural networks are constantly in play with each other, meaning that different kinds of structures are always relevant and that their relevance is always changing.

Perhaps most important, it means remembering that our work as scholars plays a role in these questions: Like an atomic detector that changes particles in the very act of observing them, the various techniques we use inevitably validate or even constitute certain kinds of memory. Conceptually, the results of a survey of memory are not collective memory, but the knowledge produced does have the potential to become a part of it. Inquiring into the experiences of traumatized individuals may start out as an attempt to discover the role of memory in action, but it often calls up memories that would not have occurred without the researcher's stimulus and then objectifies them as part of a collective record. That record, in turn, becomes a point of reference for future remembering as well as for future perception, influencing down the road how new experiences will be coded, both neurologically and narratively. The lesson of all the excellent work done in the different fields is that we can no longer get away with these easy distinctions. This is the lesson of memory — particularly of traumatic memory — as well.

CHAPTER 3

Collective Memory and Cultural Constraint

Holocaust Myth and Rationality in German Politics[1]

In spring 1981, West German chancellor Helmut Schmidt was returning from a trip to Saudi Arabia during which he had negotiated the sale of West German Leopard 2 tanks to the Saudi government. The issue was especially delicate, not only because of the usual problems of Western Mideast policy but also because of Germany's "special" relationship with Israel (Deutschkron 1991; Feldman 1984; Wolffsohn 1988). Memory of the Holocaust had always complicated Germany's stance on Israeli problems, and the idea of Israel's sworn enemy acquiring West German tanks raised the hackles of Germany watchers the world over. Schmidt, however, was recalcitrant. For him, the opportunity to deal with another government without regard to the German past was especially important for the "normalization" of German politics that he sought both domestically and internationally. Angered by Israeli and world reactions, Schmidt reportedly proclaimed that West German foreign policy should no longer be "held hostage" to Auschwitz (Wolffsohn 1988, p. 42).

From the immediate postwar period to the present, powerful images of the Nazi past have shaped West Germany. Virtually every institutional arrangement and substantive policy is a response, in some sense, to Germany's memory of those fateful years. The Holocaust, moreover, has long been the standard for evaluating German political activity; indeed, as some critics have complained, Germany has a past that, for whatever reason, will not pass away (Nolte 1987).

Both Schmidt's purported statement and the general lament that the burdens of the past reach inappropriately into the present are vernacular claims about how the past affects us, or, in more sociological terms, how collective memory works. West German commentators and politicians have often regarded the Nazi past as an ineluctable burden, one beset by and working through the mystical force of taboo. This view is similar to scholarly approaches that emphasize the enduring power of traditions to shape the present (Shils 1981). In contrast, many theorists of social memory have favored a presentist approach, seeing images of the past as the strategic handmaidens of contemporary needs (Hobsbawm and Ranger 1983). Much recent work on social memory, however, argues for a more complex view of the relation between past and present in shaping collective memory (Schudson 1992; Schwartz 1991; Trouillot 1995; Zerubavel 1994): Collective memory, as in Bergson's (1990) philosophical critique, should be seen as an active process of sense-making through time.

This chapter analyzes the so-called taboos of the German past to understand more precisely how the remembered past shapes and constrains the present and vice versa. What does it mean to say that the Holocaust creates taboos in German politics? How do enduring images of the past interact with present needs to shape political opportunities and limits? In what different ways can the remembered past constrain the present, and under what circumstances are such constraints transformable?

New Political Culture Analysis and the Interpretive Turn

The following discussion proposes a distinction between different kinds of cultural constraints: (1) those that operate *mythically*, often associated with the power of the past over the present; and (2) those that operate *instrumentally*, often associated with the power of the present over the past. This distinction, the chapter argues, is necessary in order to understand more clearly the operation of collective memory — the conceptually and politically mediated past. To do this, the discussion turns to recent work on political culture, which has problematized the issue of cultural constraint in a way that can illuminate some of the murkier features of German struggles with memory and of collective memory in general.[2]

In classic works on political development, as discussed in the previous chapter, political scientists described *political culture* as aggregate patterns of psychological orientations toward political outcomes (Almond and Verba 1963, 1980). Political culture analysis, therefore, was an attempt to measure the subjective and to argue for its importance in political life — namely, for its role in maintaining democratic institutions. In an alternative view, attitudes were seen as epiphenomenal, as mere expressions of, or at the very least tools for, the more real —that is, objective — social structure.

In recent years, interpretive social scientists have reinvented the concept of political culture (Baker 1990; Berezin 1994; Brint 1994; Hunt 1984; Somers 1995). In contrast to older reductionisms — to both the subjectivism of earlier political culture theory and those who answered it by deemphasizing culture — new political culture analysis defines culture neither narrowly as subjective ideas, values, or attitudes nor disdainfully as epiphenomenal but broadly as the symbolic aspect of all social situations. Culture is regarded as intersubjective and as embodied in symbolism and patterns of meaning (Alexander 1990); it is pervasive.

In noncultural conceptualizations, politics is often modeled as a struggle over resources based on exogenously defined interests. In new political culture analysis, however, it is argued that such approaches beg the original question of interest formation (Geertz 1973). Seeing social life as an ongoing reproductive process, new political culture analysts focus not only on how political acts succeed or fail to obtain some material advantage but instead on how, in doing so, they produce, reproduce, or change identities. The struggle for position that constitutes politics, therefore, is always simultaneously strategic and constitutive.

To appreciate the constitutive role of political culture in social processes, scholars have focused on politics as claim-making, meaning both that claims are important and that even seemingly nondiscursive political acts are claims of sorts (Baker 1990; Hunt 1984). Nonetheless, the emphasis on claim-making should not be misunderstood as a limitless voluntarism: To mix metaphors from J. L. Austin and Karl Marx, people do things with words but not in circumstances of their own choosing. Both the words themselves and the situations in which they are deployed are structured in ways that transcend individual cognition, volition, and control. To understand political action as meaningful, therefore, is to look at the claims made by political actors in terms of the structure of possible claims and the structured possibility of their effects.

Political culture, as newly conceived, is thus the symbolic structuring of the claim-making that is always a constitutive part of any political moment; the analysis of political culture, then, is the attempt to understand the patterns and logics of political claim-making both for particular settings and generally. Political culture thus can be measured only crudely by survey analysis; instead, it must be excavated, observed, and interpreted in its own terms as culture. As a result, the analysis here employs an interpretive methodology, one that seeks to recover the sometimes hidden and always changing rules that constrain, and are shaped by, claims made by political actors in particular moments.[3]

Central to the effort here to understand how the German past and present shape each other is the recognition that political cultures are not static systems — that is, structures without histories. Political culture is always a historical process, not a determinate set of relations or a once-and-for-all definition of the situation. Claim-making by actors in political contexts is conditioned by significant pasts as well as by meaningful presents; it is always path-dependent, though not necessarily in obvious ways. This point calls attention to historical events of definitive importance, to how broad parameters are fixed or transformed at particular moments, and to how those moments manifest themselves or are invoked differently in subsequent contexts. Conceiving of collective memory as part of a political–cultural process thus remedies the presuppositional tendency to view it either as an unchanging and definitive past or as pure strategy, always malleable in the present.

Mythic and Rational Logics of Cultural Constraint

As mentioned already, political commentators in Germany frequently characterize the German past as imposing taboos. Often they do so to emphasize both that a particular image of the Nazi past is considered sacred (i.e., one in which Germany is a uniquely horrible and burdened historical perpetrator) and that this image works in inscrutable — read illegitimate — ways. This chapter seeks to redeem the insight provided by this taboo label while avoiding the more polemical slant; the role of collective memory is more highly differentiated than such a blanket characterization allows. To do this, it is important to specify two ways in which collective memory operates as a constraint: (1) by *proscription*, through taboos and prohibitions; and (2) by *prescription*, through duties and requirements.

Proscription: Taboos and Prohibitions

The concept of *taboo* as articulated by anthropologists includes, first of all, reference to some sort of avoidance practice (Douglas 1966; Pelinka 1994; Steiner 1956). All societies specify objects, conditions, people, practices, topics, and ideas that are avoided under certain circumstances. Moreover, such avoidance is not merely practical or morally neutral; rather, the designated object is treated as dangerous, disgusting, dirty, morally repugnant, contagious, degenerate, or embodying some combination of these qualities.

Another core sense of taboo concerns its contravention. Violating a taboo is not simply an error or an expense. It is a transgression or a pollution.

Under some circumstances it is socially, or literally, deadly; under others it is survivable, but not without some redemptive or cleansing effort.

These usages show that certain cultural elements operate as mechanisms of demarcation and constraint and that these operations play pivotal roles in maintaining the symbolic boundaries specified by a given society (Douglas 1966). Because taboos help set terms of discourse and boundaries of identity, they are central to the major concern of political culture analysis: the constraints on (i.e., the structuring of) claim-making in concrete settings.

Nonetheless, older conceptualizations must be refined in two ways before they can contribute to the problem of collective memory as cultural constraint. First, in older conceptualizations taboos are understood mainly in terms of social reproduction of already constituted and coherent systems. In contrast, the approach developed here argues, it is necessary to historicize meaning systems, to analyze them in terms of constitutive and transformative moments. The emphasis, therefore, is on the temporal dimension of taboos and their enactments. Taboos may be foundational, but to varying degrees they are developing structures: The Holocaust may create taboos in West German political culture, but these unfold along complex trajectories through time and space. Second, much literature treats taboo as if it were part of so-called "deep structure" (Steiner 1956). According to this view, taboos manifest themselves as prohibitions in concrete settings (Freud 1946). But this mapping of deep structure and manifest enactment onto the concept of taboo and prohibition is misleading. Taboos and prohibitions are not levels (i.e., deep structures versus manifestations) of the same phenomenon but refer to distinct varieties of cultural constraint.

Taboos operate through a mythic logic; such logic is especially important in defining interests because it demarcates identities and mobilizes passion about them in suasive, ritualistic forms. Taboos involve moral principles and definitional claims that are beyond debate, not because no alternatives exist but because these issues are not decided by rational argument. Taboos are usually obdurate: They may change gradually or may be transformed dramatically, but they make their claims as absolutes. One does not debate with a taboo; one either obeys or transgresses its proscriptions.

Prohibitions, in contrast to taboos, operate through appeals to calculative rationality and exogenously constituted interests. Their method is rationality, and their goals are mundane. Here the rules of advantage and maneuver apply. A major difference between taboos and prohibitions is that in the case of prohibitions positions and plans are abandoned when they are no longer tactically useful or when they are refuted with valid arguments. Prohibition is a politics of exigency, not of passion.

Prescription: Duties and Requirements

Constraint, of course, involves more than proscription. Without some ordering of the social flux, action is impossible. By constraining the range of options for actors in situations, culture also enables them to act in the first place — to make constitutive and instrumental claims. By extension we can imagine positive correlates to taboo and prohibition — prescriptions in addition to proscriptions. A taboo *proscribes* (i.e., defines what is absolutely unacceptable), whereas a duty or an obligation *prescribes* what is absolutely necessary. A prohibition restricts; a requirement enjoins. The relation of these concepts is displayed in Figure 3.1.[4]

In contrast to the common arguments that the Holocaust is taboo or creates taboos in German politics, it is useful to specify and differentiate the Holocaust's concrete operation and development and the contestation over it as a constraint in German political culture, in other words to distinguish between *taboos* and *prohibitions, duties* and *requirements,* and more generally between the operation of the past as *rational* and *mythic* constraint. In what follows, concrete examples illustrate the operations of the two types of constraint in German political culture, showing that understanding the differences between the two, as well as their perpetual overlap, is crucial for untangling the complexities of German political culture as it is realized through time.[5]

Figure 3.1 Logics of Cultural Constraint

MODE / OPERATION	Rational Calculative, interested, exogenously caused, mundane, strategic	Mythic Moral, constitutive, endogenous, projective, definitional
Proscriptions What must not be done	(–) Prohibition	(–) Taboo
Prescriptions What must be done	(+) Requirement	(+) Duty/Obligation

| **Contravention**
How the constraint is overcome | (x) Refutation | (x) Transgression |

Holocaust Myth and Rationality in German Political Culture

Although the Holocaust is frequently viewed as a theological moment beyond all comprehension, it certainly makes demands and exerts pressures on German society; despite its moral ungraspability, its operation in German politics is not ineffable. The Holocaust exerts its power in German politics both mythically and rationally.

Strategy and Morality in German Rehabilitation

In the late 1940s and early 1950s, the emerging Federal Republic of Germany encountered many serious problems deriving from the Nazi past. In addition to the pervasive physical devastation, Germans faced a moral crisis of perhaps unprecedented proportions. Allied occupation forces confronted the defeated and destroyed German populace with the crimes it had supported, in settings including early forced tours of concentration camps, "reeducation" propaganda, and the trials of leading political and military figures at Nuremberg. All Germans in the Western zones of occupation who had been of legal age during the Nazi period were required to fill out questionnaires that were used as the basis for "denazification" proceedings. A bad classification was supposed to mean exclusion from all kinds of public service, although this system was viewed as a travesty by practically all sides (Brochhagen 1994; Friedrich 1994).[6]

Despite notorious cases in which former Nazis of various stripe managed to gain political power in the new government, Germany's new leaders had largely opposed the Nazis. A central feature of the new Federal Republic's political culture was its anti-Nazi stance, at least officially. The first major manifestation of this commitment was the Basic Law of the Federal Republic, which went into effect in September 1949. In the words of constitutional historian Jürgen Seifert (1989, p. 40), "The Basic law ... manifests a rejection of the past. It was created as a bulwark that was supposed to make impossible what happened in Germany at the end of the Weimar Republic and after 1933."

The Basic Law may be read as a theory of German history. Through both its form and its content it identified "causes" of the so-called "catastrophe" of the German past.[7] These included, most prominently, electoral provisions that had allowed for fragmentation at the political center, an inadequate federalism that had enabled a concentration of power, insufficient means to fight radicalism, and provisions on human rights expressed only toward the end of the older Weimar document. The Basic Law of the Federal Republic and subsequent legislation solved these problems de jure.

Indeed, the rhetoric of early leaders — especially that of the venerable Chancellor Konrad Adenauer — emphasized that these constitutional provisions rectified the problems that had allowed Germany to be "seduced" by "bands of criminals." This new constitution, Adenauer argued, combined with a more general commitment to "Western" values and institutions and with reparations to Israel (finalized in 1953), protected the new Germany from the problems of its past. These institutional and political-cultural reorientations established the Federal Republic of Germany as a "reliable nation," a central metaphor of the center-right government of the 1950s.

West Germany as a polity could not do certain things because of the Nazi past. At first, the Federal Republic could not have an army. When the cold war began, the Allies moved quickly to rearm West Germany as a bulwark against the Soviets. Even with a new military, however, belligerence or anything but defensive operations within the territory of the North Atlantic Treaty Organisation (NATO), which was formed later, was strictly out of the question. As we will see, the complexities of a German military role became especially poignant in international conflicts in the early 1990s, specifically in debates over Germany's contribution to the Gulf War and to United Nations peacekeeping missions elsewhere.

In addition, knowledge of Nazi atrocities as well as the standards of the "community of nations" made anti-Semitism anathema to the new state. West Germany was constrained to support Israel unfailingly, although frequently it did so only under various forms of duress or with substantial complaint (Deutschkron 1991; Feldman 1984; Wolffsohn 1988). Throughout the 1950s, West Germany worked hard to establish diplomatic relations with Israel, though Israel continually refused. Only after the Eichmann trial of 1961 — in many respects a cathartic moment for Israel in accepting the Holocaust as part of its history (Segev 1993) — did a sufficient number of Israeli leaders feel ready for such "normal" relations with West Germany. By that time, however, West Germany was caught between two conflicting imperatives: its "special" responsibility to Israel, which led the Federal Republic to supply Israel secretly with weapons after 1960, and the so-called Hallstein doctrine, the principle that West Germany would not entertain relations with countries that recognized the existence of East Germany.

When the weapons deal between Israel and West Germany was discovered, Egypt sought to manipulate West Germany by threatening to recognize East Germany. Leaders of the Federal republic pleaded with Arab diplomats to allow for Germany's "special" responsibility, but Egypt nonetheless invited East German leader Walter Ulbricht for a state visit. West Germany then announced its intention to establish formal diplomatic relations with Israel — Israel now wanted relations as a sign of support against Arab countries and viewed relations as Germany's moral obligation. Indeed, West German leaders justified the move overwhelmingly in moral terms rather than in the context of international brinkmanship that ultimately led to it; the move obviously involved elements of both.

Over the years, many academic and social programs also were made difficult by the presence of the past. Anthropology, for instance, was tainted by Nazi *Rassenlehre* (roughly, "racial studies"), euthanasia could not even be discussed because of how the Nazis had used it, and medical ethics, especially concerning the rules of genetic experimentation, have been even more problematic in Germany than elsewhere over the last decades.

These constrained topics and activities are not the same, however, nor do they draw on the same logics. Sometimes they draw on instrumental rationality, aiming at either material or ideal ends; at other times they invoke constitutive and mythic foundations or evade discussion altogether. Early in the history of the Federal Republic, West German leaders pursued images of the Nazi past and the democratic present with the explicit purpose of regaining and expanding sovereignty. The institutional "remedies," as well as many rhetorical performances, may be easily understood as rational attempts to gain these ends. An issue such as reparations to Israel, for instance, can be explained in terms of calculative rationality.

On the one hand, the international weight of such a gesture is clear enough. Never before had a state undertaken such an extensive "voluntary" program to atone for the deeds of a preceding regime.[8] On the other hand, the program had a clear moral dimension. Adenauer and other supporters of the measure argued that some such gesture was necessary, not only for cynical *raisons d'état* but also for the nation's moral stature in its own eyes. Adenauer rarely failed to convince when he claimed a pedagogical purpose. But even if one were to characterize reparations to Israel as a wholly strategic maneuver, the action's subsequent life as a symbol cannot be explained entirely in terms of the instrumental rationality that might have brought it about. Symbols take on lives of their own through unanticipated consequences, unavoidable polysemy, and their subsequent power, which is irreducible to provenance. No matter how intensely disputed the plan had been at the time, later West German leaders referred to these reparations as a shining moment of German national rectitude.

In the presence of material restitution and institutional realignments (i.e., constitutional protections coupled with a vociferous commitment to Western values and security policies), leaders of the new state acted as if the concrete burdens of the Nazi period had been remedied. Indeed, the rhetoric of the 1950s is often surprisingly strident. When occasion arose to address the Nazi past, Adenauer and his associates always emphasized that this was no longer a concern for Germany. Any other position, they argued, would imply an acknowledgment of collective guilt.[9] On occasions of anti-Semitic outbreaks, Adenauer belittled accusations that there were any serious anti-Semites in Germany.[10]

It is a long-standing commonplace of political commentary and contemporary historiography that the 1950s was a period of avoidance and denial of the past (Greiffenhagen and Greiffenhagen 1993; Mitscherlich and Mitscherlich 1967).[11] Some of this behavior is clearly instrumental rationality: When the past makes one look bad — and thus restricts one's present possibilities — one emphasizes the present or the future. Much of this, however, extends to deeper issues involved with identity formation and the problematics of self-understanding.

For most people, the extent of Nazi inhumanity was sufficient reason to reject official anti-Semitism, but privately most Germans were preoccupied with their own difficult situations and losses — and old attachments died hard.[12] The degree of self-absorption and denial in the face of horrors committed "in the name of Germany" is, however, difficult to appreciate even given the circumstances.[13] Indeed, at this early point, there was a radical disjuncture in many respects between the abilities of the government and of the general population to "come to terms" with the Nazi period.[14] The government thought it had to be careful not to fall too far out of step with the people's attitudes. This is one reason Adenauer gave for rejecting theses of collective guilt: How could he gain the necessary domestic support for his new government if it loaded significant segments of the population with a burden of guilt, either legal or moral? One reason for denying collective guilt is that it was strategically a disadvantage; another is that it was an unacceptable proposition for an expertly equivocating and evasive population.

At any rate, the conditions of the Federal Republic's early years — some the result of predispositions and persistent cultural frames, some unintentional and some the products of rational planning — set the rules of the game for memory and culture for the next half-century. The unwillingness to accept collective guilt was not simply a rational attempt to avoid burdens but also reflected Germans' inability to understand their own implication in what had happened (Olick 2005). This is not to say that collective guilt is a philosophically defensible position; it is not. Most people, however, did not reject it out of philosophical conviction; rather, there is widespread evidence that many German people — often obsessed with their own victimhood — could not even imagine why anyone should think that collective guilt was appropriate.[15]

The Mytho-Logics of Identity: Perpetration and Denial

The framing of historical obligations is quite evident in a number of proscriptions that developed in regard to the representation of the past.

Acknowledgments of collective guilt are prohibited in part on rational grounds, but they are incomprehensible without an analysis of mythic structures in German culture, some of which bridged the divide of the so-called "zero hour" of 1945. These mythic structures produced instrumentally unaccountable practices.

Studies of official representations of the Nazi past in West Germany document the various ways West German leaders discussed the Nazi period (Herf 1997; Olick forthcoming). Such study reveals a peculiar phenomenon: Of all the accounts of the causes of the German "catastrophe"— including extremism, insufficient support for the institutions of the Weimar Republic, economic pressures, criminal usurpation, unemployment, and religious intolerance, among others — the most obvious cause, anti-Jewish racism, is rarely mentioned.[16] This is true regardless of the context of the speech — from the *Bundestag* to Bergen-Belsen. In all of the analyses offered in public by West German leaders, anti-Semitism as racism, rather than as simple Christian–Jewish "misunderstanding") is rarely addressed as a cause of German problems. Indeed, its absence is so extensive that the avoidance can be said to be ritualistic.

The avoidance of mentioning anti-Semitism as racism, although it contains some instrumental elements, is an excellent example of a taboo about the German past. Over the years it has emerged in different ways in different contexts, but the avoidance is remarkably consistent. In the early years, anti-Semitism in the present was quite simply denied. The anti-Semitism of the past was portrayed as a minority view, an aberration, now eliminated, that did not warrant serious consideration in other than general terms. Anti-Semitism had been solved with human rights provisions, reparations, and an official philo-Semitism. Indeed, early leaders of the Federal Republic were remarkably pro-Israel. This was not simply the result of a wish to "make good": Visitors to Israel, at first unofficial and clandestine and later official and touristic, often reported that they were deeply impressed by what the Israelis had accomplished. In comments made after such trips, Israelis were valorized in terms previously reserved for the German "master race" (Olick forthcoming).

The mythic logic involved here is made even clearer by the reversals that occurred in the late 1960s. Until the Six Day War of 1967, the German left, as well as the center and the right, supported Israel unequivocally as the oppressed underdog. When Israel became an occupying force, however, many segments of the German left quickly and totally abandoned support for Israel, as if they had been suddenly freed from an unwanted burden.[17] Indeed, this is a common characterization of the so-called sixty-eighters. In the late 1960s, the student left began to discuss and investigate the crimes of their parents' generation. Public discussion regarding the past was opened up. This process was not quite that simple, however: Such discussion was possible only because it fit with the younger generation's rejection of their parents' entire world.

Such vehement condemnation and general interest regarding the German past was possible only because the younger generation viewed itself as fundamentally different from the older generation and as unconnected to its crimes (Bude 1992; Klessmann 1987; Moeller 1996). Yet the burdens of that experience, whether acknowledged or repressed, had maintained the foundation for official philo-Semitism. The left of the late 1960s and early 1970s generalized the burdens of the past away from the specific debts understood by their parents, and apparently they seized on the Six-Day War as an occasion to remove any special claims concerning Israel.

This delegitimation and the removal of special status for Israel and the debt to Jews are as strange as the shift from anti- to philo-Semitism in the early years of the Federal Republic. This second generation's confrontation with the Nazi past resulted in a generalized moral tone, one that challenged major aspects of the contemporary world in both Germany and elsewhere. In the process, the Holocaust and the specific debt to Jews that resulted became merely one debt among others borne by this newly "moral nation."

This peculiar way of dealing with collectivities is also related to the conceptual core of German identity. *"Germanness"* as a category of belonging is articulated in very different terms from French belonging — that is, as an ethnic rather than a civic category (Brubaker 1992). Immigrants can become French or American, but although they may obtain German citizenship, they will never be accepted as "really" German. In contrast, Eastern Europeans who do not speak a word of German and have never been to Germany but who can demonstrate German lineage — sometimes, perversely, by presenting Nazi-era documentation — are automatically granted German citizenship.

Despite the importance of such absolute ethnic principles of belonging in German Romanticism as well as in Nazi racial policy, these principles remained potent even after the delegitimation of Nazi disregard for ethnic "others." The early shift from anti- to philo-Semitism is connected, in part, to this "primordial" principle of belonging. Identities are absolute; it is easier to change the evaluative prefix from *anti-* to *philo-* than to examine the principle and to discard its logic. For this reason, debates about the status of immigrants, particularly in the 1990s, were especially stubborn. Many on the left tried to play the Nazi card as a way to establish a prohibition against excluding or disregarding immigrants. They argued that awareness of the Nazis' persecution of racial "others" should prevent contemporary Germany from enacting laws to restrict immigrants' rights to due process under the law. Yet there was relatively little willingness to question the basic distinctions. The proposals were formulated mostly as desired prohibitions, but the debate was constrained by taboos against acknowledging the situational origins of collective identities.[18]

There are clearly instrumental aspects to both the anti- to philo-Semitism shift and the unsuccessful attempt in the 1990s to prohibit constitutional changes concerning immigrants' rights. In the first case, a thorough-going examination of identity in the early years of the Republic — seemingly indicated by the unmentioned and unmentionable extremes of Nazi racism — might have called into question the significantly threatened unity of a German nation. Despite the rhetoric of European identity and its seeming refutation of nationalism, however, ethnocultural national identification remained an untouchable cultural principle, even when it produced bizarre results. In the case of immigration policy, the ability to exclude self-confidently depends on the absolute quality of the collective identity. Despite frequent arguments about the inability to manage economically in the face of huge numbers, the noninstrumental dimensions were clear in the resultant expressions of xenophobia and chauvinistic nationalism.

Another major proscription for German leaders regarding the Nazi past concerned attention to perpetrators. In the early years, leaders were careful not to be too specific about German perpetrators. This position fit with the argument that the blame lay with Hitler and his henchmen, with the understandable unwillingness of a government with implicated members to delve too deeply into personal responsibility, and with the desire not to alienate those who had played minor or major supporting roles, as mentioned already. Nonetheless, the issue of individual responsibility was caught up in more complex "mytho-logics" (Apter 1985) of exculpation.

The very metaphors of political rhetoric reveal many Germans' desires to avoid facing their own possible forms of culpability, either individually or collectively. These rhetorical stratagems include the perverse absence of actors: passive formulations, such as "the crimes committed in Germany's name"; vague terms describing the period, such as "the conditions at that time," "what happened during those years," and "the Hitler-time"; elliptical references to the details, such as "what happened" and "the crimes that were committed"; and pervasive qualification, such as "others suffered, but so did Germans".[19]

Taboos and Transgression Costs: The Jenninger Affair

The strength of these taboos is revealed poignantly in their transgressions — rare occurrences. A vivid example is the speech delivered by *Bundestag* president Philipp Jenninger on November 10, 1988, during a special session of the *Bundestag* a day before the fiftieth anniversary of *Kristallnacht*, the pogrom against Jewish businesses and property that marked the beginning of the escalation of the crimes against the Jews. In his speech, Jenninger addressed the viewpoint of average Germans in 1933, when Hitler came to power. Apparently the delivery of the speech made it difficult to determine whether Jenninger was simply portraying how the situation might have seemed reasonable to average Germans at the time or whether in fact he was saying that it was reasonable. During the speech, large numbers of deputies stormed out of the chamber in protest; in the days following, Jenninger, an extremely prominent and highly respected figure, was forced to resign.

When Jenninger's speech is read in isolation, it is difficult to detect the problem. He says nothing that had not been said before in other contexts and certainly is not guilty of justifying Nazi policies, as he was accused. The problem was that in this speech, unlike in others delivered on similar occasions, Jenninger spoke of the issues confronting real Germans living in the early 1930s. In doing so, he acknowledged officially that many real people had supported Hitler for a wide variety of reasons. His focus on how Hitler had made sense to some people violated the absolute demonization of Hitler, and focusing on German problems violated the long-standing avoidance of attention to ordinary people as supporters of the Third Reich. Furthermore, the occasion of the speech conventionally required gestures of atonement rather than serious introspection, especially not about German problems. It was not that nobody knew these things; rather, even forty years after the founding of the Republic, German guilt was a difficult topic — indeed, a clear example of a taboo in political culture.

The Historians' Dispute: From Taboo to Prohibition

In practice, one cannot easily distinguish between mythic and rational logics in political claim-making, partly because most moments include elements of both. Prohibitions and taboos, duties and requirements, are ideal types. Examples are drawn from the vastly complicated reality of changing political culture in which no claim is simple, no argument univalent, and no reference clearly bounded. The argument just presented conveys how these two logics are involved and intertwined in concrete settings. Before drawing some general conclusions, one further example is offered: an elaborated debate over whether a particular set of proscriptions should be treated in practice as mythic or as rational. The historians' dispute of 1985–1986 is a perspicuous case in which public intellectuals tried to seize control of a freighted cultural field and to transform the logic considered appropriate to it. This dispute, it follows from the argument just presented, is best understood as an attempt to transform a field of taboo into a field of prohibition and thus to alter the status of the issues contained therein and the conditions under which such constraints can be overcome.

The historians' dispute began with an exchange of articles in West Germany's major newspapers by a number of prominent historians and sociologists; it concerned the status of the Nazi past in German history and its implications for contemporary German identity.[20] On one side, archconservative Ernst Nolte (1987) argues that Auschwitz, the concentration camp that has become the metonym for the Holocaust, involved no greater evil than had occurred in many other places, from Turkish Armenia to Joseph Stalin's gulags. Also, implying that the Nazis had defensive motivations, Nolte referred to a 1939 declaration by Chaim Weizmann, leader of the European Zionists, that Jews would sympathize with the British and to Nazi statements that the Soviets would commit "Asiatic deeds" against Germany. Nolte's arguments — published in the *Frankfurter Allgemeine Zeitung*, one of Germany's leading daily newspapers — challenged the dominant orthodoxy of Holocaust interpretation, whereby the Holocaust was an event fundamentally different from all others in history and implying special burdens for Germany. Nolte's original formulations employed spurious evidence and were couched in an overtly inflammatory manner; other conservative historians — such as Andreas Hillgruber, Joachim Fest (editor of the *Frankfurter Allgemeine*), and Michael Stürmer (a former advisor to West German Chancellor Helmut Kohl) — pursued more carefully the goal of alleviating the unique status of the Holocaust through comparison.

On the opposite side, philosopher and sociologist Jürgen Habermas, among others, argued against this revisionism, which he saw both as an attempt to avoid collective responsibility through a misguided comparative historiography and as an expression of a wider-ranging neoconservative conspiracy (he used the term *conspiracy* to provoke) associated with the overall tenor of West German foreign and cultural policies since Kohl took office in 1982. Nolte's (1987) attempt to establish equivalences among the horrors of the twentieth century, Habermas (1987) argues, not only was factually misleading but obliterated moral differences. In crediting claims of defensive motivations for the "final solution," Nolte went even beyond making the Holocaust seem a "normal" part of political life; he appeared to be justifying the logic that brought it about. Even aside from this latter, extreme position, the urge toward "normalization," the desire for a "normal nation," had been potent at least since Schmidt's (1981) comment in Saudi Arabia that German policy should no longer be "held hostage" to Auschwitz and characterizes the entire period of West German cultural politics at least since 1982.

The historians' dispute generated a great deal of attention, both academic and public. The debate symbolically ended when President Richard von Weizsäcker delivered a speech to German historians in 1988 in which he indirectly supported most of Habermas's positions (Bulletin of the Press and Information Bureau of the Federal Government, #131, pp. 1185-88). Von Weizsäcker stated that Germany must face its historical responsibilities (though he used much of the traditional grammar of exculpation in his speech).

How do we explain this event and the resonance of the issue both inside and outside Germany among intellectuals and politicians alike? The debate presented no new historical evidence, nor were any of the positions especially new. The debate was significant because it concerned the ontological status of the Holocaust as a cultural constraint in German politics and involved an attempt to alter that status for the widest public.

Nolte and his supporters never argued that the past should be "forgotten," however spurious their desired "contextualization" would have been. Rather, they challenged constitutive elements of German political orthodoxy by trying to minimize the power of the Holocaust as a cultural referent. In other words, they tried to transform the hold of the Holocaust from taboo to prohibition.

German political culture, as we have seen, is powerfully constrained by the dominant and heretofore unquestionable interpretation of the Holocaust as a special burden for Germany. This interpretation has required a particular rhetoric from German leaders and a ritualized politics of regret. The most basic legitimacy claims of West German leaders — for themselves, for their government, and for their people — always involve highly specific acknowledgments of the past (Olick forthcoming; Rabinbach 1988). These requirements are largely taken for granted, and their performance has a ritual quality. In addition, as we already saw, the image of the Holocaust is present in almost every moment of German politics, domestic and international. Leaders may have worked to minimize or avoid it, but these attempts usually have resulted in peculiar symptoms, ranging from discomfort to defensiveness. A violation of the Holocaust as taboo always evokes significant reaction and a struggle to cope with the transgression.

In the historians' dispute, however, the neoconservatives' achievement was to treat the dominant role of the Holocaust in German politics no longer as an unpleasant or unavoidable mythic feature but as something open to rational challenge. Though they did not succeed in eliminating the Holocaust as a major referent for German political culture, they transformed it from a constraint that could only be obeyed or transgressed to one that could be investigated scientifically, debated rationally, and ultimately discussed much more easily. The neoconservative critics brought to the foreground the realm of interests that lies behind the absolute status of the Holocaust; they thus opened up the possibility of refutation, which is a less dangerous and ultimately less costly way to contravene it than transgression. Habermas may have won the debate, but the neoconservatives, as only a part of the wider political culture of relativization at the time, won the war — to make the legacy of the Holocaust a proposition rather than a taken-for-granted foundation. Taboos cannot be dealt with calmly; prohibitions can.

As the next chapters will show, the neoconservatives' success is manifest in the comparative ease of subsequent commemorations, especially those held ten years later on the fiftieth anniversary of the end of the war. At that time, Kohl's government stepped back somewhat from its more aggressive attempts to displace the Nazi period from German identity. Yet the highly ritualized acknowledgments they offered had become so routinized that the issue no longer had the same potential for conflict as before (Moeller 1996): The Federal Republic thus achieved "normalcy" with regard to its past, not without it.

In this way, the debates about immigration and the military of the late 1980s and early 1990s depended on that prior "rationalization" in the historians' dispute. In the context of the Gulf war, for instance, the hold of the German past was clearly delegitimated. If Germany made military or financial contributions to the international coalition against Iraq, it would be accused of belligerence — a dangerous image given its past. If Germany did not contribute, however, it would be accused of unreliability and irresponsibility. Subsequent debates over German participation in United Nations peacekeeping missions demonstrated as well that the German past created often unresolvable cross-pressures. The same is true of the immigration issue: The hold of the German past over the absolute right of asylum was seen to be irreconcilable with the high costs of economic refugees entering Germany in the late 1980s and 1990s.

The power of mythic constraints, or taboos, of the German past in the face of present exigencies has thus often produced complicated turns in German public discourse and policy. The historians' dispute, however, paved the way for characterizing the hold of the past as illegitimately constraining — that is, as a veil that hides and delegitimates strategic maneuvers. From this perspective, taboos are viewed as a way of concealing "real" power. Such a characterization, however, misses the nearly ubiquitous constitutive role of collective memory in political culture.

Conclusions

The goal of this chapter was to demonstrate that political cultures operate as historical systems of meaning — that is, as ordered but changing systems of claim-making — in which collective memory obliges the present (as prescription) and restricts it (as proscription) both mythically and rationally. Through an analysis of the Holocaust as a source of taboos and prohibitions — and of their positive correlates — in German politics, the foregoing analysis has specified different ways in which social pasts interact with social presents to shape political action.

The relationship between remembered pasts and constructed presents is one of perpetual but differentiated constraint and renegotiation over time, rather than pure strategic invention in the present or fidelity to, or inability to escape from, a monolithic legacy. As regards the role of political culture in political life generally, exigency and commitment, interest and ideal — that is, myth and rationality — are not entirely independent logics. They are two sides of a coin, mutually constitutive and, at the limit, each nonsensical without the other.

At what point should or does a past pass away? The answer depends in part on how different images of the past appear in and constrain political presents. The conceptual distinction between different kinds of constraint helps us understand how rules of political claim-making can be transformed over time. The illustrations from different moments in West German history show that the impact of the Holocaust unfolds in changing constellations. The possibility of removing the Holocaust as a focus for Germany's self-understanding — and for the way Germany is perceived by others — is thus located in a contested terrain on which mythical and rational images of the past sometimes work together and sometimes do battle, but these images always shape identity and its transformation. The possibility and the style of such transformation depend on the kinds of constraint that are operating.

The effects of German unification and Germany's central role in the European Community have created new challenges to the way the past is remembered and how it works as collective memory. These challenges, however, have a long and varied history; the accumulation and transformations of this history lie at the center of Germany's ongoing work to define what it is, what it can do, and what it should do. The analysis of political culture, as newly conceived, helps us to appreciate and untangle the complexities of that work, which involves a continuous negotiation between past and present. Collective memory is this negotiation rather than pure constraint by, or contemporary strategic manipulation of, the past. In response to Helmut Schmidt, therefore, it may be said that Germany is held hostage not by a taboo arising from Auschwitz but by the changing shapes of collective memory — the interplay of myth and rationality in shifting constellations — that give German political culture its particular, though changing, character.

CHAPTER 4

Genre Memories and Memory Genres

A Dialogical Analysis of May 8, 1945,
Commemorations in the Federal Republic
of Germany[1]

According to commemorative rhetoric, the past makes the present. Commemoration is a way of claiming that the past has something to offer the present, be it a warning or a model: In times of rampant change, the past provides a necessary point of reference for identity and action (Shils 1981). In contrast, the literature on social memory often emphasizes the importance of contextual factors in shaping commemorative practices and symbolism (Olick and Robbins 1998). Images of the past are malleable. Traditions are "invented" and memories are altered for instrumental reasons in the present (Hobsbawm and Ranger 1983). Social memories are subject to, and are products of, preproduction conflict and purposeful memory entrepreneurship (Wagner-Pacifici and Schwartz 1991). Producers, moreover, cannot control the ways in which images of the past are perceived (Savage 1994). Scholars therefore look at how people use memory to create identities and at how dominant narratives suppress alternative ones and view the past as a terrain on which competing groups struggle for position (Bodnar 1992; Foucault 1977). These accounts emphasize that commemoration is explainable in terms of its contemporary circumstances: The present, from this perspective, makes the past.

In reaction to this overwhelmingly presentist emphasis on the politics of memory and commemoration, some recent scholarship argues that mnemonic practices express neither the past nor the present but the changing interactions between past and present: Past meanings are malleable to varying degrees, and present circumstances exploit these potentials more or less. Schudson (1989, p. 105), for instance, argues that "the past is in some respects, and under some conditions, highly resistant to efforts to make it over." The structures of available pasts, of individual choice, and of social conflict limit our abilities in the present to alter images of the past. By exploring the potentials of past meanings for relevance in combination with an analysis of the needs of the present, we can explain why some pasts are suppressed whereas others are recovered or even invented, why some pasts persist little changed whereas others are altered beyond recognition. Outcomes reflect both the nature of the signified past and the needs of the present.

Changes in historical images, however, are not just one-time interactions between the meanings of the distant past and the needs of the present. Rather, from the moment being remembered, present images are constantly being reproduced, revised, and replaced. Many authors therefore trace the history of representations of the past over time. In doing so, however, we must not treat these histories as successions of discrete moments, one present-to-past relation after another; images of the past depend not only on the relationship between past and present but also on the accumulation of previous such relationships and their ongoing constitution and reconstitution.

Nevertheless, asserting in this way that images of the past are path-dependent is only the first step. What are the mechanisms of this path-dependency? How are images of the past constituted and reconstituted through time? Many authors (e.g, Schudson 1989; Schwartz 1991; Shils 1981) have identified relevant institutional mechanisms. Here I highlight the role of cultural processes in their own terms. To do this, I examine the history of one commemorative occasion — anniversaries of May 8, 1945, in the Federal Republic of Germany — through the lens of Mikhail Bakhtin's (1963, 1985, 1986; Bakhtin and Medvedev 1978) ideas about dialogism.[2] This approach, I demonstrate, provides useful concepts for specifying the cultural mechanisms of commemoration's path-dependency.

May 8, 1945, has long served as a decisive referent in German political culture. It poses a central question for German identity: Was Germany defeated or liberated on that date? Answers to that question have entailed an elaborate discourse within Germany's developing political–symbolic landscape and go to the heart of Germany's domestic and international image. The historical record of May 8, 1945, commemorations in the Federal Republic of Germany exemplifies commemoration's complex cultural path-dependency and is thus a perspicuous case with which to develop such a theory.

Immediately striking, for instance, is how sedate and unproblematic the fiftieth anniversary was compared with the fortieth: In 1985, commemorative issues erupted into an international controversy known as the Bitburg affair, and in the surrounding months West German public culture entered a period of profound moral and intellectual crisis. By 1995, however, the end of the cold war had radically altered the context of German identity: Though unified Germany faced a host of new problems, the circumstances of *Geschichtspolitik* (history politics) were less vexatious.

Changed context thus explains much about the change in commemoration. But this straightforward observation begs the question of how we separate commemoration from context, for part of the context for any new commemoration is the residue of earlier commemorations. Commemoration in 1995 was not only different from commemoration in 1985; it was also different in reference to 1985, although this reference was more implicit than explicit, more specter than spectacle. Bitburg was the name no official speaker dared utter for fear of awakening the demon, and even journalists drew the connections with great care. This does not change the fact that the 1995 commemoration was in part a reaction to the 1985 controversy as well as to earlier moments.

The 1995 commemoration of May 8, 1945, was not only a present product but also was a moment in an ongoing discourse, although the path of that discourse was far from straightforward. As discussed in previous chapters, "Each individual utterance," Bakhtin (1986, pp. 93–4) writes, "is a link in the chain of speech communion. Any utterance, in addition to its own theme, always responds (in the broad sense of the word) in one form or another to others' utterances that precede it." How, in particular, can we specify this central Bakhtinian claim in a case in which the response is silence?

Genre Memories and Memory Genres

As already discussed in chapter two, the central idea in Bakhtin's work is that of dialogue — the ongoing addressivity and historicity of language. All utterances take place within unique historical situations while at the same time containing "memory traces" of earlier usages, meaning not that any utterance can be decoded to reveal earlier usages but that the specificity of every term is the product of a long historical development. For Bakhtin, dialogical analysis requires taking into account both the span of "great time" as well as the "prosaic" unfolding of particular dialogues. Without the former, the historicity of the basic terms of the discourse is underemphasized; without the latter, their contingency is neglected. For Bakhtin, and for many sociological theorists who seek to balance or overcome the contradiction between determinism and contingency, historical trajectories are constitutive, but their influence is "unfinalizable": Path dependence is never path determination.

In regard to explicitly mnemonic practices, "great time" has been addressed by what is commonly called the *history of memory and commemoration*. Many authors call not for the history of specific traditions or images but for the history of mnemonic practices per se (Hutton 1993; Le Goff 1992; Matsuda 1996). How have our modes of historical apprehension changed? What forms are available? What do different technologies and media offer? Which are preferred? Differences between commemorations are not only a function of the politics of the present or of immediate historical precedents but also of the forms and media available in different moments. Comparing commemorations in terms of the history of memory thus helps explain their differences and leads to epochal insights about the status of commemoration as a social practice within particular societies. These are themes I take up again in the chapters constituting part two of this book, as well as more briefly here.

The second aspect of Bakhtin's dialogism concerns the prosaic unfolding of particular dialogues in and through time. Applying this principle to the sociology of memory, I identify what I call the *memory of commemoration*, and, by extension, *memory of memory*. Commemorations are not usually onetime occurrences but are often conceived from the beginning to endure (e.g., a "first annual" event) (Hobsbawm and Ranger 1983). The periodicity of a commemoration (e.g., once only, occasional, annual) is an important feature of its temporality, as are the numbers and sorts of occasions for remembering a particular past. Such features define in part how the commemoration relates to the present and the past. That past includes not only the history being commemorated but also the accumulated succession of commemorations, as well as what has occurred between those powerful moments.

In addition to these formal aspects, later commemorations often include more or less explicit references to or echoes of earlier commemorations. As already mentioned, Schwartz (1996) shows that John F. Kennedy's funeral was replete with symbolism from Abraham Lincoln's funeral. Sandage (1993) shows that Martin Luther King Jr.'s appearance at the Lincoln Memorial was reminiscent of Marian Anderson's appearance. Speakers often quote — with and without acknowledgment — speeches given by their predecessors on that or other occasions.

But references need not be explicit or conscious for earlier moments to affect later ones. For this reason, Bakhtin (1963) distinguishes *influence*— the explicit awareness of an earlier text by a subsequent one — from what he calls *genre contact*—the sharing of a common "way of seeing" between texts. "A genre," he writes, "possesses its own organic logic, which can to a certain extent be understood and creatively assimilated on the basis of a few generic models, even fragments" (ibid., p. 157). This understanding of genre highlights commemoration's role in producing its own circumstances, for earlier commemorations shape later ways of seeing, whether or not subsequent speakers are aware of any specific earlier commemoration. This does not mean that speakers are "cultural dopes" manipulated by or simply carrying out discourses but that the materials available to them in any context — materials they may transform — are historical accretions, the results of long developmental processes as well as of relational contexts rather than formally defined features of an atemporal system.

Bakhtin develops a concept of *genre* to identify "kinds" of utterances, which are historical accretions rather than ideal forms, the results of "a continuous and generative process implemented in the social-verbal interaction of speakers."[3] He distinguishes between "primary" genres like exclamation, apology, and demand and "secondary" genres like novel, play, and poem. I extend Bakhtin's *genre* concept to identify historically accrued types of utterances of a somewhat different order: patterns of speaking structured as a set of conventions against which or within which those utterances are produced and read.

Elsewhere (Olick 1999a, forthcoming), I have demonstrated that official images of the past in the Federal Republic of Germany developed into four distinguishable patterns centered around different occasions, taking place in different contexts, and employing distinct vocabularies, tropes, grammatical forms, and so on. Specifically, I identified *"normal legitimation," "German suffering," "German guilt,"* and *"German traditions"* genres structuring official German commemoration. In the present chapter, I treat May 8, 1945, commemorations as emblematic moments in the "German guilt" genre and explore the continuities and transformations in the way of speaking about, on, and through that occasion. This usage remains true to Bakhtin (1986, p. 152) because these groups or kinds of objects are, as he puts it, "practical" types defined "by the object, the goal, and the situation of the utterance" and because my account specifies the dialogical nature of the commemorative process: Genres are the central mechanisms of dialogue, "the drive belts from the history of society to the history of language" (ibid., p. 65).

Bakhtin's approach — with its axiomatic emphasis on dialogue and on genre as its central mechanism — thus provides a way of studying commemoration (and other processes) that simultaneously takes into account its conjunctural (politics of commemoration), developmental (history of commemoration), and dialogic (memory of commemoration) dimensions, all of which are essential to understanding long-standing discourses like

May 8, 1945 commemoration. To understand commemoration "generically" is to appreciate the organization of language and action without reifying or making it permanent, to see it as a fundamentally historical accomplishment: "A genre lives in the present, but always remembers its past, its beginning. Genre is a representative of creative memory in the process of literary development" (ibid., p. 121). By demonstrating a genre effect, we counter the tendency to see commemorative texts as wholly constituted either by the history to which they refer or by the present context in which they are produced.

May 8, 1945, in West German History

Many theorists of social memory and nationalism have demonstrated that recollection is a central part of defining and legitimating identities (Olick and Robbins 1998). For leaders in the Federal Republic of Germany, the Nazi past poses a significant rhetorical and institutional challenge: How do you speak for a nation held accountable not only for two devastating wars in one century but for what many consider to be the worst atrocities in human history? The different genres of official German speech about the Nazi past responded to the different aspects of the problem posed on different occasions and in different contexts.[4] Though all the genres have provided significant challenges — as well as solutions — to Germany's leaders, denying charges of collective guilt has been the most pressing task for every German leader over the last fifty years; it has been the linchpin of German legitimacy, both domestically and internationally (Olick 1999a, 2005; Olick and Levy 1997). The "German guilt" genre — including ways of speaking on anniversaries of November 9, 1938 (*Kristallnacht*), and September 1, 1939 (the invasion of Poland), as well as on official visits to concentration camps and to Israel — has thus been central. Within this genre, May 8, 1945, anniversaries are especially poignant because the occasion's central question — "May 8, 1945: Defeat or Liberation"— defines not only how to view the Nazi past but also how to view everything that came after it as well.

The events marked by the eighth of May pose a central paradox. World War II was an ever-increasing horror for the German people as well as for the rest of the world. With the unprecedented devastation wrought by the Nazi regime for Germans and for others, ordinary Germans felt released by the war's end, freed from tyranny or the suffering of war. At the same time, the fatherland they had patriotically defended and for which they had sacrificed so much lay destroyed, and the ruins of the Reich were at the mercy of a world it had mercilessly abused. The hardships of the immediate postwar period, combined with the military occupation and collective

Table 4.1 May 8, 1945: Defeat or Liberation?

Defeat		Liberation	
Benefits	**Costs**	**Benefits**	**Costs**
Justifies soldierly enthusiasm as ordinary patriotism	Associates ordinary Germans with Nazi regime	Distances ordinary Germans from Nazi regime	Disallows focus on German postwar suffering
Understand postwar suffering and division as victimization	Prevents satisfaction with postwar settlement	Makes Germans during the war victims of Nazis	Binds Germany to Western détente, sometimes at Germany's expense
Focuses attention on crimes committed by East after war	Implies burden of reparations	Places Germany clearly in the West	Delegitimizes proud German national identification
Allows pride in German patriotism and identity		Allows claim that Germany had a subterranean liberal tradition	

accusations of what to many seemed like a victor's justice, made defeat the obvious characterization for most people.[5]

According to the discourse (Table 4.1), if Germany was defeated then the Federal Republic is continuous with the Nazi regime that led the war and is responsible for its deeds. On the other hand, if Germany was liberated then the Federal Republic denies responsibility for the war but sacrifices the claim to patriotic duty that would exculpate the loyal soldier. Defeat leaves a traditional national identity intact, but that identity is associated with the Nazis; liberation makes Germans both victims of the Nazis and part of the victory against them, thereby erasing identification with the West but discrediting complaints about suffering that were essential to Germany's postwar self-perception (Moeller 1996).

This formal matrix, however, misleadingly freezes what has in fact been a living discourse. In what follows, I identify five moments in the generic development of the May 8 commemoration: (1) victimhood and the balanced trope in the 1950s; (2) the emphasis on liberation in the 1960s; (3) the demand for normalcy in the late 1970s; (4) relativization in the 1980s; and (5) a rhetoric of the new Germany in the 1990s (Table 4.2). These moments are comprehensible only as a combination of conjunctural, developmental, and prosaic factors, that is, in terms of the politics, history, and memory

Table 4.2 Periods of West German Rhetoric about the Commemoration of May 8, 1945

Period 1: Defeat, Liberation, and the German Victim
1949: Federal President Theodor Heuss
1955: Chancellor Konrad Adenauer
Period 2: Liberation and the Pan-European Future
1970: Federal President Gustav Heinemann and Chancellor Willy Brandt
Period 3: Normalcy and Normalization
1975: Federal President Walter Scheel and Chancellor Helmut Schmidt
Period 4: Normalization through Relativization
1985: Chancellor Helmet Kohl, U.S. President Ronald Reagan Federal President Richard von Weizsäcker
Period 5: Commemoration in the New Germany
1995: Federal President Roman Herzog and Chancellor Helmut Kohl

Chancellors	Federal Presidents[a]
Konrad Adenauer (CDU) 1949–1963	Theodor Heuss 1949–1959
Ludwig Erhard (CDU) 1963–1966	Heinrich Lübke 1959–1969
Kurt-George Kiesinger (CDU) 1966–1969	Gustav Heinemann 1969–1974
Willy Brandt (SPD) 1969–1974	Walter Scheel 1974–1979
Helmut Schmidt (SPD) 1974–1982	Karl Carstens 1979–1984
Helmut Kohl (CDU) 1982–1998	Richard von Weizsäcker 1984–1994
Gerhard Schröder (SPD) 1998–	Roman Herzog 1994–

[a] As symbolic leaders of the republic, Federal presidents give up their party affiliations.

of commemoration, respectively. This irreducible combination, I argue, is the central message of Bakhtin's dialogism, his response to both formalism and sociological reductionism in the analysis of discourse.

Period 1: Defeat, Liberation, and the German Victim

Speeches concerning May 8, 1945, were not common in the early years of the Federal Republic.[6] The history of German memory shows that any look at the past was exceedingly problematic for the early Federal Republic, given the taint of Nazi associations. Indeed, the Nazis' heavy reliance on public display discouraged postwar ceremony and symbolic politics. What to do about a flag or national anthem, for example, was contested (Hattenhauer 1990; Ortmeyer 1991); celebratory impulses pointed toward the future and the tasks of rebuilding. Indeed, avoidance of the past by focusing on the future characterizes the entire 1950s, a period referred to as the "economic miracle."[7] The miracle was not only that the society moved ahead economically but that in doing so it distracted itself from its past. This seemed to many at the time to have been a political necessity.

Of course, as Karl Marx pointed out, even — or precisely — in the most revolutionary moments new programs inevitably refer to old symbols and discourses. The defeat or liberation trope was one example of what Herf (1997) refers to as the "multiple restorations" of German society after the war. How to characterize May 8 was tied up with older memories: of the defeat in 1918 that resulted in the legend that Germany had been "stabbed in the back" by the Treaty of Versailles signatories; of pre-1945 political traditions that were touchstones for the ideologies of Germany's new leaders; of perceptions of Germany held by its former enemies before and during the war; of the still-relevant Nazi rhetoric about the need to defeat Bolshevism. Genres, including the "German guilt" genre, clearly have no absolute beginning or end.

The trope of defeat or liberation was widespread in public discourse in various forms immediately after the war and drew on these older memories. Nevertheless, because I deal with official rhetoric of the West German state, it makes sense to start at its beginning: the closing of the *Parlamentarischer Rat* (constitutional convention) on May 8, 1949, which lay the foundation for the new West German State. In his concluding speech to the convention, future Federal president Theodor Heuss stated, "In essence this eighth of May remains the most tragic and questionable paradox of history for each of us. But why? Because we were at once saved and destroyed...." At the time, however, there was no official marking of the occasion, certainly no celebration. In the context of postwar depredations, few saw May 8 as a happy occasion, despite Heuss's careful assessment.[8] Moreover, the third reading and final approval of the Basic law occurred on the same date; thus, attention was focused forward rather than backward. This is an example of what Reichel (1995, p. 276) refers to as "the grace of the calendar," implying that this displacement of an opportunity for commemoration by a celebration of the future was too much and too often a part of German symbolic politics in this period to have been a mere coincidence. Indeed, West German leaders discussed whether to celebrate May 8 or September 7 (the day in 1949 on which the *Bundestag* assembled for the first time) as the national holiday, deciding in favor of the latter. September 7 was celebrated until 1954, when it was replaced by June 17, marking the 1953 uprising in East Germany.[9] In a speech on the first national holiday on September 7, 1950, Heuss expressed regret over not using May 8 as a way to connect the defeat of 1945 and the achievement of 1949, but his perspective was unusual; others preferred to avoid such connections.

The tenth anniversary of May 8 in 1955 also saw no official commemoration.[10] In the intervening years, the Federal Republic had pursued a course of faithful integration into the Western alliance, negotiated a reparations agreement with Israel, and played up its present reliability as evidence that West Germany deserved equal status in the "community of nations." In 1955, the political leadership was preoccupied with the end of the occupation and the return of sovereignty, which took place on May 5, 1955. Once more, contemporary events and an orientation to the future overshadowed the pull of recollection.

This moment, however, was a unique opportunity for synthesizing both defeat and liberation into a more productive narrative for the Federal Republic: 1945 was a defeat, whereas 1955 could be seen as the beginning of liberation. In his memoirs, Chancellor Konrad Adenauer (1966, p. 432) wrote about the 1955 occasion as follows: "I considered the day of winning back sovereignty to be a great day in German history. Ten years before, Germany collapsed and ceased to exist as a self-governing state. It was the darkest hour of our fatherland." This formulation preserved the advantages of defeat while implying coming benefits of liberation. Allocating the two sides of the trope to different dates allowed the Federal Republic a proud place in the Western alliance and a new history of West German diligence without precluding complaints about the occupation years and the benefits of a victim identity. This formulation of the Federal Republic's sovereignty as a liberation — albeit a liberation from postwar occupation as much as from the Nazis — provided an important reference point for later May 8, 1945, speeches that view German suffering as belonging to an earlier and no longer relevant era. At the same time, viewing the return of sovereignty as liberation reproduced the basic conceptual framing of the day as a paradox.

The first official published statement about May 8, 1945, after Heuss's speech — and the only one before the coalition changes of the mid 1960s — was an unsigned article in the *Bulletin of the Press and Information Agency* in 1965 — the twentieth anniversary. This article also presents Heuss's paradox as the defining feature of this date for Germans: "Re-winning of Freedom and national collapse with all of its consequences — both are connected to this day." The statement argues that "no good German could have wished for the victory of the National Socialists. But the approval of the defeat as prerequisite for a worthy continued existence demanded the readiness to accept that the entire hate fomented by the crimes of the regime also falls upon the innocent." This statement combines costs and benefits in a rather bitter formulation: "Good Germans" have to accept liberation in principle, but in doing so they make themselves martyrs, as Germany's former enemies condemned these "good" or at least "innocent" people along with the "real" perpetrators. For a German to do the right thing — to accept the liberation thesis — meant an almost heroic forbearance of history's injustice as manifest in reeducation, denazification, division, and expulsion.

Period 2: Liberation and the Pan-European Future

By the twenty-fifth anniversary in 1970, the Federal Republic had emerged from its first period, which was characterized by its focus on German suffering, avoidance of individual and collective guilt, integration with the West, a hard line toward the East, absolving the debt to Israel and Jews (accompanied by an official philo-Semitism), and an emphasis on economic recovery that conceived of 1945 as a "zero hour," a decisive caesura between old and new. This core of the first epoch's character had been eroding since the late 1950s. A wave of anti-Semitic vandalism in 1959–1960, combined with the celebrated stage adaptation of the *Diary of Anne Frank* and the grisly Frankfurt Auschwitz trials of 1963–1966, contributed to a generational frisson, awakening those born during or after the war to the burdens of their parents' cohort and the associated historical aversions of the 1950s. This new generation demanded a thoroughgoing reevaluation of their state's political identity, questioning the issue of responsibility and the metaphor of the "zero hour." Social structural changes associated with this new generation's coming of age led to demands for a more radical democratization that included attacks on the elitist educational system, much like those in the rest of Western Europe at this time. Perhaps most important, the erection of the Berlin wall in 1961, combined with a general economic downturn, delegitimated Adenauer's policy of strict integration with the West.

These conditions, among others, overdetermined the political changes of the mid 1960s. In 1963, the Social Democrats entered a grand coalition with the ruling Christian Democrats, and their young charismatic leader, Foreign Minister Willy Brandt, clearly overshadowed the old-fashioned Christian Democratic chancellor, Kurt-Georg Kiesinger.[11] By 1969, the Social Democrats had taken over the leadership in coalition with the liberal Free Democrats, and Chancellor Brandt pursued a new *Ostpolitik* — aiming at rapprochement with the East, even if it meant renouncing immediate unification and claims on former territories — that he had begun as foreign minister. Additionally, the new president, Gustav Heinemann, had been a vocal pacifist since the rearmament debates of the early 1950s and had been critical of Adenauer's policies.

The 1960s generation and its leaders were not prone to the same sense of loss and victimization that had dominated their parents; they related to the events differently.[12] Shifts in generation, policy line, and leadership thus allowed for a new interpretation of May 8. Indeed, the new leaders took May 8 as a particularly good venue for articulating their rejection of the earlier profile, and they officially commemorated the date for the first time. Although it was new to mark the occasion with a direct commemoration — rather than with a reference in another context — that direct kind of commemoration was not without generic resources that were available from other discursive contexts and from the indirect discourse.

The lack of an official commemoration earlier, moreover, was part of the general tendency to avoid symbolic politics in the first period of the Federal Republic's history, a consideration deriving from Bakhtin's call to examine the "great time" of genres. Over time, all four of the different official commemorative genres were more clearly demarcated, more directly associated with particular dates, and marked with increasingly ritualistic regularity. On the other hand, the high costs of both the defeat and liberation arguments in the 1950s contributed in a unique manner to the lack of official commemoration: German guilt was certainly harder to discuss in the 1950s than, for instance, German suffering, which did not raise the same kinds of moral problems for ordinary Germans.

In 1970, in the first official speech commemorating May 8, Federal president Gustav Heinemann clearly locates the horror before 1945, not after as had been common in the 1950s. In pointing to the future, Heinemann rejected the defeatist position, arguing that mourning the past is a useless and outdated enterprise:

> We know today that it does not lead forward to mourn what is lost and that it is now above all a matter of bringing the task of reconciliation also with the East to completion. This applies for those who themselves experienced the Second World War with its horrors as well as for the members of our young generation for whom this is only an historical but no longer a personal memory.

Without spending much time attributing causes or describing historical realities, Heinemann pointed to the general imperatives of pursuing a politics of peace, stating that "only in that way can we stand up in face of the meaningless death of all victims of the last war and of the terror." Like earlier speakers on a variety of occasions, Heinemann included Germans among the victims. But in contrast to his conservative predecessors, he neither placed them first nor seemed concerned with the particularities of victimhood, German or otherwise (Moeller 1996). This generalization of victimhood responds to the earlier focus on German suffering by making it as inexplicit as that of the Jews. Thus, he prepared the ground for a reformulated *grammar of exculpation* in the 1980s, one based on a relativization not only of the victims but of the perpetrators as well.

Brandt also delivered a significant address to the *Bundestag* on this occasion in 1970. Like Heinemann, he spoke less about the past than about the present and future. In a remarkable departure, Brandt acknowledged a connection between suffering during the war and suffering after the war, although he characterized victimhood as universal. Brandt then turned to his general goal of peace by discussing the pressing situations in Southeast Asia and the Middle East, making clear that he saw the warning of World War II in much more than its German–Jewish dimensions. Although not as unequivocal as Heinemann, Brandt saw May 8 primarily as a day of liberation: "For the majority of Germans … the chance for a new beginning, for the creation of a constitutional and democratic relation grew." Nonetheless, according to Brandt, 1945 was a terrible time for Germany: "Seldom was Germany a more difficult fatherland than in the year 1945."[13]

One of Brandt's main concerns while pursuing rapprochement with East Germany was the implication for German national identity. Though rejecting ethnocultural categories of the German people or "*Kulturnation*" (cultural nation), Brandt nonetheless emphasized the continued perception among the populace that some German national identity persisted, despite the difficulties of 1945. He characterized it as an achievement that this perception is still strong. Brandt's assertions of continued national identity went to his argument about the importance of rapprochement with the East. In an explicit attempt to connect this occasion to contemporary geopolitical debates — while echoing a widespread portrayal of World War II in its international context as the product of what conservatives referred to as a "European civil war" — Brandt stated, "The two world wars of our century had their origins in the rivalries between the European powers." Therefore, the Federal Republic vigorously pursued European cooperation, which is " … the most promising result of the tragic occurrences of the year 1945." And, he added, "only a European peace order will be able to draw a final line (*Schlußstrich*) under the history that is for us Germans connected to the year 1945."

Thus, Brandt used this commemorative occasion to argue for his general foreign policy agenda, constructing May 8 as a resource for his position, the symbol of a turn in German history that is only now being realized. In contrast to earlier, conservative rhetoric, Brandt characterized May 8, 1945, as a tragedy rather than an injustice, avoiding any overtone of belligerence. His words thus responded ("in the broad sense of the word") to earlier formulations, reproducing the matrix of possibilities the genre poses even as he favors previously avoided choices.

Period 3: Normalcy and Normalization

By the thirtieth anniversary in 1975, Brandt, but not the Social Democrats, had fallen from power. His chancellorship was, at least in part, the victim of great trepidation about making concessions to the East. The new chancellor, Helmut Schmidt, was a thoroughgoing pragmatist who pursued a more moderate strategy of reform within a climate much less optimistic than that surrounding Brandt's accession to power.[14] Schmidt often characterized the problems facing West Germany as identical to those facing other Western states; this characterization was the beginning of a rhetoric of "normalization" that became pervasive in the 1980s.

Additionally, Walter Scheel had succeeded Heinemann as Federal president in 1974, only nine days after Brandt's resignation. Like Schmidt, Scheel employed a more moderate tone. However, in stark contrast to Heinemann's very reserved stance toward the development of the Federal Republic, Scheel injected a tone of pride in both German and West German history. Moreover, he matched Schmidt's emphasis on the "normalcy" of the Federal Republic in facing the global problems of the welfare state in the 1970s. More than Schmidt, however, Scheel introduced emerging neoconservative elements into his rhetoric, including the exhaustion of the welfare state, moderate to strong patriotism, and the importance of historical consciousness.

Scheel's thirtieth anniversary speech received much less notice — indeed, not much notice at all — compared with that of President Richard von Weizsäcker ten years later, though it was in many ways similar, and von Weizsäcker drew on Scheel's speech explicitly. This difference in reception demonstrates vividly the importance of timing and context, but it also shows that ideas and arguments that are at some point successful or praised, or vilified, do not spring from thin air. They are instances in longer-standing genres that provide a horizon of terms, positions, and general precedents. Like von Weizsäcker's speech, Scheel's speech is but one moment in an ongoing dialogue, sharing perceptions with both prior and subsequent statements in the genre.

In his 1975 address, Scheel provided a carefully balanced assessment of Germany's defeat and spends at least as much time examining the past as the present and future. For Scheel, Germans must be ambivalent about their nation's defeat. He acknowledged that Germany's former opponents celebrate the day and argues that "we were freed from a terrible yoke, from war, murder, bondage, and barbarism. And we exhaled when the end came." However, " … we do not forget that this liberation came from outside … " According to Scheel, too much of importance for Germany was destroyed along with the Third Reich for Germans to have wished for that defeat:

> ... [O]n the eighth of May not only the Hitler dictatorship fell, the German *Reich* fell too. The German *Reich* was not a work of Hitler's, it was the state of the Germans, the work of a great German statesman [Bismarck]. It was for generations of Germans the fatherland that we loved as every person in the world loves his fatherland.

Scheel's point is that German patriotism is no different from patriotism elsewhere in the world and that it was right to have wanted to protect that fatherland, no matter who was at the helm: "Should we love it less because a dictator took it over, or because it now lay destroyed on the ground?" Germans have no occasion to celebrate; the paradox of the day remains potent.

Scheel called the day one of self-examination. It was important, he said, that Germany acknowledge its entire history. He began in 1933, the year in which, he said, " ... the German tragedy begins ... not in 1945," thus indicating a greater willingness than earlier speakers to accept the Nazi regime as part of German history. Adolf Hitler's victory in 1933, he said, " ... was no inescapable fate. He was elected." This admission is a departure from most earlier speakers, who emphasized that Hitler never gained a majority of votes in "free" elections. Scheel also denied the argument that people were not aware of the dangers in the years leading up to 1933: "The shaky hope that an all-promising seducer could nonetheless perhaps help us out of the worst suffering got the better of the perceptual ability, of critique, and also of fear." In a significant departure, Scheel thus acknowledged that the general populace played a role in the horrible machinery of war and destruction. There was some responsibility for having closed eyes and ears, but not for more insidious motives. Thus, Scheel rejected collective guilt, but not the possibility of individual guilt, which earlier seemed to have been swept away with the former: "The question of guilt? Whether he wants to feel guilty about it, or ashamed of it, this every German who lived as a responsible person in this time may alone as an individual settle with himself."

Scheel addressed those who " ... want to hear nothing more about our dark past." Such a position had gained popularity among conservatives, who saw themselves as finally having the courage to respond to the so-called sixty-eighters, whose fascination with the past and with the complicity of their parents' generation had produced a tremendous discourse on German guilt. Many conservatives in the 1970s saw calls for a "mastering" of the past (*Vergangenheitsbewältigung*) as an insidious feature of New Left ideology — a sort of national self-flagellation — and sought to reformulate this term as a code word for German self-hatred, a condition that undermined a positive identity.

In response to those who claim that historical commemorations like May 8 involve having young Germans "run around in sackcloth and ashes because crimes were committed in which they had no part," Scheel argued that such critics missed the point. Though it would not make sense, he said, to demand that young Germans atone for things that happened before they were born, "all words of a national dignity, of self-respect remain hollow if we do not take on ourselves the entire often enough pressing weight of our history." To win back the national honor lost in 1933, the contravention of all that was "good and noble in the history of our people," Scheel argued, "Germany must accept this dark history." Thus, Scheel's speech was a sharp rebuke to the extreme calls for forgetting that had appeared in the public discourse, just as von Weizsäcker's would be ten years later in the context of Bitburg. But, according to neoconservative principles, Scheel also sought positive elements of German tradition, including concepts like the German Reich. Scheel offered a multifaceted formulation that incurred the costs and enjoys the benefits from both liberation and defeat arguments.

In 1975, Schmidt also gave a brief commemorative address. By this time, the issues for such a speech were well established. Schmidt began by characterizing the day as one of " ... liberation from National Socialist domination." However, he was more defensive than Scheel. Though taking almost verbatim from Scheel an acknowledgment that Germany's former opponents are justified in celebrating the day, he did not say that Germany cannot celebrate as well. Rather, he characterized May 8 as an occasion to inquire into what Germany has made out of the catastrophe, echoing the displacement of defeat to history and liberation to the future seen in 1955 interpretations.

Schmidt's assessment was, not surprisingly, overwhelmingly positive, though defensively so. For instance, Schmidt argued that it is " ... a mistaken judgment if some few still suspect us or impute that we understand the day of unconditional capitulation as a day of mourning for the defeat of Hitler." Instead, Schmidt argued that Germany did indeed mourn on that day, but for the victims rather than for Hitler or even, as Scheel did, for the Reich.[15] Nonetheless, Schmidt expressed the wish to move away from the costs of this mourning: "We Germans," he said, "therefore do not need to go around in hair shirts in perpetuity."[16] He placed greater emphasis here on a generational defense than other speakers did, though all recent speakers included it, if more briefly on this occasion than elsewhere. He said, "The great majority of the Germans living today were born only after 1933; they can in no way be burdened with guilt." He pointed out as well that no member of the presently sitting government was old enough to vote in 1933.

Focusing on the long-term generic features of commemoration, the lack of reaction to this comment is telling. In 1984, during a trip to Israel, Chancellor Helmut Kohl set off an international controversy when he claimed during a speech to have the "grace of a late birth" (*Gnade der späten Geburt*). In this context, Kohl was accused of claiming that he, and Germans younger than he, bore no responsibility for history.[17] This comparison shows that reaction is not always proportional to novelty. Part of a very different context, Schmidt's comments were apparently not as portentous. Nevertheless, the similarity between Kohl's and Schmidt's formulations shows that Kohl's comments cannot be interpreted solely in terms of their context: The formulation was a more general and long-standing genre resource.

In conclusion, Schmidt emphasized "that element that today binds us with the former war opponents of National Socialist Germany; the peace politics that arises from the knowledge that war as the continuation of politics by other means is a useless, an inhumane instrument." Schmidt thus echoed Adenauer's Western integrationist rhetoric from the 1950s, responding, in part, to powerful anti-American and anti-North Atlantic Treaty Organisation (NATO) sentiments in his own party, although he coupled this rhetoric with Brandt's *détente* rhetoric. In comparison to Brandt, however, Schmidt's focus on the past was more defensive and included German victimhood more prominently. And though Brandt used the occasion as a resource in arguing for his *Ostpolitik*, Schmidt appeared to understand any particular attention to the occasion as a constraint, at least insofar as it raised guilt feelings within Germany or special suspicions from others about Germany's "normal" foreign policy role. Schmidt used May 8 to argue the Federal Republic's claim to equal partnership. The long-standing liberation trope helped shape that argument, but Schmidt seemed to prefer that the entire issue disappear.[18]

Period 4: Normalization through Relativization

The Schmidt government and the Scheel presidency did not survive the continued economic downturn and the increased tensions between the United States and Soviet Union in the beginning of the 1980s. In 1982, Christian Democrat leader Kohl became chancellor, in part by advocating a broad-ranging change of tone that included proposing two new historical museums, courting ultraconservative fringes, renewing a strong rhetoric toward the East, and using a general language of patriotic pride. Kohl pursued a symbolic rehabilitation of German identity and history that demanded from Western powers a gesture of forgiveness for the Nazi past — indeed, of forgetting it.

Events surrounding the fortieth anniversary of May 8, 1945, were centrally involved in this neoconservative cultural program. The main issue here is the so-called Bitburg affair, although the matter spread into the surrounding public discourse.[19] The beginning of the controversy goes back at least to June 1984, when the Western Allies from World War II celebrated the fortieth anniversary of D-Day in Normandy. Chancellor Kohl was not invited to participate in that ceremony. From the perspective of West Germany's neoconservative leadership, this symbolic exclusion provided an undesirable image, indicating continued limitations on Germany's equal status. After forty years of democratic stability, this seemed unfair to many West German politicians and commentators: History should no longer limit West Germany's political equality. With this ceremony in mind, Kohl sought a gesture to indicate West Germany's upgraded stature, its freedom from the constraints of a burdened past.

One such symbolic demonstration came in September 1984, when French president Francois Mitterrand and Chancellor Kohl conducted a ceremony at the World War I French–German military cemetery at Verdun. Mitterrand and Kohl held hands over the graves to show that their countries had overcome the antipathy that had been so horribly expressed in World War I.

During a trip to Washington, D.C., in November 1984, Kohl suggested to U.S. president Ronald Reagan that, as part of a trip to an economic summit in Europe in the spring of 1985, Reagan should visit a German military cemetery — and perhaps also a concentration camp — as a gesture showing that the alliance between the United States and West Germany was one of equals, unencumbered by residues of past conflicts. This occurred after Kohl had fought hard, against substantial internal opposition, for deployment of intermediate-range nuclear missiles on West German soil. In that meeting, Reagan said that he did not want to go to a concentration camp: "I don't think we ought to focus on the past," he said, "I want to focus on the future. I want to put that history behind me" (Hartmann 1986, p. xii).

At the end of January 1985, the White House announced that President Reagan would commemorate the fortieth anniversary of V-E day together with Chancellor Kohl during Reagan's trip to Europe. German and American officials settled on the military cemetery at Bitburg, which was near a U.S. air base. A bit later, Reagan announced that he would not be visiting a concentration camp as part of the "reconciliation" with Germany. Reagan argued that young Germans who had not lived through the Nazi period were saddled with an unnecessary sense of guilt that he did not want to reinforce with such a visit.

Reagan's comments in this announcement offended many. In the United States, Jewish groups and veterans' groups objected strenuously to Reagan's plans, which were immediately placed under White House review. In response, Kohl cabled Washington to point out that the original discussion between him and Reagan had included plans for a visit to Dachau. But the problem became more difficult: It was revealed that in addition to "normal" *Wehrmacht* soldiers, members of the *Waffen-SS* were also buried at Bitburg.[20]

Reagan's response to the controversy was to agree to lay a wreath at a concentration camp. At about the same time, fifty-three U.S. senators petitioned him not to go to Bitburg. In a press conference, Reagan responded in harsh terms, arguing that "those young men are victims of Nazism also ... They were victims, just as surely as the victims in the concentration camps." Despite all the years of denial, defense, and construction of Germans as victims in the German discourse, such a bald elision of distinctions was something that would never have been dared by a West German leader, whatever the sentiments. Reagan thus made even clearer than Kohl exactly what was at issue here, though Reagan's remarks cannot be disconnected from the long discourse on the German past.

On April 21, 1985, Kohl gave an unusually forthcoming address during an unrelated visit to Bergen-Belsen. This speech, of course, cannot be separated from its context, a context in which it was important that Kohl make a gesture to critics. In contrast to the repressive rhetoric of the 1950s (which sought to limit responsibility) and that of the 1960s (which accepted a highly generalized responsibility), this speech indicates a new solution—to "accept" responsibility while emptying it of political content. In other words, Kohl seemed to accept — as Scheel did ten years earlier and as von Weizsäcker would perfect a month later — all of the options shown in Table 4.1 without seeing the contradictions, arguing that the costs have long since been paid.

Kohl thus uncharacteristically specified Jews as victims and mentioned German indifference to the crimes as they were happening. "Reconciliation with the bereaved, and the descendants of the victims," he said, "is only possible if we accept our history as it truly was: our shame, our responsibility before history." Kohl spoke of a "never expiring shame," but he connected this to a view of German suffering as well by stating clearly that May 8, 1945, was a day of liberation. And he employed characteristic equivocations: Germans risked their lives to help Jews; Germans themselves suffered under the Nazis — suffering occurred "not only in the concentration camps" — the Nazi period was just one "chapter" of German history; the "holocaust" was a human, not a German or Jewish, tragedy ("... that merciless war that man basically declared upon himself"). Germany acknowledges its historical responsibility, but it is unclear how Germany differs in this regard from all members of the "community of nations."

In a subsequent address to the *Bundestag* defending the upcoming Bitburg visit, Kohl gave an account of the controversy's history. He began with the Allied celebration of D-Day and said that he understood why he was not invited and had no interest in taking part. Nevertheless, in discussing the matter with his French colleagues, Kohl said, he inquired about the possibility of acknowledging through some symbolic gesture — some form of "reconciliation over the graves"— that the antipathies of past generations had been overcome through great achievements in recent European history. This, according to Kohl, was the origin of the Verdun ceremony; it was not supposed to answer Germany's exclusion from the Normandy celebration. These remarks, then, appear to be an attempt to control the memory of commemoration, which can be variable and contested.

The idea of a similar ceremony with the United States, according to Kohl, came about because he and Reagan wanted "to honor the fallen of all peoples at a military cemetery, not only the fallen of our people, not only the fallen young Americans, rather all victims of the Second World War." About the *Waffen-SS* soldiers buried at Bitburg, Kohl argued that such soldiers are buried at virtually every German military cemetery and that it is necessary to avoid generalizing judgments, even regarding the SS. Kohl argued that most of the members of the *Waffen-SS's* fighting units were draftees, many of them extremely young. Therefore they bore, according to Kohl, no special responsibility for the horrors of the Holocaust. He argued vociferously against " … undifferentiated judgment … [and] unbearable collective accusations …."

It is important to note what Kohl means by "undifferentiated judgment." Adenauer used this term in the 1950s to argue against collective guilt. It implied that grouping together ordinary Germans, opportunists, enthusiastic Nazis, and the major decision makers — the only ones, in Adenauer's argument, who were rightfully held responsible — was illegitimate and vindictive. In the present context, Kohl had thus revived an argument from the immediate postwar period, but he had refined the argument through the crucible of universalizing rhetoric from the 1960s and 1970s. Where Heinemann, Brandt, and Schmidt avoided differentiating the victims, Kohl then built on their formulations — by echoing Adenauer's — to avoid differentiating the perpetrators or even differentiating perpetrators from victims in general: "Reconciliation between former war adversaries has been reached when we are capable of mourning for people independently of which nation the murdered, fallen and dead once belonged to. We demonstrated this at Verdun. We want to demonstrate it at Bitburg."

On May 5, 1985, Reagan's visit to Bitburg came off as planned, including the addition of a brief wreath-laying ceremony at Bergen-Belsen. The addresses included remarks by both Reagan and Kohl at Bergen-Belsen, a statement by Kohl at the Bitburg cemetery, and one by Reagan at the American air base. All appearances were met with significant protests, but all followed the script laid out in the previous weeks. The differences between Kohl's restrained rhetoric and Reagan's seemingly indiscriminate historical view is interesting and probably not entirely accidental. Reagan does his job with flying colors, saying what Kohl might have wanted to say but did not dare. In sum, Kohl seems to have gotten what he wanted. On the other hand, the preceding controversies, the on-site protests, and the memory of it as a debacle combined to demonstrate exactly the opposite of what Kohl was trying to establish: the "normalcy" of German history.

Three days after Bitburg, Federal president Richard von Weizäcker delivered a major address in the *Bundestag* during a ceremony commemorating the fortieth anniversary of May 8, 1945. This address became perhaps the most noted of all the speeches on the past in the forty years of West German history. More than 1.5 million copies were distributed, and the speech garnered an enormous public response, both domestically and internationally. The speech was comprehensive, touching on most of the major interpretive issues in debates about the Nazi past. Von Weizäcker argued for truthfulness about the responsibility for history. The speech offered something for everyone — a catalogue of themes and images from previous commemorations — and provided a useful formula for future commemorations as the speech integrated previous solutions while avoiding their difficulties. Like Scheel, and more like Kohl than commentators acknowledged, von Weizäcker made it seem unnecessary to choose among the alternatives that the prior discourse offered.

Von Weizäcker began with the basic question of Germany's attitude toward the unconditional surrender and its aftermath. He argued that different nations necessarily bear different relations to May 8. "For us," he said, "the 8th of May is above all a date to remember what people had to suffer. It is also a date to reflect on the course taken by our history. The greater honesty we show in commemorating this day, the freer we are to face the consequences with due responsibility. For us Germans, May 8th is not a day of celebration." Nonetheless, it is also a day of liberation. He argued explicitly against judging the day on the basis of how much Germans suffered: "Nobody will, because of that liberation, forget the grave suffering that only started for many people on May 8th." On the other hand, he followed Scheel in rebuking those who "regard the end of the war as the cause of flight, expulsion, and deprivation of freedom. The cause goes way back to the start of tyranny that brought about the war. We must not separate May 8th, 1945, from January 30th, 1933."

If May 8 is not a day of celebration, von Weizäcker argued, it is a day for remembering the vast suffering associated with the war, although German suffering still comes first. "Today," he said, "we mourn for all the dead of the war and tyranny." He listed the Jews, all the nations who fought (including the Soviet Union) German soldiers and citizens, the gypsies, homosexuals, the mentally ill, those who were politically persecuted, resistance fighters in occupied lands, as well as the many different kinds of German resistance. Thus, he grouped all the victims together under one umbrella, but his inclusiveness sounded more like Brandt's than Kohl's — that is, he was more interested in commemorating suffering than in eliminating the commemoration.

On the one hand, von Weizäcker struck a balance between attributing blame to a small clique and to the population at large: "At the root of the tyranny was Hitler's immeasurable hatred against our Jewish compatriots." And, he said, "the perpetration of this crime was in the hands of a few people. It was concealed from the eyes of the public." Von Weizäcker thus echoed the simplistic "intentionalist" thesis of the 1950s. On the other hand, he was not willing to stop here, as so many other speakers over the years had. Nor is what he added an exculpation. Indeed, he began by saying that "Hitler had never concealed this hatred from the public, but made the entire nation a tool of it." He then went on to offer an indictment of all those who claim that they did not know:

> ... [E]very German was able to experience what his Jewish compatriots had to to suffer, ranging from plain apathy and hidden intolerance to outright hatred. Who could remain unsuspecting after the burning of the synagogues, the plundering, the ceaseless violation of human dignity? Whoever opened his eyes and ears and sought information could not fail to notice that Jews were being deported.... When the unspeakable truth of the Holocaust then became known at the end of the war, all too many of us claimed that they had not known anything about it or even suspected anything.

Thus, von Weizäcker did not follow the easy road of distancing that so many of his generation pursued. These were harsh words assaulting many a repressed memory, echoing Scheel's unnoticed effort ten years earlier.[21] Kohl, as well, made similar statements at Bergen-Belsen, but there is a crucial difference between making such a statement in a concentration camp and addressing it to the nation and world.

What is the implication of this acknowledgment, which targets a basic national memory myth? It is not, according to von Weizäcker, to embrace notions of collective guilt, for guilt is an individual matter: "There is no such thing as the guilt or innocence of an entire nation. Guilt is, like innocence, not collective but personal. Everyone who directly experienced that era should today quietly ask himself about his involvement then." Of course, the younger generation is not subject to this call for self-examination: "No discerning person can expect them to wear a penitential robe simply because they are Germans." Who was demanding a penitential robe and what that would entail is not entirely clear, although the formulation had been around for a while.

Nevertheless, von Weizäcker did not argue that the past is no longer relevant to the younger generations: "All of us, whether guilty or not, whether old or young, must accept the past. We are all affected by its consequences and liable for it." Thus, there could be no final adjudication, no so-called *Schußstrich* (final line): "It is not a case of coming to terms with the past. That is not possible. It cannot be subsequently modified or made not to have happened. However, anyone who closes his eyes to the past is blind to the present. Whoever refuses to remember the inhumanity is prone to new risks of infection." Von Weizäcker thus promised that the revisions of the previous year would not mean an end to ritualistic acknowledgment.

Von Weizsäcker's address had an eloquent moral tone and was highly praised around the world as a fresh wind in a West German discourse that had attracted criticism for its apparent attempts to minimize the past. The center hailed the speech as particularly honest, balanced, and even courageous. However, some argued that there was nothing special in it. Grosser (1985, p. 340), for instance, writes that "every time it is said that there is finally true consciousness in the Federal Republic, whereby it is forgotten every time that this consciousness had already existed before—and at particular points in time especially intensively."[22] Public commentary has a short memory, whereas speakers seem well attuned to the generic resources and constraints of commemoration.

The speech was well received by the moderate left, which hypothesized that it indicated a split between von Weizsäcker and Kohl. That is, von Weizsäcker's argument for the importance of continued painful memory was seen as a rebuke to Kohl's "grace of a late birth" comment. To maintain this reading, Kohl's Bergen-Belsen speech, which resembled von Weizsäcker's in many respects, was dismissed as a strategic move in the context of Bitburg, or as Maier (1988) puts it, evidence of Kohl's willingness to use history for immediate purposes no matter what the contradictions, forming a malleable postmodern hodgepodge rather than a consistent theory of history. But von Weizsäcker's theory appears to be the true hodgepodge: Where Kohl replaced one set of blinders for another when expedient, von Weizsäcker attempted to hold all arguments simultaneously in view.

For many, the speech settled the disturbances of the previous months of providing a formula for an older, more mature Federal Republic to get on with things. The new commemorative regime was now past the struggle: "Responsibility before history" was a palatable trope and could be deployed without the fuss of old struggles — it demands nothing other than ritual acknowledgment. Indeed, this is what happened through German unification in general, and on the fiftieth anniversary of May 8 in particular. But this smoother ritualism was possible only after the difficult moment of 1985 had passed. In that moment, von Weizsäcker settled the internal contradictions and external costs of the genre by providing a new synthesis in which no one felt left out. On this basis, commemoration could occur without opening up so many partisan wounds.

Period 5: Commemoration in the New Germany

By identifying this new ritualism, I am not implying that every subsequent official commemoration came off without controversy. The major difference is in the way that the German leadership responded to such controversy. Whereas in 1985 leaders often exacerbated conflict, after Bitburg they seemed to recognize that they could carry out relativization while pleasing critics. As the previous chapter showed, this was the case in 1988, when Bundestag president Philipp Jenninger delivered an ill-fated speech in which he discussed how it might have seemed reasonable to average Germans in 1933 to vote for the Nazis. Misunderstood as implying that it actually had been reasonable, Jenninger faced an onslaught of criticism. Instead of defending this venerable party figure — who, incidentally, had a strong record in regard to history politics and diplomacy with Israel — the Christian Democratic leadership accepted his resignation rather than face the kind of criticism they had faced in 1985. Several moments during the course of reunification engendered placating responses as well (Olick 1998). The new formula seemed to minimize the costs of acknowledgment; it was no longer necessary for the revision to be so strident.[23] The new formula combined powerfully with Germany's new stature after unification to shape a more quietly ritualized official memory in the 1990s.

This same placative ritualization marked the fiftieth anniversary of May 8 as well, but the commemorations in 1995 were not without problems. These problems fall into three major categories: (1) conflict over the role of Poland in the events (the invasion of Poland on September 1, 1939, had started the war); (2) a major challenge in the name of German victims to the official rhetoric's emphasis on liberation; and (3) the anti-Semitic arson attack on the newly consecrated Lübeck synagogue. When Polish leader Lech Walesa insisted on participating in what had originally been planned as a purely German affair — but which had expanded to include French, American, and Russian leaders after France's ailing president Francois Mitterrand asked to use the occasion for a final visit — the Kohl government defused the crisis by inviting the Polish foreign minister to a special session of the Bundestag. Poland, moreover, was in no position to object, given its need for German support. When the conservative German parliamentarian Alfred Dregger took out ads in leading newspapers objecting to what he saw as disrespect to German veterans implied in the ubiquitous liberation argument, the Kohl government simply ignored him. The contrast to ten years earlier, when Dregger was a powerful voice defending the Bitburg visit, is significant. And when the newly consecrated synagogue in Lübeck was firebombed, the government responded quickly and unequivocally with condemnations. In comparison to the events of 1985, then, the ceremonies of 1995 went off without a significant hitch, demonstrating that the Federal Republic had solidified the ritualistic "normalcy" for which Kohl's Christian Democratic Union government had worked so hard and to which von Weizsäcker had contributed even as he reined in Kohl's more aggressive efforts.

At the same time, Federal president Roman Herzog, in an address he claimed to have written himself, called May 8 a day on which a door into the future was opened but acknowledged that it might appear as such only in hindsight. He began by saying that one has to have experienced the day to really understand what happened. He marked the distance of the crimes when he talked about the different sorts of suffering. He said he was not mentioning all the different aspects "to allow the guilt of the German rulers to disappear behind the picture of a general ruin or to make it smaller." This is an explicit commentary on earlier formulations. Herzog believed his predecessors had adequately acknowledged the fact that crimes were committed against many people by Germans: "about that we really don't have any more to discuss." And therein lies the true message of the fiftieth anniversary: After 1985, there may indeed be nothing more to discuss; the hurdle may have been high and there may have been injuries, but the road ahead is clear as long as some gesture is offered.

Kohl's official declaration was no more controversial. Consistent with his long-standing pattern of relativizing suffering, of treating all victims equally, he declared that there is no common denominator for the different memories and feelings the day raises, actually meaning exactly the opposite. "We should," he continued, "respect them as existential experiences of each individual and shouldn't talk them to death (*zerreden*).... Exactly in the respect for every individual fate is the conviction expressed that all people share a common inalienable dignity." Among these different experiences, he apparently included just about everyone, including soldiers and expellees. He said we must mourn everyone who suffered, both non-German and German. The thorough individualization of guilt and suffering at this late stage makes possible the advancement of a less problematic national identity. Kohl was clear that for him May 8 is, in the last analysis, a day of liberation, a day that deserves to be marked. But the tough self-examination that accompanied the transitional moment ten years earlier is no longer necessary. Moreover, to have the new style appear normal, it was necessary to forget the struggle involved in achieving it. Thus, the normalized commemoration on May 8, 1995, included a double reformulation — of the commemorated event in 1945 and of the later struggles with it.

Conclusion

There is much to be said for a contextual account of the differences among commemorations of May 8, 1945. Lack of reactions, for instance, to Scheel's speech or to Schmidt's generational denials in 1975 when compared to von Weizsäcker's major speech and to Kohl's "grace of a late birth" comment in the 1980s clearly demonstrate the conjunctural basis of reception. On the production side, Brandt's and Heinemann's emphasis on liberation in 1970 was tied up with their desire to legitimate the new *Ostpolitik*, in which an emphasis on German suffering during negotiations with Poland and the Soviet Union would have been a major stumbling block; Kohl's neoconservative program of historical revision was tied up as well with the search for new sources of legitimacy for the fading West German welfare state; the emphasis on German suffering in the 1950s, combined with the overall avoidance of commemoration in that period, fit with the perceptions of the population and the needs of the state too, as did the new rhetoric of the 1960s.

Though these examples show that circumstances shape commemorative choices and reactions to them, however, those circumstances also include the ongoing discourse. It makes little sense to say that either political context or discursive history was decisive. Instead, it is the inextricable interplay of past and present, discursive history and contemporary context — accomplished through "genre memory" — that produces images of the past and reactions to those images. Though specific issues, themes, formulations, and sets of choices appear again and again, order mattered a good deal. Intellectual and political leaders in the 1980s, for instance, struggled to overcome the discourse of the late 1960s and early 1970s, which they perceived as moving from the 1950s' preoccupation with German defeat and victimhood to denying it altogether. In doing so, however, they adopted the universalism of New Left rhetoric to escape the specificity of German defeat. In contrast to the 1950s, German victimhood was no longer a way of looking back, of making claims about past injustices; it was now a way of looking forward, of showing that all past injustices were basically irrelevant for contemporary politics, except in the most general ways. This would not have been possible without the generalizations of the

1960s and 1970s, and it is in this way not a strict return to the formulations of the 1950s.

In this light, the 1995 commemoration of May 8, 1945, takes on an entirely different profile. Without attending to genre memory, we can neither assess how much of a departure the 1995 commemoration was (departure in comparison to what?), nor can we see its central feature — its response to 1985's commemorative difficulty. Indeed, this composure in 1995 was the essential lesson of the paroxysmic struggle in 1985. Kohl and his neoconservative supporters realized they had propagated their revisionist history in 1985 rather expensively. Within the context of East–West brinkmanship, West Germany's pursuit of more symbolic markers and levers for its growing power had to be seen as a disturbance. That West Germany in the process challenged a fundamental orthodoxy of the contemporary epoch — German guilt — and demanded Western complicity was simply too much.

Within the German discourse, Christian Democratic image makers sought to recapture the May 8 anniversary and to link it to their more general program, but it was not possible to replace one framework with another without containing the contradictions. This is why von Weizsäcker's synthesis was so significant: His speech contained the contradictions of the discourse within a grand framework. Von Weizsäcker asserted liberation without denying defeat; accepted responsibility without dishonor; learned lessons without assuming practical constraints. In the wake of Bitburg, an assurance of ritualized commemoration — one that did include some unusual acknowledgments in addition to old exculpations — sufficed for most critics while providing an acceptable burden (i.e., rhetorical and not practical) for neoconservative leaders.

Kohl's government and its intellectual supporters continued in their rhetorical vein of relativizing the past and seeking a "wider" historical vision, but they did so more quietly after 1985, largely having accepted von Weizsäcker's solution. Everything had been laid open in 1985 as part of the struggle to alter the commemorative landscape, and after that difficult transition the issue no longer required such analysis as long as Germany avoided any overt provocations. This formula for ritualized acknowledgment — perhaps only possible after the difficult struggle over Bitburg — shaped both the reactions in 1995 and the silence about 1985: To acknowledge the struggle would have been to question the formula, which dictated that Germany could move beyond the costs of commemoration by accepting a generalized "responsibility" to commemorate; the commemorative regime allowed not only no controversy about the past but also no memory of earlier controversies.

None of this analysis denies the role of the political moment in 1995, when profound changes had occurred in the world order and the symbolic issues of *Geschichtspolitik* (history politics) appeared less important in light of Germany's new size and political role. It is merely to appreciate the simultaneous continuities and departures in the rhetoric and to show that the commemorative situation in 1995 was understood through the lens of developing genre memories. Moreover, it points out that the new commemorative composure of 1995 was a result of the major transformation in the German guilt genre that occurred before unification as well as the different context after unification.

My account in this chapter thus demonstrates that commemoration is an ongoing dynamic process involving social and political contexts and genre memories. Viewing commemoration from this historical perspective reveals general patterns in the history of German commemoration. Over the more than fifty years since May 8, 1945, for instance, strategies of commemoration became increasingly codifed. I have shown, for instance, an allocation of specific issues to specific days and places: Kohl, for instance, delivered very different speeches in the different moments and locations surrounding the Bitburg event; in the 1990s, the government solved the commemorative problem of the multiple referents on November 9 by establishing one special holiday for the victims of National Socialism on January 17, the anniversary of the liberation of Auschwitz, and one special day for celebrating unification on October 3, the anniversary of unification. More generally, alterations occurred in the connections between politics, personal memory, and collective memory: From an early avoidance of ritual in the 1960s and 1970s there came an attempt to instrumentalize commemoration for immediate political purposes, and then in the 1980s an attempt to use commemoration to generate proud identity.

Disputes about how to commemorate the Nazi past continue. This was seen in the recent debates over a Berlin monument. Nevertheless, the ability of such debates to encroach on Germany's political reputation has, I think, been substantially diminished. It is important to recognize, however, that 1995 was not the end of German commemoration but is only one moment in its ongoing life course. What direction that process has taken since then has depended not only on what may come but also on what has gone before — on both the event and its accumulated history and memory of commemoration.

In conclusion, the case study presented here is an example for social studies of commemoration generally: The complex reflexive dynamics of commemoration are especially visible here and stand as a model for other studies of commemorative processes, which are always fundamentally dialogical. Views of commemoration as a mirror of history or tool

of exigency are outdated, and this case study identifies the mechanism
— genre or, more precisely, genre memory — through which commemoration works instead to create meaning through time. Moreover, this case
study demonstrates the value of dialogism as a principle for the study of
all sorts of cultural productions: Speech, ritual, symbolism, ideology, and
other cultural practices are shaped as much by the ongoing mediations
between past and present, context, and utterance as are commemorative
practices. Bakhtin's call for a prosaics of culture, in contrast to formalism
or sociological stylistics, provides a solid theoretical foundation for analyzing such processes without reducing or reifying them. To elaborate such
a program is the ambitious task of the next chapter.

CHAPTER **5**

Figurations of Memory
A Process-Relational Methodology,
Illustrated on the German Case

Introduction

The sociological term *collective memory* has become a prominent part of public vocabularies in many places. It has appeared on the front page of newspapers like the *New York Times*, in the rhetoric of politicians, as a rallying cry for various kinds of groups making identitarian claims, and as a focus for artistic and literary efforts to articulate the spirit of such groups. It has been an organizing principle for academic conferences, for numerous essay volumes and special issues of journals, and even for a journal of its own — *History and Memory*.[1] As we already saw, the sociologist Herbert Blumer (1969, pp. 153–82) makes a useful distinction between operational and sensitizing concepts, the former delimiting a fixed and measurable phenomenon and the latter indicating an evolving field of purview and mode of perception. It should be clear that collective memory is not an operational concept: There seems to be very little agreement on what it is — if indeed it is anything — or on what sort of a metric would apply. The question, then, is what kind of a sensitizing concept collective memory is. To what does it sensitize us? And what kind of a sensitivity is it?

Numerous different social forms, locations, and practices have been included under the rubric of collective memory, ranging from explicit recollection to general forms of pattern-maintenance (Olick and Robbins

1998). The term collective memory has been employed in regard to aggregated individual recollections, to official commemorations, and to collective representations in the Durkheimian sense; it is said to be located in tradition, myth, style, language, art, popular culture, and the built world. Some authors see collective memory as shared images that bind a society together (Shils 1981), whereas others see it primarily as a field of negotiation and contestation (Foucault 1977; Sturkin 1997). Sometimes collective memory is seen as an important living form of history (a goal for historiography) (Hutton 1993), and sometimes it is seen as an inferior and degraded mode of retrospection (in epistemological contradiction to historiography) (Yerushalmi 1982). This variety raises questions about both the potential objects of the term (i.e., what it sensitizes us to) as well as about its mode of reference (i.e., what kind of a sensitivity it implies).

Collective memory has featured most prominently in recent analyses of group identity, and it is here that its sensitivities have been clearest.[2] Collective memory in scholarly work on identity has been used to refer to representations of the past and mnemonic practices produced in the service of solidifying the sense of belonging of a group, as well as to a disembodied frame of reference — part of a society's unique cultural essence — for the community's shared "imagining" of itself (Anderson 1991).[3] As Bellah et al. (1985, p. 153), as we have already seen, put it in *Habits of the Heart*, "Communities... have a history — in an important sense are constituted by their past — and for this reason we can speak of a real community as a 'community of memory,' one that does not forget its past. In order not to forget that past, a community is involved in retelling its story, its constitutive narrative." Collective memory thus refers to the group's sense of itself as a continuous entity through time, as well as to the manifestations of, and efforts to enhance, that sense of continuity.

Paramount among the groups that operate in these ways, of course, are nations, or at least nation-states, and it is in the context of theorizing the nation that the term collective memory has been especially prominent (Gillis 1994; Olick and Robbins 1998). Research on nationalism has focused on collective memory as a tool — indeed, a particularly powerful one — in the ideological arsenal of nationalists for articulating national boundaries and establishing the legitimacy of national principles. Hobsbawm's (1983) notion of *invented tradition* is perhaps the most cited of such approaches: In the late nineteenth century, Western European states propagated numerous forms of artificial retrospection to shore up legitimacy, perceived to be in decline years after heroic golden ages of revolution and reformation and in the face of expanding demand. At the time, Nietzsche (1997) bemoaned this seemingly indiscriminate proliferation of what he called *monumental history* — which he feared would become "the gravedigger of the present."

But most "scientific" historiography as well as vernacular forms of historical consciousness willingly served the needs of the nation in what has been
labeled the age of historicism (Iggers 1983).

Overall, the literature on nationalism has thus bequeathed to us a
largely instrumentalist concept of collective memory: what memory can
do for identity. There are, of course, debates about the degree to which the
past can be remade in the present for contemporary purposes (Schudson
1989; Schwartz 1991), but even those who maintain that the past resists
such efforts to be remade work within a framework that sees memory —
durable or malleable — as doing something for the group, whether it is
what the group wants it to do or not (Shils 1981). In contrast, it is possible
to ask a very different kind of question about memory — not what memory
does for the group, but what the group does for memory. "Memory," Matsuda (1996, p. 16) writes, "has too often become another analytical category to impose on the past; the point should be to rehistoricize memory
and see how it is so inextricably a part of the past." This relatively new line
of inquiry has been called the *history of memory* and has yielded a number
of important insights.

In the first place, it is virtually impossible to discuss the history of memory without highlighting developments in the material means of remembering.[4] Important here is the long-term shift of memory from the mind to
external loci, though memory has always been externalized in the form of
storytelling and transmitted patterns of behavior. In a now classic study,
for instance, Francis Yates (1966) traces the decline of *ars memoria* — the
art of memorization — from Roman times to the Renaissance, when it was
largely, though never completely, supplanted by written forms through the
advent of the printing press. For a later period, Ian Hacking (1995) refers to
a basic shift in the so-called "sciences of memory" from a focus on memory
how to a focus on memory that: "The art of memory was truly a *techne*, a
knowing how...not a science that delivered knowledge about some object of
study, 'the memory'" (ibid., p. 202). Indeed, this increasing externalization
and objectification of memory in "artificial" sites, mainly print, is a crucial
condition for recognizing that memory is a social activity — that is, for
developing a concept of collective memory — though of course memory
is already a social activity even where it is not pervasively externalized or
conceptualized as such.

Another key point in many histories of memory, which we will see in
much greater detail in the papers composing part two of this book, is that
a significant transformation in the experience of time occurred at some
debatable point between the Middle Ages and the nineteenth century.[5]
Many authors describe an existential crisis arising out of an increased
possibility for abstract thought, out of accelerating change resulting from

increased industrialization and urbanization, as well as out of the associated decline of religious worldviews and traditional forms of political authority. Within these contexts, the very nature of memory — as part of the general forms of perceiving time[6] — was transformed as well. Many note, for instance, the rise of new calendars and the ways in which they unified societies by standardizing temporal frames of reference (Dohrn-van Rossum 1996; Zerubavel 1981). Walter Benjamin (1968) describes such a transformation in almost apocalyptic terms when he referred to the rise of the "empty, homogeneous time of the nation-state" (p. 261). In this tradition, critics have argued that "statist ideologies involve a particularly potent manipulation of dimensionalities of space and time...[by] invoking rhetorically fixed national identities to legitimate their monopoly on administrative control" (Boyarin 1994 pp. 15–16). As Prasenjith Duara (1995) writes, "National history secures for the contested and contingent nation the false unity of a self-same, national subject evolving through time" (p. 4). Indeed, it is exactly this falsely unitary subject that demands nationally unified historical consciousness (Iggers 1983).

As Maria Alonso (1988) puts it, "Historical chronologies solder a multiplicity of personal, local, and regional historicities and transform them into a unitary national time." It is important to recognize that precisely this context of "empty, homogeneous time," — has shaped our understanding of collective memory, just as it gave us nationalist historiography and historical consciousness. Modern historiography is in significant measure the product of Romantic German nationalism and its emotional reverence for the powerful central state (Berger 1997; Iggers 1983). Indeed, the earliest use of the term *collective memory* I have ever come across was by Hugo von Hofmannsthal in 1902, who referred to "the damned up forces of our mysterious ancestors within us" and to "piled up layers of collective memory" (Schieder 1978, p. 2). Interest in memory generally, however, was pervasive all over nineteenth-century Europe. Not only German nationalists, but also writers like Marcel Proust, Henri Bergson, and Sigmund Freud excavated, theorized, diagnosed, and even propagated what many have called a *memory crisis* (Terdiman 1993). The existential uncertainties of this period were widely understood as problems of memory, paradoxically just when the world seemed saturated by the past.

As already discussed in chapter two, however, contemporary usages of the term collective memory are largely traceable to Emile Durkheim (1961), who writes extensively in *The Elementary Forms of Religious Life* about commemorative rituals, and to his student Maurice Halbwachs, who published a landmark study on "The Social Frameworks of Memory" in 1925 (translated and edited by L. Coser in 1992). Durkheim and his students, of course, have often been criticized for an organicism that neglects difference and conflict. Indeed, as we saw, Durkheim did write *Society* with a capital S, and collective representations in his work do take on something of a life of their own. Halbwachs was somewhat more careful, employing *groups* in place of Durkheim's *Society,* and indeed characterized collective memory as plural, showing how shared memories can be effective markers of social differentiation (Coser 1992). But although there are as many collective memories as there are groups for Halbwachs, and although Halbwachs emphasizes that it is only individuals who remember, there remain some echoes of Durkheim's *collective representations* as phenomena sui generis.

The Process-Relational Critique

Whether or not these charges are fair to Halbwachs, it is clear that the concept of collective memory, though sensitizing us to important aspects of social life, risks doing so in a rather insensitive way, a way that reifies, overtotalizes, and hypostatizes. This is the mark of its social origins as a concept in a period in which states concentrated power by forging unitary, fixed, and exclusive identities through "monumental history." As a result, we often write of collective memory as if it were one distinct thing reflecting past experiences; the archetypal collective memory is the architectural collective memory — tangible, monolithic, recognizable, permanent, literally carved in stone. Use of the term collective memory, it seems, is thus often tempted by what I would call, following Charles Tilly (1984), at least four "pernicious postulates":

1. Unity: Collective memory is one, unitary, and consensual (or at least imposed), rather than multiple and essentially contested.
2. Mimetic directness: Collective memory in some way or another represents or mirrors a prerepresentational past, rather than being from the very first embodied in representational form.
3. Tangibility: Collective memory is a thing, rather than a process or activity, despite the fact that it may be embodied in, or represented by, a thing.
4. Independence: Collective memory is distinct, separable from other kinds of culture, rather than intricately tied up within constellations of other meanings and general purposes.

Collective memory, of course, is not the only concept that manifests these tendencies, and the critical discourse provides some suggestions for avoiding these dangers. A number of theorists (Abbott 1988; Bourdieu 1993; Elias 1968, 1978; Emirbayer 1997; Mann 1993; White 1992), for instance, revived a neglected tradition of critique to argue that the problem may lie at the very foundations of sociological — and, indeed, vernacular — thinking in general, affecting many of sociology's central concepts. In the 1920s, the German philosopher Ernst Cassirer (1953) named the problem "substantialism." Cassirer labeled alternative approaches "functionalism," but that term is too specifically associated with a particular variety of British social anthropology and the later structural-functionalism of Talcott Parsons to serve as a good label for contemporary efforts. The recent critique of substantialism (Abbott 1988, 1992, 1996; Bourdieu 1990, 1996; Bourdieu and Wacquant 1992; Emirbayer 1997; White 1992) has therefore usually gone under the labels "relationalism" or "processualism," which I combine as *process-relationalism.*[7] Given the tendency of work on collective memory to adopt one or more of the pernicious postulates previously outlined — postulates that, I show, are essentially substantialist — my goal in what follows is to rethink collective memory in a more thoroughly process-relational manner.

According to the process-relational critique, conventional sociological approaches are largely substantialist insofar as they assume that social life comprises preformed entities or substances in which "relation is not independent of the concept of real being; it can only add supplementary and external modifications to the latter, such as do not affect its real 'nature'" (Cassirer 1953, p. 8). Such reifications, these authors argue, are built into the very language of social science, which, as Pierre Bourdieu (1994, 1996) puts it, is better suited to express things than relations, states than processes. Norbert Elias (1978, pp. 111–12), influenced by Cassirer and influencing Bourdieu, puts it this way:

> Our languages are constructed in such a way that we can often only express constant movement or constant change in ways which imply that it has the character of an isolated object at rest, and then, almost as an afterthought, adding a verb which expresses the fact that the thing with this character is now changing...This reduction of process to static conditions, which we shall call "process-reduction" for short, appears self-explanatory to people who have grown up with such languages.

Research on collective memory often shares in these assumptions, particularly when it treats collective memory as either an independent or a dependent variable, asking when memory causes changes or what causes changes in memory. Such approaches assume that collective memory is a thing or set of things isolable from, and exogenous to, the processes being measured, rather than being their very medium. Additionally, as I discussed in the introduction, we refer more commonly to *memory* rather than to *remembering,* often associating it with a place, in either the brain or in society, or locating it in and as an object rather than seeing it as a process, occurring through a variety of practices.

In contrast, process-relationalists "...reject the notion that one can posit discrete, pregiven units such as the individual or society as ultimate starting-points of sociological analysis" (Emirbayer 1997, p. 287). Rather, "the very terms or units involved in a trans-action derive their meaning, significance, and identity from the (changing) functional roles they play within that trans-action. The latter, seen as a dynamic, unfolding process, becomes the primary unit of analysis rather than the constituent elements themselves" (ibid.). As Bourdieu puts it, playing on Hegel, "the real is the relational: what exists in the social world are relations — not interactions between agents or intersubjective ties between individuals..." (Bourdieu and Wacquant 1992 p. 97). Elias refers to social figurations — enacted and reenacted networks of relations rather than atomistic individuals — to capture the flux of life in time; figuration is understood on the model of the dance, a work in motion where the whole in time is reducible neither to the parts (i.e., dancers) nor to the moments that comprise it. In this way, process-relationalism is more profoundly sociological than substantialism, which presumes presocial categories or entities which endure across social interactions rather than ongoing social projects and processes.

From this perspective, the analytical goal of research on collective memory should be to understand *figurations of memory* — developing relations between past and present — where images, contexts, traditions, and interests come together in fluid, though not necessarily harmonious, ways, rather than to measure collective memory as an independent or dependent variable, a thing determined or determining. Where the substantialization of the memory as an entity or place suppresses the processual-relationality of remembering, figuration preserves fluidity and calls attention to ongoing structuration and practice. In what follows, I thus articulate four counterconcepts — field, medium, genre, and profile — in contrast to the aforementioned pernicious substantialist postulates — unity, mimesis, tangibility, and independence, respectively. Each of these counterconcepts is fundamentally relational, and taken together they sensitize us to the varieties of *collective remembering* without the reification, hypostatization, and overtotalization attached to much previous use of the term. This methodology for collective memory research, moreover, demonstrates the value of processualism generally, for remembering, as will become clear, is a paradigmatic example of processual thinking. I illustrate each dimension of mnemonic figuration with examples mainly from my own systematic empirical research on the Federal Republic of Germany, where problems of collective memory, as we have seen, have been especially poignant.

Four Process-Relational Counterconcepts

Field

The concept of *field* responds to the first pernicious postulate, unity, and its overtotalizing presumption that collective memory is unitary, a shared cultural heritage that unproblematically transcends social divisions. Social scientists, of course, have used the concept of field in both common-sense as well as highly theorized ways. The basic metaphor refers to a place where a battle or sporting contest occurs. By extension, it can be used to refer to a particular segment of society, such as politics or the arts — that is, particular institutional locations. Indeed, scholars of collective memory have developed such ideas at length to indicate that there are many different kinds of social memory produced in different contexts. Michael Schudson (1992), for instance, argues convincingly in his study of Watergate in American memory that it is important to investigate the ways different social institutions produce different versions of the past and how they often compete with each other both over these versions as well as through them. Also, John Bodnar (1992) argues against overtotalizing collective memory by definitionally limiting it to official accounts of one sort or another, such as government or academic versions of the past. According to Bodnar, it is important to distinguish between *official* memory and *vernacular* memory, in part because reconceptualizing a vernacular memory notes analytically the power of ordinary people to shape and challenge dominant ideologies.[8]

Along these lines, indeed, notions of different kinds of social memory have proliferated, including family memory, group memory, historical memory, cultural memory, official memory, dominant memory, and folk memory. The German Egyptologist Jan Assmann (1992), among others, even argues explicitly for different version as a way to avoid the overtotalization that seems to inhere in the very concept of collective memory; Assmann writes of material, social, and cultural memory, among others. He critizes Halbwachs's (1992) account along lines that are long familiar to critical neo-Durkheimians, namely that it assumes too much consensus. There are thus many collective or social memories, partly because they are produced in different fields and partly because there are multiple contenders within particular fields. There is not one collective memory, nor does one sort of social memory count as the real one in contrast to other failed contenders or imitators. The social production of the past is almost always more complicated than invocations of *the collective memory* imply.

Though scholars of social memory have long argued for the importance of differentiating and specifying institutional origins of images of the past, Pierre Bourdieu's (1996) conceptualization of field helps us resist the tendency to hypostatize these institutional locations. Bourdieu defines *field* as follows:

> Field may be defined as a network, or a configuration, of objective rela-
> tions between positions. These positions are objectively defined, in their
> existence and in the determinations they impose upon their occupants,
> agents or institutions, by their present and potential situation (*situs*) in
> the structure of the distribution of species of power (or capital) whose
> possession commands access to the specific profits that are at stake in
> the field, as well as their objective relation to other positions.

Furthermore, and more directly to the point, "In a highly differentiated society, the social cosmos is made up of a number of such relatively autonomous social microcosms, i.e. spaces of objective relations that are the site of a logic and a necessity that are specific and irreducible to those that regulate other fields."

These definitions clearly highlight field's contribution to thinking about memory relationally, but what of the processual, temporal dimension? According to Bourdieu (1996, ibid.), the internal structure and operation of any particular field is never completely fixed. Indeed, insofar as the field is a place of struggle, its very nature and its rules of operation are always either reproduced or changed and thus cannot be taken for granted. One major object and result of the struggle is not just the internal structure of the field, but the very boundaries of the field itself, its borders with and relations to other fields. As Bourdieu (1996) puts it, "The question of the limits of the field is a very difficult one, if only because it is always at stake in the field itself, and therefore admits of no a priori answer.... Thus the boundaries of the field can only be determined by an empirical investigation." So though we may talk about official memory or vernacular memory, historical memory or literary memory, public memory and private memory, we need to keep in mind not only that these categories themselves — and the institutions with which they are associated — are ever shifting but also that the struggle over memory within them may in fact play a role in their configurations, both internal and external. A valid approach to social memory along these lines sensitizes us to the fact that different fields produce different kinds of pasts according to different rules, that remembering is a different activity in different fields, and that different kinds of remembering are involved in constituting and reconstituting the boundaries between fields. "To think in terms of field," Bourdieu (Bourdieu and Wacquant 1992, p. 96) therefore writes, "is to think relationally."

Moreover, different social fields, Bourdieu points out, have different implications for the *field of power*, which, in his account, is a sort of metafield. On the one hand, this means that to speak about one kind of collective memory as especially powerful is to make no a priori claim about it being the real collective memory and others being either failed contenders or something else entirely. On the other hand, it also means that we can empirically determine which field is dominant at any particular moment, though keeping in mind that as the relational structure in terms of the field of power shifts, so too do the hierarchical relations among, and indeed the very boundaries of, the different fields.

Some more concrete discussion should serve to clarify this appropriation of Bourdieu's relational ontology as a methodological guide for studying social memory. In the course of researching the ways Germans have constructed and dealt with the social memory of the Nazi period, for instance, as in other cases, one faces a number of boundary problems. Is it possible to characterize the way a whole society deals with its past? Such blanket characterizations, of course, are the bread and butter of political commentary. In Germany, for instance, it has long been a commonplace that the 1950s were a period of repressing the past. Indeed, we often make such generalizations about an entire society — such as that the United States has never come to terms with the genocide of indigenous American peoples or that it was long unable to assimilate the Vietnam War into its "collective conscience." Such generalizations work through multilayered reifications, for example, of the nation as a collective actor, of the event as singular, of the memory as a thing, of the victims and perpetrators as distinct.

Before, and ultimately instead of, making such generalizations, which risk sinking into the polemics of ideological memory makers, process-relationalism demonstrates that we need to engage in prior, systematic empirical efforts that look at the many different images of the past produced within social contexts: Neither isolated case studies nor static overviews will suffice. Virtually all fields within German society produced images of the Nazi period, often very different from each other. Politicians produced images of the past, and so did artists, novelists, historians, commentators, communities, schools, architects, journalists, families, individuals. Sometimes there seemed to be a division of labor, sometimes merely a different form of expression, and sometimes an outright contradiction. No general picture of the mnemonic landscape is possible without dangerous reductions or as polemic, nor will narrowly defined efforts be likely to appreciate the contingency of their case-constituting categories.

This is clearly more than a call for research over opinion. It is necessary to attend systematically to, and to appreciate analytically, the disjunctures among the kinds of images produced in different places in the society. It is not just that a poet evokes images of the past whereas a journalist reports facts and a politician proclaims, though this is part of it. There are things that could or would be said in one field and not another. For instance, a

German novelist is freer to accept collective guilt than a politician: They have different constituencies, among other things. An opposition critic can be less careful or more provocative than a political incumbent. The rules of international commemoration are rather different than those of barroom nostalgia, though there have occasionally been some striking similarities. In the history of West Germany, and elsewhere, there were clear distinctions between what could be said in public and in private, both across fields and within them. The point is that each of these categories makes sense only in relation to the others, and that relation is in constant flux, though that flux is more or less radical.

A good example is the issue of reparations payments (*Wiedergutmachung*) from the Federal Republic of Germany to the State of Israel, negotiated and debated between 1951 and 1953. From early on, Chancellor Konrad Adenauer considered such a gesture mandatory for numerous reasons, ranging from Christian notions of grace and moral principles of political obligation to calculations about West German standing in the "community of nations." In contrast, public opinion was largely opposed to any such agreement. A December 1952 survey, for instance, revealed that 54 percent of West Germans felt neither guilty for what was done to the Jews during the Third Reich nor responsible for compensating these wrongs; 44 percent still believed there was more good than evil in National Socialism (Merritt and Merritt 1980, p. 198). A 1951 survey (Noelle and Neumann 1967, p. 146) showed that only 31 percent of the population agreed that Germany was responsible for the war. In another 1951 survey (Deutschkron 1991, p. 47), 68 percent of respondents agreed that Jews and other groups should be helped, but 17 percent of those assigned Jews the smallest amount, and 49 percent thought the Jews deserved the same as other groups; 21 percent rejected any reparation to Jews altogether. To the question of which group had the biggest claim, respondents ranked Jews in last place, behind war widows and orphans, the bombed out, and expellees. Altogether, only 11 percent of the population approved of the final negotiated agreement for more than three billion marks.

Even, indeed especially, within his own party and cabinet, Adenauer faced significant opposition as well. Opponents argued that the negotiated amount was excessive given the Federal Republic's needs for rearmament, debt payments, and reconstruction as well as that any such agreement was vigorously opposed by members of the Arab League, which threatened to cut off relations if the agreement was ratified. Vice Chancellor Franz Blücher went so far as to suggest that the agreement would produce anti-Semitic reactions (Wolffsohn 1988, p. 25). On March 18, 1953, the *Bundestag* did ratify the agreement, but the very different ideas about the issue demonstrate both divisions within the field of politics as well as between the fields of politics and public opinion and that different fields operate by different rules with different results for memory. Adenauer's concerns and responsibilities were clearly different from those of ordinary people. And though the fact of reparations payments may have subsequently served to change some public memories — indicated in part by increasing public acceptance of German culpability and of the appropriateness of payments — it can in no way be said to have settled the collective memory. Moreover, the various positions in the debate reflected different understandings of the proper role of the West German state, and one result was the propagation of a particular image of governmental responsibility for the past.

In addition to the different practices in different fields, therefore, the very structures and relations of fields change over time. For instance, in West German history as elsewhere, there was a clear professionalization of commemoration within different fields. So though the social organization of commemoration was rather diffuse in the 1950s, with much interpenetration and blurring of boundaries across fields, as time went on different fields developed rather elaborate apparatuses for producing and controlling their memory work. Organizations of many kinds took official positions on the past and became increasingly organized in their production of representations. Speech ghost writing, for instance, became a much more elaborate enterprise over the course of time: in the 1950s, Federal president Theodor Heuss wrote many of his own most important speeches, indeed frequently improvised his remarks; in the 1990s, a national leader did not even attend interviews without "talking points" prepared by a staff of advisors.

Though politicians in the 1950s often had close connections to the intellectual classes — indeed, the first Federal president of West Germany, Heuss, was a prominent intellectual — the relations between intellectual life and politics changed dramatically over the decades. Sometimes these shifts resulted from changes within and among fields, like to a Social Democratic government in the 1960s, which sought a much more active intervention in social life than earlier regimes. And sometimes shifts within and among fields resulted from more general changes, for instance the mediazation of society. Indeed, this latter process is Janus-faced: The mass media now make a greater claim in the field of power and have the potential for much more control; at the same time, politicians have become quite adept at managing their images and media gatekeepers.

Following Bourdieuian ontology, we need to look at how the very status of the political field, both internally and in relation to other fields, has altered over time. To conduct research without overgeneralizing as public polemicists do, it may be necessary to direct attention to one particular field, perhaps official memory because of its dominant position in the field of power or local vernacular memory for its contrast to the official line. But in doing so, we need to be careful not to treat official memory as the collective memory or vernacular memory as the authentic memory. Neither of these can be understood without attending to other forms of memory and other elements of the situation. Additionally, we must make no assumption that official memory as an aspect of the political field or vernacular memory were constant categories. The very forms of official memory — indeed, the internal structure and external boundaries of the political field — for instance change over time, as do distinctions between public and private, local, cosmopolitan, and national in multifarious ways with important implications for the representation of the past.

Medium

Attention to the media of memory responds to the second pernicious postulate, mimetic directness, insofar as it calls into question the presumption that an ultimate historical truth comes before its embodiment in form. The mimetic postulate focuses our attention on the problematics of representation, thereby treating memory as a repository for past experiences and remembering as the better or worse access to those preserved pasts (e.g., re-present-ation). In contrast, we need to recognize that memory is not a vessel of truth, but a crucible of meaning. That does not mean that "what actually happened" is irrelevant, but only that what actually happened is at least difficult to decide finally and that what actually happened is not the only issue of importance.

Historians, of course, have long disdained memory as subjective and unreliable, but historians and social memory scholars make a similar assumption about representation. Historians presume there is some fact, usually in the form of an "event" that can be captured through "objective" historiographical procedures; it is on such a basis that they defend the "truth" of their accounts. Similarly, though memory may distort or reconstruct the past, honest memories are authentic because they derive from some "genuine" experience. Though history and memory thus relate to the event in the different postures of truth and authenticity, they both presume that, to paraphrase Gertrude Stein, there is a there there.[9]

This presumption has not gone unchallenged in recent years. First, theorists of history have argued forcefully that historiography constructs as much as uncovers the "truths" it pursues; history is written by people in the present for particular purposes, and the selection and interpretation of "sources" is always arbitrary in this regard. The distinction between history and memory in terms of truth thus loses some of its force. Second, as historiography has broadened its focus from the official to the social and cultural, the "evidence" of memory has become central.[10] The recorded memories of no-longer-living ordinary people lead to a more inclusive historical account, and the memories of living ordinary people, including the historian, help shape the historian's reading. Additionally, memory sometimes employs history in its service, where historians seek to ground authenticity through truth: Professional historians have often provided political legitimation for nationalism and other more reconstructive identity struggles, and this involvement raises questions not just about the success of historians in being objective but also about the very notion of objectivity (Novick 1988).

Recent work from a postmodernist perspective has thus challenged the "truth-claim" of professional historiography by questioning the distinction between knowledge and interpretation, and derivatively between history and memory at the very moment of their genesis (i.e., the "event"), all as part of a larger program to dismiss "foundationalist" or "representational" (i.e., mimetic) accounts of knowledge (White 1973). There is no perception without interpretation; there is no event that is not constructed as such through social forms; there is, more generally, no unmediated reality. Historiography, in this account, does not begin with a prerepresentational occurrence that can be separated from all points of view on it — from the meaning-making activities of the participants who experience it as an event or from the interpretation of the participants and others after the fact — but has available as its object of study only representations, not because there are realities that it cannot get at but because there are not.

Whether we agree with this postmodern turn or take it merely as an intellectual historical event of questionable merit, it is clear that the representational forms through which memory mediates experience are of central importance. For if there is no prerepresentational experience, the media of memory are everything, and even if there is some ultimate truth of events, representational media clearly shape its delivery to us. To be more concrete, the past always comes to us through some representational medium. To remember, moreover, is to mediate temporal distance, to relate past and present. A process-relational concept of memory, therefore, both attends to the media of memory as well as conceptualizes memory as mediation. Media of memory are definitive of and not merely secondary to the message; these media are fluid forms, inextricable from, and changing with, the messages they carry; remembering is an ongoing process of mediation rather than of storage and retrieval.

To be concrete about a particular field, politicians employ many different kinds of mediation in their repertoire of historical representation; different media not only allow the politician to accomplish different tasks, but they also make different demands: on the politician, on the audience, as well as on the past. In the mid 1980s, for instance, the neoconservative government of Helmut Kohl sponsored two museum projects: one to German history as a whole, and one to the history of the Federal Republic. The projects, however, met with tremendous opposition because, critics charged, museums naturalize a vision of the past in a way quite different than a political speech, which is more transitory in its impact. Museums and speeches not only have different effects but also construct different pasts, more and less inclusive, more and less direct, more and less evocative, more or less malleable. As a result, we should understand media in terms of what they do, not in terms of what they are. *"Speech," "gesture," "museum,"* and the like are not permanent things but changing forms of communication and sociation.[11] Even within the short term, there can be vast changes in what they can do and what we mean when we refer to them. Representational media are thus not isolable forms existing apart from the social relationships they shape but are abstractions of those encounters.

Not only do available media change, but mediation itself also changes: Not just the pasts, but the pastness represented, for instance, in a museum is different than that presented in, say, a parade. Some media produce permanence, others repetition, some constant change; some unify collectivities, others mark off particular fractions; some strive for supremacy (e.g., some versions of academic historiography) whereas others celebrate multiplicity. Remembering as the mediation of past and present changes with context, technology, and epoch. Which pasts are remembered is thus only one question next to the more basic one of what remembering is and does.

The landscape of memory in the Federal Republic of Germany comprises many different occasions and places, including political festivals, anniversaries, ruins, monuments, museums, autobiographies, photographs, statues, films, historiography, oral history, archives, laws, amnesties, reparations agreements, and treaties. In his study of the politics of memory in Germany, Peter Reichel (1995) differentiates among these as differences in media of memory, particularly in terms of their criteria of validity and the problems to which they respond. He identifies four types: (1) political festivals and official anniversaries use emotion to produce identity and integration (affective media); (2) memory places, including ruins, monuments, museums, as well as autobiographies, letters, pictures, photos, are judged on authenticity as representations or images (aesthetic-expressive media); (3) historiography, documentation, and analysis are judged in terms of truth in their contribution to knowledge, explanation, and meaning (instrumental-cognitive media); and (4) punishment, amnesty, reparations, and so forth are evaluated in terms of justice and produce legitimacy, rehabilitation, and integration (political-moral media). These types are represented in table 5.1.

Table 5.1 Mnemonic Media

Criterion	Medium	Function
Emotionality (Affective)	Political Festivals, Anniversaries	Identity and Integration
Authenticity (Aesthetic-Expressive)	Memory Places: ruins, historic sites, museums, photos, letters, films	Representation, Imagination
Truth (Instrumental-Cognitive)	Historiography, Documentation, Oral History, Analysis	Knowledge: Explanation and Meaning
Justice (Political-Moral)	Punishment, Amnesty, Reparations	Legitimacy, Rehabilitation, Integration

Adapted from Reichel (1995).

The value of such a typology is that it grasps the fundamental differences among media in terms of both their forms and their functions. And though Reichel's categories are provisional and fluid, we can nonetheless appreciate through them the importance of representational media, not just in terms of what they do to the past but also what they do with it.

The unique powers of various media are quite clear in the example of Willy Brandt's famous visit to the Warsaw Ghetto Memorial in late 1970. In 1969, the West German Social Democrats formed a coalition with the liberals to establish the first left-center government in the history of the Federal Republic. The new chancellor was Brandt, the charismatic young socialist whose autobiography stood both as an exemplar of moral courage to the younger generation and as grounds for suspicion from the right. During the war, Brandt had been involved with Socialist opposition circles before fleeing to Scandinavia when the situation in Germany became untenable. During his exile, he renounced his German citizenship, thus for some casting doubts on his patriotism.

Brandt began his chancellorship with a bold appeal for Germany to "Dare more democracy!" speaking the language of the anti-establishment New Left. His program included an anti-elitist stance, wide-ranging social entitlements, and a generally engaged language. Most importantly, Brandt called for a new opening to the East in response to the failures of earlier Western integration policies to bring about unification and as an expression of Germany's moral responsibility to her former enemies — first in the West, but now in the East as well, despite cold war divisions. Through a program known as the new *Ostpolitik* (Eastern policy), Brandt sought rapprochement with the Soviet Block, with Poland in particular. On numerous occasions, Brandt articulated the ongoing responsibility Germany had toward its former enemies deriving from the suffering it had brought to them under the Nazis. In this way, his rhetoric differed markedly from that of his predecessors, who spoke of responsibilities from the past as strictly circumscribed and as mostly accomplished through reparations to Israel and Western integration. Brandt's official stance was close to that of the younger generation, who were at the time demanding a new openness about their parents' crimes — crimes they accused the older generation of repressing, though this openness was certainly easier for a generation not itself culpable (Bude 1992).

Brandt spoke often of German responsibility, seeing the new *Ostpolitik* in its terms as a moral imperative. But it was one particular moment that expressed his image of German responsibility in a way and to a degree — because through a different medium — that he had not previously achieved. In December 1970, Brandt paid the first official state visit of a West German chancellor to Poland as part of negotiations over the so-called Warsaw Treaty, which sought to "normalize" relations between West Germany and Poland. The events that interest us here are perhaps best related through Brandt's own words:

> The screens and newspapers of the world featured a picture showing me kneeling — before the memorial dedicated to the Jewish ghetto of the city and its dead...

> I had not planned anything, but I had left Wilanow Castle, where I was staying, with a feeling that I must express the exceptional significance of the ghetto memorial. From the bottom of the abyss of German history, under the burden of millions of victims of murder, I did what human beings do when speech fails them.

> Even twenty years later, I cannot say more than the reporter whose account ran: "Then he who does not need to kneel knelt, on behalf of all who do need to kneel but do not — because they dare not, or cannot, or cannot dare to kneel (1992, pp. 199–200).

With this simple gesture, Brandt created a symbol that condensed multiple dimensions of European history, German responsibility, and contemporary politics in a way that would not have been possible in conventional political media. Gesture expressed what speech could not, not least because it left open to interpretation the goal of Brandt's atonement: Was it aimed at Jews, at Poles, or at victims of aggression generally? Was it purely memorial or was it an indication of West Germany's desires for the future? The gesture was sufficiently polysemic that it coalesced many issues and satisfied many audiences, though it angered others.

Perhaps the most important development in the mediation of history in recent times, of course, has been that of electronic broadcast, particularly

television. Indeed, a number of theorists have demonstrated the important implications for memory of the so-called "mass" media. For an earlier period, the eighteenth and nineteenth centuries, writers like Benedict
Anderson (1991) and John Thompson (1995), among others, ascribe to
print unique capacities for binding diverse people together as a collectivity.
In his studies of nationalism, Karl Deutsch (1966) argued that nationali-
ties are defined in part as strongly bounded networks of communication,
networks made possible over wide territories only by the mass media.
The capacities of large groups to conceive of themselves as communities
— which, as we saw, means seeing themselves as communities of memory
— require such unifying media.

Addressing the relations between television and memory, Dayan and
Katz (1992) argue that television is uniquely able to produce a sense of
simultaneity of historical experience across populations, thus enabling
a particular kind of social memory — namely shared autobiographical
memory of events. Moreover, they argue, television employs a number of
different narrative frames in its presentation of "media events" — "conquest," "coronation," and "contest," according to their analysis: frames that
have an enduring and significantly homogenizing effect on the collective
audience. Television thus provides a sense of immediate experience to
individuals, but it encourages those individuals to interpret that shared
experience in a relatively homogenous way. This simultaneous atomization
and homogenization of experience is the hallmark claim of the long tradition of mass media criticism (Gans 1974; Rosenberg and White 1957).

The power of the mass media for German memory was demonstrated
vividly in the 1979 broadcast of the American miniseries *Holocaust* on
German television, which attracted perhaps more attention than any other
single mnemonic event in West German history. West Germany's leading news magazine, *Der Spiegel*, for instance, covered the event under the
headline "Catharsis of a Nation" (*Der Spiegel* 26, 22/6/98, p. 27; Zielinski
1986). Though many features of the political and social context in Germany and the world at the time contributed to the increased interest in
the Nazi past in the late seventies and early eighties, *Holocaust* served as a
uniquely unifying moment for public discussions, attracting an enormous
audience and galvanizing public attention. According to both supporters
and critics, it was the "Hollywood" conventions of melodrama that created
a unique sense of identification with the victims, an identification that had
been noticeably absent in German society, which was much more aware of
its own victimhood (Moeller 1996). It is clear from the commentary that
the sorts of mnemonic activities embodied in and surrounding *Holocaust*
were possible only through the mass appeal and homogenizing rhetoric of

television. This is just one example of the ways different media available for remembering decisively shape both what and how we remember.

Just as important, though less obvious, is that what is being remembered can have a decisive effect on the media of memory as well. In a historical study of how the American mass media cover State of the Union addresses, for instance, Michael Schudson (1982, p. 97) observes that "while it is true that a new technology can condition politics and society, a new technology appears and comes into use only in certain political and social circumstances. The way the technology is used has a relation to, but is not fully determined by, the technology itself." Television thus adapts itself as a medium to certain journalistic conventions that predated its introduction as well as to the kinds of events it is expected to report. In a study of press coverage of the John F. Kennedy assassination, Barbie Zelizer (1995a) makes the point even more explicit: Not only was the Kennedy assassination an opportunity for journalism to make its claim as an important field for the production of memory, but particular journalistic conventions and techniques — features of television as a medium, rather than as a field — also were defined in the process of covering that event. The media of memory thus both construct and are constructed by the events they mediate, developing new capacities from their historical experiences.

Attending to the different rhetorics of different media both within and across institutional fields is thus crucial to any general picture of social memory, as well as to understanding the social process and life embodied in any particular image. What media are available to which fields at what times? How do those media and their types of frames change through their use by those fields to convey particular issues? Along these lines, much has been written about the so-called crisis of representation the Holocaust — the event, not the miniseries — engenders. What forms are appropriate or capable of representing an event of such proportions? Many critics argue that the only coherent lesson from the Holocaust is our inability to comprehend or to represent it adequately. Walter Benjamin (1968) had already located such a crisis of representation, and thus of memory, as the result of the First World War and the twentieth century generally: "...Never has experience been contradicted more thoroughly than strategic experience by tactical warfare, economic experience by inflation, bodily experience by mechanical warfare, moral experience by those in power." These cataclysms, according to Benjamin, left people not only without the conditions for telling stories but also without communicable experiences to tell. For others, the importance of preserving memory makes clear the great expansion of particular mnemonic media like video testimony, oral history, and documentary film. Indeed, such efforts to preserve Holocaust memory have had a ripple effect, contributing to the spread of victimization as an identitarian principle and to the postmodern valorization of memory in other contexts as well, a theme I take up in the second half of this book (Huyssen 1995). Media of memory are thus not only relational mechanisms but are themselves also caught up in complex relational figurations of fields, themes, and contexts. Not only do the media of memory change with the "events" they mediate, but memory as mediation — the demand or even hope for representation — also changes as well: The media of memory decisively shape not only specific memories but also memory's mediating functions. This, too, is an important implication of process-relationalism, which presumes neither that past and present are independent nor that remembering is an unchanging practice.

Genre

The concept of *genre* responds to the third pernicious postulate that social memory is a thing rather than a process, tangibility, illustrated perhaps best by our pervasive strategy of reifying memory in and as objects: Not only do we treat the memory as a thing, but we also treat memories as clearly bounded entities representing or embodying a distant historical past. In contrast, conceptualizing memories as forming ongoing genres recenters memory's work in, as well as on, time, thus avoiding "process-reduction."

Social studies of memory have attended to the processes that go on before an image is produced as well as to the variety of subjective reactions people have to it after it is produced. There may, for instance, be a struggle over the meaning of the past and over how to represent it, such as in the debate over the Enola Gay exhibit at the Smithsonian (Zolberg 1998), and we can see that even after the past is "fixed" or embodied for example in a monument, exhibit, or image, viewers may react to it in a variety of ways (Wagner-Pacifici and Schwartz 1991). But between the production of culture and the reception of culture is the text of memory itself: The production and reception of memory occur through the textuality of memory, which is comprehensible only by attending to its intertextuality with other issues and earlier memories.

Whereas social studies of memory often describe images of the past as determined either by the past they represent or by the present in which they are produced, as we saw in previous chapters, recent work has argued that mnemonic practices are made wholly neither in the past nor in the present but in the ongoing and reflexive interactions between them: remembering as meaning-making in time rather than as the production of static objects (Olick and Levy 1997; Schwartz 1991, 1996). As I developed similarly in the previous chapter, from the very moment being remembered, present images follow one after another, being constantly reproduced, revised, and replaced. We are by now familiar with Bakhtin's (1986, p. 93–4) mantra:

"Each individual utterance is a link in the chain of speech communion. Any utterance, in addition to its own theme, always responds (in the broad sense of the word) in one form or another to others' utterances that precede it." The past being remembered thus includes not just the history being commemorated but also the accumulated succession of commemorations: the memory of commemoration. Remembering, in Bakhtin's terminology, is dialogue, a processual and relational activity.

There are several aspects to this "chain of speech communion," this essential reflexivity of mnemonic practices. In the first place, as we saw, commemorations are not usually one-time occurrences. Indeed, they are often explicitly conceived from the very beginning to endure, as when we talk of a "first annual" event (Hobsbawm and Ranger 1983). The periodicity of a commemoration (e.g., once only, occasional, annual) is an important feature of its temporality, as are the numbers and sorts of occasions for remembering a particular past. In the Federal Republic of Germany, as we saw, there were several occasions that were marked again and again on more and less regular schedules. Round-number anniversaries of particular historical events make it difficult for political leaders to remain silent about them or at least make their silence loud. The temporal frameworks of commemoration are thus an important part of its dialogical trajectories.

Second, as previously mentioned, many scholars have pointed out that later commemorations often include more or less explicit references to or echoes of earlier ones. As already mentioned, Barry Schwartz (1996), for instance, shows how Kennedy's funeral was replete with symbolism from Abraham Lincoln's. Later speakers often quote, both with and without acknowledgment, speeches given by their predecessors on the same or other occasions. More loosely, as already mentioned, Sandage (1993) shows that Martin Luther King Jr.'s appearance at the Lincoln Memorial was reminiscent of Marian Anderson's. Such potential echoes can be the objects of more or less direct planning. On a spring 1998 trip to Poland, Social Democratic chancellor candidate Gerhard Schröder avoided visiting the Warsaw Ghetto Memorial not, according to observers, to escape acknowledging the events commemorated there but to prevent too close an association with the memory of Brandt's gesture; anything Schröder could have done would have paled in comparison, which is never helpful for a candidate in the midst of a campaign.

But, as also discussed in the previous chapter, references need not be explicit or conscious for earlier moments to affect later ones. In his book on Fyodor Dostoevsky, Bakhtin (1963) distinguishes *"influence"* from what he calls *"genre contact,"* the former indicating explicit awareness of an earlier text by a subsequent one and the latter referring to the sharing of a common "way of seeing" between texts. "A genre," Bakhtin (ibid., p. 157) wrote, "possesses its own organic logic, which can to a certain extent be understood and creatively assimilated on the basis of a few generic models, even fragments." Earlier texts, insofar as they produce and reproduce the genre in a long chain of discourse, set the stage and provide the materials for later ones. This means not that speakers are "cultural dopes" manipulated by or simply carrying out discourses but that the materials available to them in any context — and which they may thereby transform — are historical accretions, the results of long developmental processes as well as of relational contexts rather than as formally defined features of an atemporal system.

It is important to note, as Bakhtin did in his critique of formalism, that genres are not ideal forms, transcendental grammars that are instantiated in speech acts: To treat them in this way would lose their processuality — the importance of order, their resultant path-dependency, their fundamental dialogism. Genres, rather, are practical types defined "by the object, the goal, and the situation of the utterance." Genres are historical constructs, the results of "a continuous and generative process implemented in the social-verbal interaction of speakers," — thus fundamentally relational — the residues of past behavior that shape, guide, and constrain future behavior. "As the culture's congealed events and crystallized activity," Morson and Emerson (1990, p. 292) write, "...genres constitute an important part of its memory and carry a great deal of its wisdom." By demonstrating the power of genre — including its explicit and implicit workings — we thus counter the tendency to see commemorative texts as wholly constituted either by the history to which they refer or by the present context in which they are produced. In this way, genres reflexively mediate between past and present. And by seeing these genres as historical accretions rather than as ideal forms, we avoid the temptation of transcendentalism, without at the same time giving up typological analysis. Elias (1991) made a similar point when he criticized Max Weber; according to Elias, there are no "ideal types," only "real types."

As the previous chapter outlined, official German speech about the Nazi past has developed a number of memory genres in the fifty years since the end of the war. Different occasions and issues have provided distinct objects, goals, and situations for official commemoration. As a result, speakers have employed particular, though by no means entirely exclusive, vocabularies, tropes, grammatical forms, and other rhetorical devices to accomplish different purposes depending on the how the occasions have traditionally been understood as well as on the contemporary contexts.[12] Indeed, the nature of the contemporary context is defined in part in reference to earlier definitions and traditions; this is part of what is meant by a genre effect. Important to note here is that though different genres may be associated with different media and take place in particular fields, they are not reducible to these other categories. A particular genre can take place in different media at different times and places, such as the celebration of German traditions in a speech, a parade, or a monument. Additionally, such a genre can be part of discourse within families, schools, and sporting events as well as in politics. Again, this is the value of the concept of figuration, which emphasizes the ways these structurings come together, like a traffic flow through a complex intersection.

Collective memory — or more properly collective remembering — is an ongoing process rather than a product of some other process, "continuous and generative," implemented in "the social-verbal interaction of speakers," as Bakhtin puts it. It is thus crucial to investigate the different genres on which specific utterances draw and to which they contribute, as well as how these practical types are defined and understood with the changing "objects, goals, and situations of the utterance." Such frameworks, moreover, are not to be seen merely as constraints, for they provide the necessary form and content for every new production. Genres are fluid constructs, changed with the memory of each new addition, which can merely reproduce it in a new context or change it fundamentally. What genres do images of the past draw on and contribute to? What is the position of any image within an ongoing dialogue? These are central questions for work on social memory that aims, from a process-relational perspective, to avoid the postulate of tangibility, the treatment of memories as isolable objects, things determined or determining, rather than as links in the ongoing processes of relating text and context, past, present, and future.

Profile

The concept of *profile* responds to the fourth pernicious postulate, independence, that collective memory is a clearly demarcated object in political cultures, in some sense independent of them. This postulate underlies approaches that ask either what effect collective memory has or what determines collective memory, as if collective memory were not an integral part of political cultures without which they would be conceptually impossible. Despite the emphasis on genre trajectories — on memory's discursive historicity — it is clear that memory should be viewed as part of more general relations of meanings and within historical conjunctures as well, though a conjuncture is more a regularity over time than a monolithic and unchanging synchronic structure (Abbott 1996). Of course, some points in time are more conjunctural than others, and the identification of conjunctures must take into account differences within fields as well as various generic trajectories.

Because collective identities are constituted in part by their sense of continuities through time, images of the past are almost always in one way or another definitive features of political cultures, though they can play more and less leading roles in different cases; in the German case, images of the past have obviously been quite central, though in different ways at different times. I use the concept of profile to describe the unique contours, more and less smooth, of political meaning systems at given points in time. These comprise diverse meaning elements, including images of the past, identitarian claims, rhetorical styles, attributions of present responsibility, policy characterizations, types of heroes, styles, sense of inside and outside, moral and practical purposes, and procedures. The notion of profile is used to capture the irreducibility of these meaning systems to their discrete elements, the necessity for viewing them as wholes greater than the sums of their parts. Indeed, it is this generalized and irreducible character of epochal profiles that makes it possible for a period to be represented in powerful "condensation symbols," or emblematic images. Epochs are thus often characterized powerfully by photographs, which are easily reproduced, widely distributable, and immediately graspable (see the previous discussion of media).

Approaching meaning systems in this way, of course, has a long history. French structuralism, for instance, has as its hallmark claim that the meaning of any given symbological element comes about only as part of a system of meanings, the structure of which is "arbitrary" in regard to what is being signified in external "reality." By extension to the discussion of social memory, to remove presented images of the past from their contexts to treat them either as identifiable causes or separable products is to reify remembering — by objectifying its embodiments and fixing their meanings in a substantialist manner. Rather, remembering is an ultimately irreducible feature of the dynamic political meaning systems through which identity and legitimacy are articulated and contested. Additionally, social movement theorists have often employed the concept of "*frame*" to emphasize this irreducibility of interpretative wholes to their symbolic elements. However, the notion of frames or framing can imply a monolithic cognitive structure, and new frames often replace old ones in these accounts willy-nilly. In contrast, I intend the concept of profile to indicate more emergence and fluidity than the framing concept, with particular emphasis on the path-dependency of profile change.

This emphasis on irreducible "profiles" clearly contrasts with conventional interest-based conceptualizations of politics. Focusing on profiles begins from the premise that politics is about much more than who gets what, where, when, and how, because such questions often neglect both the symbolic dimensions of politics and the constitution of political interests in the first place. At best, they imply that symbols — and historical images as particularly prominent ones — are merely tools in the struggle over resources (Edelman 1967). To explain political symbols as representations of or tools for pursuing interests, interests are seen as exogenous to political culture, and symbols as merely expressive.

In contrast, a process-relational approach to mnemonic conjunctures views meaning and identity as the ends of politics, not simply its means or context. Collective memory is thus not just cause or product of what is really going on, but part of the self-definition process that is at the very heart of politics, even when politics appears to be about some more tangible result. Neither a tool for pursuing interests nor the "foundation" of identity, remembering is a central medium in which identity and interest are negotiated and contested. A process-relational perspective thus necessarily rejects the ontological distinction between interests and identities.

As will become clear, the meaning of any particular image of the past or mnemonic practice is not available outside of its contemporary context, just as the genre concept demonstrates that meaning is not available outside of history: To treat it as such would be to see representation as a logical rather than a social process, all denotation rather than connotation, unproblematically transposable from one context to another. Even symbols or images that remain ostensibly the same over time may in fact change quite a bit in their import, range of reference, applicability, comprehensibility, and appropriateness. The very act of remembering is as unique as the situation in which it is taking place, and the images or objects produced by it are not only uninterpretable outside of it but are part of its definition. Treating profiles as in this way irreducible in no way contradicts attention to the different fields, media, and genres of remembering. Attention to profile points out the total relations of fields, media, and genres — the figurations of memory. Profile thus reinforces the relationalism inherent in the concept of figuration, and, as long as we keep in mind that, as Michel de Montaigne put it, "Stability is nothing but a more languid motion," does not negate its processuality.

According to my analysis, there were three major official profiles in West Germany form 1949 to 1989 (figure 5.3). In each, images of the past are essential, though in different ways at different times. First, the "Reliable Nation" spanned from the founding of the Federal Republic in 1949 into the Grand Coalition of the mid to late 1960s. During this period, the Nazi past was constructed as a bounded aberration from the true course of German history. The rhetorical style of leaders talking about that period was thus defensive, exculpatory, and repressive. The problem was identified as a faulty constitution and an unstable first German democracy. These problems had been "solved" with the (albeit temporary) founding of the Federal Republic. West Germany's leaders therefore claimed that their state and society were reliable, which they sought to demonstrate with the legal gesture of reparations to Israel and the political insistence on Western integration and human rights, though they resisted and criticized various forms of "de-nazification," political cleansing, and legal prosecution. During this period, images of the past thus formed a central, though circumscribed, node in the political culture. On the basis of that profile, there was a purported reorientation of other aspects of political culture, a redesign of institutional controls and priorities, and a redirection of policy. The changes were both dramatic at the same time that they were minimal: The rhetoric of caesura belied numerous restorations (Herf 1997).

The profile of the reliable nation is embodied strikingly in an image from the founding of the Republic (figure 5.1). On September 21, 1949, a formal ceremony took place at which the Allied High Commissioners were to hand over the Occupation Statute and at which Adenauer was to introduce his cabinet. Adenauer and his cabinet were expected to wait at the edge of the carpet on which the three High Commissioners — Sir Brian Robertson, André François-Poncet, and John J. McCloy — stood, indicating his subordination. Instead, Adenauer stepped directly onto the carpet, demonstrating his unwillingness to acquiesce in that definition of his position: The past was not to be a limitation on his government, which claimed a decisive ideological and institutional break with the Nazis as well as with older traditions of Central European antipathy toward the West. This literally strident posture marked Adenauer's work and rhetoric until the Occupation Statute was lifted in May 1955 and throughout his entire chancellorship, a posture that came to be known as *"carpet politics"* (*Teppichpolitik*).

Second, the "Moral Nation" began with the Social Democrats' assumption of at first shared governmental responsibility in the Grand Coalition of 1966–69 and reached its epitome under Chancellor Brandt's Social-Liberal coalition of 1969–1974. In this period, the Nazi past was seen as an essential feature of German history, one whose structural as well as cultural manifestations had not been totally expurgated. In this period, leaders drew a generalized responsibility to the world as a whole as the legacy of Germany's crimes. The historical rhetoric in this period was generalizing and diffuse and pointed to long-term social–structural patterns. During this period, however, the complexities of memory were minimized as the political culture was stamped by generational demands and the politics of reform. The past, or at least its rejection, was a motivating background and a frequent topic, but not, seemingly, the focus in and of itself.

The central image of the "Moral Nation" — both positive and negative — was the dramatic photograph of Brandt's previously discussed kneeling at the Warsaw Ghetto monument (figure 5.2). As already mentioned, this gesture combined Germany's distinct historical debts — to Jews, to Poland, and to peace in general — in an effort to advance a progressive program of reform, both domestically and internationally. For supporters, who seemed to be in the majority, this image indicated an appropriate distancing from the denials and stridency of the Adenauer era. For later

Figure 5.1 Carpet Politics: Konrad Adenauer introduces his cabinet, September 1949.

Figure 5.2 Willy Brandt at the Warsaw Ghetto Memorial, 1970.

conservative critics, it embodied everything wrong with the so-called politics of sixty-eight: Germany on its knees. Whether positively or negatively assessed, however, this image crystallized for many the "spirit of the age" or, in my terms, the *profile* of the era — including a generalized sense of responsibility, new attitude toward old structures, ideas, and allegiances, and a progressive policy agenda.

The "Normal Nation" began after Helmut Schmidt took power in 1975 and, despite important changes when Kohl's Christian Democrats came into power in 1982, continued and intensified through the 1980s. In this period, the Nazi past was viewed as one historical epoch among many in a long and venerable German history. The rhetorical style of historical discussion was relativizing, normalizing, and revisionist, as it became in vogue to compare Germany's burdens with those of other countries. In this period, the neoconservative leadership worked for changes in historical consciousness as part of a program of cultural reform aimed at enhancing legitimacy through identity.

Perhaps the central moment of this period, as we saw, was the Bitburg affair. To review, to mark the fortieth anniversary of the end of the war, Chancellor Kohl invited U.S. president Ronald Reagan to participate in a ceremony of reconciliation over the graves at the military cemetery at Bitburg. Opposition to the visit and its implication that it was time to lay

Figure 5.3 Retired U.S. General Mathew Ridgeway (center left) and German General Johannes Steinhoff (center right) along with U.S. President Ronald Reagan (far left) and German Chancellor Helmut Kohl (far right) at Bitburg, May 5, 1985

history to rest, however, reached crisis proportions when it was revealed that forty-nine soldiers of the *Waffen-SS*, an organization declared criminal at Nuremberg, were also buried at Bitburg. But the ceremony was very important to neoconservative supporters of Kohl — who had recently fought hard for the deployment of American mid-range nuclear missiles on German soil — as well as for ordinary Germans who had always wanted to see their lost fathers, sons, and brothers as normal patriotic soldiers. The image of a German and an American World War II general shaking hands at a German military cemetery while Chancellor Kohl and President Reagan stood behind them (figure 5.3) thus symbolized for many a long-hoped-for new status for West Germany — one in which this loyal partner was to be given "proper" respect and "proportionate" power without regard to this terrible yet distant past in which, according to the words of Chancellor Kohl, the lines between perpetrator and victim were blurred and no longer relevant.

The essential relationship between memory and profile is even more apparent if we look more closely at the ways images and practices make sense only within their contexts. Certain words, for instance, can serve as mnemonic lightning rods within one profile while not attracting particular attention in others. One such example is that of *Vaterland* (fatherland), which has taken on different roles in different epochs of German history. In the Nazi period and even earlier, the word called up an elemental Romantic ethnic identification and distinguished the German idea of belonging from that of the more rationalist West, whose intellectual proponents — mostly Social Democrats — were referred to as *vaterlandlose Gesellen* (rootless cosmopolitans). In the Adenauer era, however, the term *Vaterland* was used in a much less polemical fashion, indicating a natural patriotism and sense of civic responsibility, and evoked no particular notice. By the 1960s and 1970s, the political integration of the Federal Republic with the West had grown into an intellectual integration as well, and the term *Vaterland* appeared much less frequently than before. This is demonstrated perhaps most vividly by efforts of the Social-Democratic government in the early 1970s (mentioned in chapter two) to measure feelings of national unity with a survey (Schweigler 1975). Instead of being a presumed form of identification — beyond the subjective will of individuals — national identity was thus reconceptualized in liberal terms as a "daily plebiscite," as Ernst Renan, following John Locke, put it. By the 1980s, however, *Vaterland* had returned with a vengeance, as described vividly by Ralf Dahrendorf (1990) in *Reflections on the Revolution in Europe*:

> Helmut Kohl likes few words as much as "fatherland." When he speaks of the *Vaterland*, the deep, almost Wagnerian sound resonates through his not inconsiderable frame, so that often, and characteristically, he tries to sweeten it a little by adding an adjective like wunderschön. "Our wondrously beautiful fatherland" is what he is about. What exactly it means is not so easy to tell; but certainly the language annoys more critical minds.

This return of *Vaterland* in Kohl's rhetoric — and he used it frequently — is part of the more general profile of proud German identity through revived historical consciousness.

Historical epochs thus display distinctive discursive profiles, including images of the past, legitimacy claims, as well as other political–cultural meanings, in which mnemonic practices are comprehensible only as part of an irreducible totality. In the 1950s, a particular set of images of the past gave a decisive stamp to new institutions and new policy orientations, indeed was an irreducible part of those new institutions and policies. In the 1960s, generational changes constituted and were constituted by a mnemonic revolution. In the 1980s, a more general institutional and cultural malaise turned toward the past for consolation, indeed was felt as a lack of a "usable" past. It should be clear, then, that images of the past are not simply products of political cultures and contexts or causes of them. Rather, official memories shape, and are shaped by, a complex cultural process in which elements are integrally connected. The sociological study of collective memory is thus not just a question of what determines collective memory, or even of what collective memory as an identifiable variable does — it does lots of things at once — but also of how it works within symbol systems as a constituent of meaning and identity, though in different ways at different times. The same images may take on different meanings in different contexts, and different images may serve the same function in new situations. This kind of situated account of official memories as integral elements in political–cultural profiles thus avoids the reductionist dangers of more conventional approaches, as well as instrumentalist and substantialist presumptions about the independence of discrete symbolic elements or "variables."

Viewing commemorative politics in terms of political–cultural profiles therefore does not allow for the absolute analytical disentangling of discrete elements and their clear causal relations. This is further grounds for dismissing the independent–dependent variable form of analysis with which many social scientific studies of memory proceed. The concept of profile contextualizes commemorative significance within a total moment, which includes noncommemorative and nondiscursive conditions as well. It is thus impossible, at the limit, to say when memory is a cause and when it is an effect. Memory does do things, but it does those things within contexts, not to them.

Conclusions

My goal here has been to suggest a number of different ways to reduce the tendency to reify and overtotalize collective memory, to reconceptualize collective memory in a way that highlights its essential processuality and relationality. "Logical method and form," writes Oliver Wendell Holmes, "flatter that longing for certainty and for repose which is in every human mind..." Nevertheless, he added, "certainty is generally an illusion, and repose is not the destiny of man." Memory, many of its historians have pointed out, comes to particular prominence in times when certainty and repose seem increasingly uncommon experiences, when the past, as David Lowenthal (1985) puts it, has become "a foreign country." The desire for memory is thus a symptom of its own impossibility. "Collective memory...," as Robin Wagner-Pacifici (1996) puts it, "is existentially committed to being provisional, whether or not the memorizers in any given case are aware of this." And scholars of memory have occasionally seemed no more sensitive to this than the memorizers.

My reformulation of the concept of collective memory in the foregoing pages has thus had two goals. In the first place, and primarily, I have sought to demonstrate the advantages — indeed, the necessity — of a process-relational approach to collective memory for empirical work that seeks to understand mnemonic practices while remaining analytically distinct from — though not necessarily irrelevant to — mnemonic politics. I have offered the outlines of a transposable methodology for scholarly work on social memory that is appropriate to memory's fundamental historicity and complexity, referring to multiple mnemonic forms and practices rather than to a monolithic phenomenon. At first glance, this effort has involved a seemingly vast proliferation of additional concepts — like *field*, *medium*, *genre*, and *profile* — as well of empirical categories like official, vernacular, public, and private memory; affective, aesthetic-expressive, instrumental-cognitive, and political-moral media; the normal legitimation, German traditions, German victimhood, and German guilt genres; and the reliable, moral, and normal profiles. But at second glance, it should be apparent that these concepts and categories involve less obfuscation than their monolithic alternative.

The four counterconcepts thus respond to the reifications and overtotalizations of a substantialist collective memory concept by calling attention to the relational and processual figurations of memory. Both the verb and noun forms of the word *figuration* — a figure, to figure — are relevant here. Fields (and the relational system of fields) media, genres, and profiles all shape — indeed, constitute — mnemonic practices. The distinct structuring forces at work here have often been missed both conceptually and empirically, particularly in the rather sterile debates between presentist and traditionalist positions in the sociology of memory (Olick and Robbins 1998; Schudson 1989; Schwartz 1991). Indeed, this sterility extends to the sociology of culture generally, which usually attends alternatingly to the production and reception of culture, effacing culture's textuality and the mutual constitution of text and context (Bourdieu 1996).

In the foregoing, I have sought to show how mnemonic practices are structured by, and structured as, distinct yet imbricated fields, media, genres, and profiles by calling attention to the unique results of these patternings, seeing those "structuring structures" (Giddens 1984) not as ideal forms but as empirical historical accretions. Fields, media, genres, and profiles are not different things, or indeed things at all, but different ways of structuring practices. Together, they produce figurations of memory in the sense of mulitplex and constantly shifting patterns of images and meanings reducible neither to any given figuring mode nor to present context or past occurrence.

In linking process-relationalism to collective memory, moreover, my goal has been to demonstrate the relevance of work on collective memory to recent sociology in the process-relationalist vein generally. Though the process-relational critique has appeared in many areas, it has perhaps been most prominent in historical sociology of late. A recent volume of essays on the so-called historical turn in the human sciences (McDonald 1996), for instance, argues that a general social scientific turn toward history, though salutary, has largely failed to historicize its own concepts. Sewell (1996, p. 246) puts it this way: "If historical sociology is merely the sociology of the past, it is valuable above all because it increases the available number of data points...But is history just a matter of more data points? Doesn't making sociology historical imply introducing ideas of temporality that are radically foreign to normal sociological thinking...?" Historical sociology, Sewell demonstrates, though in different terms, has been no less subject to process-reduction than other branches of the discipline.

Having developed, partly on the basis of Elias's work, a more genuinely historical understanding of historical sociology, Philip Abrams (1982, p. 2) argues that "sociological explanation is necessarily historical. Historical sociology is thus not some special kind of sociology; rather it is the essence of the discipline...whatever reality society has is an historical reality, a reality in time." A number of scholars who could be labeled *"new temporalists"* — most prominently Andrew Abbott— have in similar ways critiqued the conventional vocabulary of sociological analysis, including most importantly *"variables"* and *"causes"* as ahistorical reifications. In contrast to a "standard model" of "general linear reality" — in many ways another name for substantialism — Abbott argues for a sociology that adequately appreciates the fact that social processes are inherently temporal. Time is not an exogenous context for social life; social life is in all of its manifestations temporal.

It is not, therefore, just history that is important for sociology, but also historicity. And this is why memory is so important. For not only is memory, as I have demonstrated, processual and relational; social processes and relations also are mnemonic. Indeed, this is what it means for social processes to be temporal. As Abrams puts it, "Doing justice to the reality of history is not a matter of noting the way in which the past provides background to the present; it is a matter of treating what people do in the present as a struggle to create a future out of the past, of seeing that the past is not just the womb of the present but the only raw material out of which the present can be constructed." Memory — relating past and present — is thus the central faculty of being in time, through which we define individual and collective selves: "I, entelechy," as James Joyce's Stephen Daedalus thought it, "form of forms, am I because of memory..."

Empirically, as we have seen, this all means noting first rather than as an afterthought the contingency, path-dependency, and relationality of our major categories of social organization and conceptualization. In regard to the German case and to others as well, it means taking as axiomatic, for instance, the contingency of field categories like public and private, domestic and international, official and vernacular and that the different kinds of remembering in these fields are implicated in the very construction of those categories. It means recognizing the shifting figurations of media available to those provisional fields, the shifting ways different media of remembering contribute to the constitution of those fields, and the shifting ways those fields constitute the media. It means recognizing both short- and long-term generic resources and constraints for remembering in those different fields with those different media. And it means recognizing that mnemonic practices are not special activities apart from their contexts but are parts of our efforts at making meaning and organizing life generally. Remembering is not an activity that can be bracketed out as either an independent or a dependent variable: It is both the medium and the outcome of social figurations generally. Appreciating historicity is thus a central part of understanding what it is to remember — and how what it is to remember changes — just as appreciating the constitutive role of memory is central to understanding what historicity — and an historical sociology along these lines — entails.

PART II

CHAPTER **6**

The Politics of Regret

Analytical Frames [1]

... only under certain historical circumstances does frailty appear to be the chief characteristic of human affairs.

Hannah Arendt, *The Human Condition*

In the past several years, major world newspapers have run front-page stories reporting apologies and other expressions of regret by world leaders. Examples include Pope John Paul II's remarks about both the Catholic Church's treatment of Galileo and Catholic individuals' behavior during World War II; British prime minister Tony Blair's acknowledgment of an English role in the Irish potato famine; U.S. President Bill Clinton's public consideration of an official apology for slavery; and an official, though limited, Japanese recognition of wartime atrocities in Nanking and elsewhere. A variety of redress movements have demanded — and, frequently enough, won — material reparations for numerous historical injustices. We have also seen widespread acceptance of a "universal human rights" paradigm, with concrete institutional manifestations like the expanded powers of international tribunals to prosecute war crimes, as well as the growth of trans- and nongovernmental watchdog organizations. And from South Africa to Latin America, Guatemala, and Central and Eastern Europe, postauthoritarian governments have placed an open discussion of the past at the heart of their legitimation efforts.

In many places in the world today, the past is very much present on the public agenda, but it is more often a horrible, repulsive past than the

121

heroic golden ages so often part of public discourse in previous centuries. Political legitimation depends just as much on collective memory as it ever has, but this collective memory is now often one disgusted with itself, a matter of "learning the lessons" of history more than of fulfilling its promise or remaining faithful to its legacy. Observing this transformation, this chapter identifies a new principle of legitimation, which I call the *politics of regret*. I include under this rubric a variety of practices with which many contemporary societies confront toxic legacies of the past. Many analysts distinguish apology, reparation, and criminal prosecution, among others, as distinct genres of retrospective practice (Hayner 2001; Kritz 1995; Minow 1998; Offe 1997; Teitel 2000). Though the differences among these types are many and important, here I am concerned with what they have in common.

Recent literature offers two distinct frames for understanding the politics of regret: a philosophical–jurisprudential discourse centered around the concept of universal human rights, and a comparative–political study of regime transitions now often referred to as *transitology*. These two frames are well developed and ubiquitous, yielding much insight into varieties of contemporary political regret and problems faced by practitioners. Nevertheless, they are often less interested in explaining what is unique and new about regret as a political principle, either denying its novelty or seeing it merely as the result of contingent historical events — most often Nuremberg or the transformations of 1989.

In contrast, this chapter seeks to explore ideas for a genuinely developmental[2] sociohistorical account of political regret. Where has the politics of regret come from? What social structural and cultural developments have made it possible, and which developments does it in turn make possible? To answer these questions, it is necessary to retheorize the historical dimensions of this phenomenon. In what follows, I begin by looking more closely at the two dominant frames just mentioned to evaluate their fitness for this sociohistorical task. The chapter then explores a number of other theoretical resources which I believe provide better tools for understanding the politics of regret historically. In particular, the chapter lays the groundwork for placing the politics of regret in the context of a more general consciousness of progressive temporality that is a central, constitutive feature of modernity and is implicated in a variety of major institutional transformations over centuries — the subject of the remaining chapters. This exploration of theoretical resources, it should be clear, is a framework for ongoing research, not its end product.

Moral Philosophy and the Discourse of Universal Human Rights

The first analytical frame available for understanding the politics of regret is a philosophical–jurisprudential discussion about universal human rights.[3] Philosophers of the Enlightenment and their revolutionary political counterparts in France and the United States often articulated theories in terms of basic guarantees to which human beings, merely by virtue of being human, had a legitimate claim. At the time, obviously, there were important minor exceptions, variously including women, Africans, the non-propertied, and so forth! But the relevant point here is that these arguments were made in terms of "human rights," often illustrated by demonstrating what modern man has in common with his "natural" ancestor. Basic humanity, in this account, remains basic humanity throughout the transition to civilization, though this history can be presented alternately as one of gradual perversion (e.g., Rousseau) or realization (e.g., Hegel).

Despite some tentative formulations in the late nineteenth century and later in the wake of World War I, it was not until after World War II that a discourse on "universal human rights" became quite so dominant a frame in world politics. Since then, with a special gaze directed at the Nuremberg Tribunals,[4] human rights entrepreneurs have pushed to develop international legal and political instruments for guaranteeing universal human rights and have pressured governments both to improve their records and to deal harshly with other states that do not. In the immediate aftermath of World War II, the most important early achievement of this movement was the Universal Declaration of Human Rights of 1948. Since then, numerous nongovernmental agencies, such as Human Rights Watch and Amnesty International, have become vibrant institutional forces on the world stage.

Accompanying this advocacy work have been efforts to articulate these claims of universality in theological, philosophical, and jurisprudential terms. A significant academic literature on universal human rights has grown alongside the political work. Here the goal is to specify and elaborate the concept, to argue for its importance, and to demonstrate its necessity. R. H. Tawney (1972) describes the basic principle this way: "The essence of all morality is this: to believe that every human being is of infinite importance, and therefore that no consideration of expediency can justify the oppression of one by another.... But, to believe this it is necessary to believe in God." Not all — perhaps not even most — human rights advocates would agree with this last deduction, but Tawney and others point out that the discourse of universal human rights, even its philosophical versions, often takes on a tone of irrefutable conviction. The task for such work, as a result, is most often exegetical or a matter of identifying conceptual and political obstacles.

One of the most important philosophical works in this vein, though it does not center on the universal human rights trope, is Karl Jaspers' (1965) *Die Schuldfrage* (*The Question of Guilt*), originally written in 1945–46. Within a discussion about German collective responsibility for National Socialist crimes, Jaspers articulates four distinct varieties of guilt — criminal, political, moral, and metaphysical — each of which entails different forms of accountability. Indeed, the German case — and the precedents established at Nuremberg — remain an important touchstone for the human rights literature. The important points here, however, are that Jaspers' articulation of metaphysical guilt is strongly connected to the concept of original sin and that he sees the question of guilt in many ways as a permanent part of the human condition. A more recent example along these lines is Donald Shriver's (1995) *An Ethic for Enemies: Forgiveness in Politics*, which outlines a principle of forgiveness — founded in Christian ethics — as the basis for peace in human affairs.

On the jurisprudential side, efforts aim at solving practical dilemmas. One good example is the discussion that surrounded the case of former Chilean president Augusto Pinochet. What are the relevant jurisdictional limits? What role should the passage of time play (e.g., Should there be a statute of limitations on crimes against humanity)?[5] What value do such limits have? At a more general level, both philosophers and legal theorists have debated the age old question of utility versus right: Do we pursue former leaders after they relinquish power if doing so will make others in similar circumstances hesitate to go peacefully? Indeed, this issue of principle versus consequence — which I discuss later, and in the next chapter, in Max Weber's terms of an *"ethic of conviction"* versus an *"ethic of responsibility"* — is a central question for theorists of human rights: Are we morally obliged to pursue human rights as a principle regardless of whether doing so decreases the likelihood of realizing them in practice, or is it acceptable to do business with dictators if doing so will improve political realities?

Many theorists in the tradition of universal human rights have sought to specify the psychological, social, cultural, and political costs of failing to prosecute perpetrators.[6] They do so in reaction to those, ranging from Friedrich Nietzsche to Henry Kissinger, who argue that amnesty and forgetting are the only ways to ensure peace. There is a difference, human rights advocates argue, between peace and temporary quiescence, and many such theorists speak in terms of a Freudian return of the repressed.

For all its evocative language and practical success, however, this frame has two major deficiencies. First, it tends to be ahistorical. This is not to say that it does not offer an historical account of itself: Quite the contrary, many participants in this discourse expend considerable energy specifying the lineage of the concept. A recent compilation of readings (Ishay 1997), for instance, includes "sources" as wide-ranging as the Bible, Epictetus, the Magna Carta, the English Bill of Rights, Immanuel Kant, Karl Marx, as well as Woodrow Wilson and Frantz Fanon. But tracing the lineage of a concept and specifying its developing role in changing social circumstances are not the same things. The lineage, moreover, often takes on Hegelian overtones: "The History of the World," Hegel wrote in the "Introduction" to *Lectures on the Philsophy of History*, "is none other than the progress of the consciousness of Freedom." And so it is with universal human rights. The lineage of universal human rights thus does not truly historicize the concept — for indeed, from this perspective, the concept is transhistorical — but focuses on its realization in practice and on "the coming to consciousness of itself" of the principle. According to the standard account, human rights, after all, are universal, which means not only that they are applicable all over the world but that they are valid principles for evaluating past societies as well. Missing, however, is an explanation of the historical circumstances that make it possible —- and indeed necessary — to think universalistically.

Additionally, and often as result of its ahistoricism, the literature on universal human rights is frequently unscientific, violating conventional distinctions between normative and empirical concerns. The question of why such rights exist in some places and not others — the identification of conditions of possibility[7] — is solely at the service of increasing and solidifying claims on behalf of the idea. In many respects, for all its talk of the value of unique cultures and rights to self-determination, the philosophical–jurisprudential literature on universal human rights commits the same conceptual sins its practitioners reject in modernization theory (i.e., assuming only unilinear and teleological model of moral and social development). The strong position on human rights dismisses historical or cross-cultural contextualization as either theologically unacceptable (i.e., to see the universality of human rights as contingent on kinds of social organization is to deny what makes us all human) or philosophically dangerous (i.e., sociological contextualization leads directly down a slippery slope to cultural relativism, thus vitiating the concept's legitimacy claim in practical politics).

These issues have been fought out partly under the rubric of a so-called "Asian Values" debate, in which critics charge that the human rights concept illegitimately universalizes what are in fact specifically Western values. The Western preference for liberal individualism, critics claim, is no more inherently universal than putative Asian preferences for collectivism.

Criticisms of this and other sorts resulted in the 1993 Bangkok Declaration, an explicit response to documents like the 1948 *Universal Declaration of Human Rights* — and to the more recent politics carried out under its banner — questioning the Western priority of rights over duties and individuals over collectivities (Bell, Nathan, and Peleg 2001; Habermas 2001). As Jürgen Habermas (2001) and others argue, however, the stark dichotomy between universal human rights and Asian values acts as a straightjacket: For it is possible to entertain doubts raised by critics of universal human rights without capitulating to the apparent relativism of the Asian values position.[8] My call here to investigate the historical conditions of possibility of universal human rights, therefore, should not be read as an embrace of moral relativism. Rather, it is part of an effort to make the politics of human rights more supple conceptually, indeed to recognize the sociohistorical achievement this frame of reference represents. Focusing on historical conditions of possibility, in sum, reframes the question as a sociological rather than philosophical one.[9]

The discourse of universal human rights is tied directly to a politics of regret because its advocates believe that only gestures of reparation, apology, and acknowledgment can restore the dignity of history's victims and can deter new outbreaks of inhumanity. The retrospective gaze of this discourse is thus part of an anticipation of the future. Hannah Arendt (1958, p. 237) puts this most eloquently when she binds forgiving and promising:

> The two faculties [forgiving and promising] belong together in so far as one of them, forgiving, serves to undo the deeds of the past, whose 'sins' hang like Damocles' sword over every new generation; and the other, binding oneself through promises, serves to set up in the ocean of uncertainty, which the future is by definition, islands of security without which not even continuity, let alone durability of any kind, would be possible in the relationships between men.

Nevertheless, this argument remains at an abstract philosophical level. Arendt does offer some considerations on the rise of the "politics of pity" after the French Revolution and on the unique conditions for the *Vita Activa* after the Holocaust, but the appeal of regret here, as elsewhere in the discourse on universal human rights, remains rather general.[10] The question remains of why the wave of regret is taking place now, however salutary these theorists see that wave or however advocates celebrate its triumphs.

Transitology

The second major frame for analyzing public apology is work, particularly by political scientists, that has come to be known as *"transitology."*[11]

Following the demise of authoritarian regimes in Latin America in the 1980s and the breakup of the Soviet Union following 1989, social scientists, legal scholars, and politicians alike have focused a great deal of their attention on problems of "transitional justice." How do new regimes deal with the legacies of their predecessors' past misdeeds? What solutions — including show trials, "political justice," "lustration," compensation, truth and reconciliation commissions, general amnesties, memorialization, and organized amnesia, among others — are most likely to provide a solid foundation for a peaceable future? Who is responsible for the crimes of the past, and what does that responsibility entail? What are its limits? Where legal scholars and politicians debate solutions normatively, social scientists observe the various choices and attempt to correlate them with differences in circumstances.

One of the earliest entries in this tide of studies is Samuel Huntington's (1991) *The Third Wave*. There Huntington lays out a number of basic empirical issues, raising questions of the correlation among various transition variables and possible outcomes. In his analysis of post-1989 transitions, Huntington places great emphasis on the timing and personnel involved in the changes. Were old elites agents of the change or objects of it? Did old elites remain in power, hand it over peacefully, or resist violently? Did the transformation come at the beginning of an international wave, and did the particular country and its leaders advocate the transformation or resist it? All of these factors, according to Huntington, contributed to the nature of the post-transition settlements.

Perhaps the most important goal of transitology is *typological*. Another work in this vein, by Claus Offe (1997), reveals this goal in its title, *Varieties of Transition*. A major three-volume compilation edited by Neil Kritz (1995) consists of case studies of the transition process and the solutions offered in a variety of cases, most prominently from Eastern Europe and Latin America. Another recent book — sitting at the borderline between the philosophical–juridical and transitological frames (as is the Kritz volume) — is called *Human Rights in Political Transitions: Gettysburg to Bosnia* (Hesse and Post 1999). Several other volumes have drawn comparisons between American Reconstruction after the civil war and recent transitions in Latin America and Eastern Europe. A number of other studies have compared Japan and Germany, many of them returning to the theory of shame versus guilt cultures Ruth Benedict advanced fifty years ago (e.g., Buruma 1994). I will return as well to Benedict's theory, but for its historical rather than typological dimensions.

In such inquiries, many scholars argue that the questions of transitions from authoritarian regimes are not just widespread in the modern world but are perennial ones, facing every society that has developed principles of justice based on anything more abstract than instantaneous retribution. In a programmatic statement for contemporary studies of transitional justice, for instance, Jon Elster (1998) uses an example from ancient Greece to demonstrate this permanence. In *The Constitution of Athens*, Aristotle describes an agreement between the Athenian oligarchs — the so-called "three thousand" — and the democrats in exile at Piraeus, drawn up under Spartan supervision. Most remarkable here was a provision that granted a general amnesty for everyone but the top leadership, who were nevertheless to become immune from prosecution once they had rendered their accounts. "A striking feature of the Athenian reconciliation treaty," Elster writes, "is that so many of the general themes of justice in the transition to democracy are already found in the very first well-documented instance" (ibid.).

One major difference between the Athenian case and contemporary ones, however, is the scope and purpose of reconciliation. In Athens, as Donald Shriver (1995) points out, vengeance was indeed limited for the purpose of preserving the community, but this did not lead to a universal human ethic against vengeance per se — quite the contrary at Nuremberg or in the current debate concerning jurisdiction over Pinochet. In contrast to ancient Athens, where the concern was largely for the continuity of the community, and to the age of heroic nationalism, where even the slightest vacillation was rejected as blasphemous (Hobsbawm 1990), today a great number of cases demonstrate a willingness to admit historical mistakes and even to try to make up for them.

Central to this new politics of regret is a more general moralization of political conflict.[12] Though the idea of *"just war"* is ancient, for instance, contemporary definitions are rather strict in comparison to earlier ones, and contemporary remedies are rather different. Premodern conflicts were often understood as contests between kings, who did not necessarily hold each other morally responsible for their conquests or defeats. And when acts of war were seen as illegitimate (e.g., when Charles V's armies sacked Rome in the sixteenth century), this involved the personal honor and responsibility of the king rather than the obligation of one people to another (e.g., in the sack of Rome, most of the soldiers were foreign mercenaries and the battlefield was not the object of the conflict, which was between a Spanish king and a French king). Solutions to premodern conflict most often involved bribes, trades, marriages, territorial transfers, and the like but rarely expressions of remorse, reparation to civilian victims, reeducation, or prosecution of "war crimes." And though premodern blood feuds may have been born of moral indignation, there are stark differences between premodern and modern political conflict and between blood feuds and collective responsibility. Though there are thus earlier precedents and models for reparation and apology, regret as a sine qua non of postconflict peace building, is a preeminently modern phenomenon; indeed, in many ways, the principle of political accountability defines contemporary politics.

In sum, principles of political justice, vengeance, compensation, and so forth have been around as long as there has been law: They were central in the Athenian example; they were present in the code of Hammurabi; they were formalized as principles of an international "system" by Hugo Grotius in 1625; and they have played out in twentieth-century institutions. According to transitologists, the more cases we can include in our models, the clearer will be our typologies and the better our predictions. Many important works in this tradition therefore adduce cases from widely divergent times and places into one vast model of transition. Where the transitology frame is to be admired for its analytical clarity and scientific impulse, however, its "variables" approach removes much of the context from the analysis, erasing the peculiarities of specific cases. In this literature, virtually any case is grist for the analytical mill.

In what sense can we speak of a transition to democracy in both ancient Athens and modern Hungary? In what sense can we speak of problems of restitution as comparable in Rwanda and Argentina? The very meaning of the terms and the units of analysis can be radically different — not just the conditions or orders in which universal variables operate. The transitology frame is thus no more help than the philosophical–jurisprudential frame in answering the question: Why regret, why now? Seeing the problems of transitional justice as basically perennial is to miss the profound ways in which both the questions and the answers have changed over the course of history.

The Historical Sociology of Political Regret

How can we explain this proliferation of collective regret?[13] One account emphasizes the postmodern demise of legitimating narratives: Within societies, disenfranchised groups produce alternative historical narratives that call elites to account for historical wrongs; across societies, subjugated peoples in the periphery challenge the arrogance of the center. Other accounts point to the morally shattering experiences of total war and genocide in the twentieth century: The Holocaust was a decisive refutation of the idea of progress and makes us all guilty, or, as Walter Benjamin (1968) argues so persuasively, World War I destroyed the bases of genuine experience, ending all claims to innocent national purpose (of course, more commonly the myth of the war experience stoked an even more bellicose nationalism). Still others point to the role of the mass media: Aryeh Neier (1998), for instance, argues that a decisive moment in the development of principles of political justice was the emergence of war correspondents in the mid nineteenth century, who were able to present the horrors of modern warfare to their readers at home (see also Boltanski 1999). In another important statement, which I will discuss shortly, Michel-Rolph Trouillot (2000) argues that the apologetic state extrapolates from the apologetic liberal individual; in a sort of inversion of Habermas, Trouillot could be said to be arguing for a colonization of the system by the life-world.

Most of these theories, however, though intriguing, seem to be merely descriptive or partial. They share a presumption that the emergence of regret is only a symptom of modernity — or of its demise — perhaps an interesting result or window but not at the heart of the process. In contrast, the remainder of this chapter explores resources for a more general developmental account that places regret at the center of modernity. In the process, I bring classical concerns of sociological theory into greater contact with the concerns of social theorizing outside of sociology: Though the concept of *collective memory* comes from sociology (Halbwachs 1966, 1992), within sociology its study is considered a special interest of the sociology of culture or the sociology of knowledge; outside of sociology — in history, literary criticism, anthropology, and elsewhere — in contrast, the concept has attracted some of the most fertile theoretical minds and has become a central preoccupation at the highest levels.[14] This chapter argues, in turn, that those important efforts outside of sociology suffer from a lack of attention to social–structural and cultural developments understood sociologically. We find leads for a sociological account of memory and regret in different theoretical traditions, ranging from Emile Durkheim and Norbert Elias on differentiation and density to Weber and Jürgen Habermas on rationalization. In what follows, I review these and others as resources for a theory of political regret, laying ground for a theory that attends to historical transformations in temporal perceptions leading to a rise in "historical consciousness," which I develop in chapters eight and nine. This perspective, I will argue, places memory and regret properly at the center of its sociological account of modernity

Regret and Responsibility

The two central questions for a sociohistorical theory of regret concern the ways regret is modern and the ways modernity is regretful. Beginning with the first, I turn to William James (1981) for some basic considerations. In *Principles of Psychology*, James writes, "An act has no ethical quality whatever unless it be chosen out of several all equally possible." Perhaps we might modify this just a bit by adding that the perception of alternative possibilities is important as well. And precisely this is what has developed to a radically different order in modern societies: Modernity makes the individual master of his fates and opens up to him a range of possibilities; at the same time, it also introduces a clearer sense of personal and collective responsibility, both theoretically in terms of philosophical and legal principles and practically as it involves him in matters of politics and war. Only under these conditions can one be aware of, and thus regret, not having acted otherwise, and only thus can one be held accountable — in all the senses of that word — for one's own acts of commission and omission as well as for acts committed "in one's name." This is as true for contemporary collectivities and their agents as it is for individuals.

In many ways, the problem of collective regret is synonymous with the problem of collective memory, and indeed of collectivity per se. In premodern societies, the space between individual and collective experience was easily bridged. In complexifying societies, however, people from different milieus congregate in urban settings, leaving behind both their earlier contexts and to some degree their earlier selves; the labors of life are more highly differentiated than in rural households; classes and guilds and interest groups form. Hence, the bases of agreement, the bonds of commonality, are much less obvious, requiring vast new efforts and conceptual frameworks (themes developed more extensively in chapter nine).

This is, of course, a Durkheimian account. Missing from many cultural accounts of collective regret, as already hinted, is a sense of the social–structural transformations just mentioned — the kinds Durkheim (1984) highlighted in his argument about the rise of individualism. Also important here are Durkheim's ideas about the growing functional requirements for contractual obligation and consistency in increasingly interlocked commercial societies. For instance, as I discuss in chapter eight, the idea of reparations is strongly based on an extrapolation of tort law and other institutions for generating consistency in commercial relations (e.g., insurance). This is one reason why Japan, whose cultural resources and identity might, and do, work against participating in the politics of regret, has made some gestures, albeit reluctantly: Reparation of past injustice maintains restitutive norms essential for contemporary forms of international commerce (see note 8).

But a social–structural account such as this can describe more than just a commercial order, to which the current discourse on reparations is sometimes reduced. In Elias's (1994) account, for instance, increasingly dense networks of relations give any single action a wide and unforeseeable circle of implication. As a result, actors need to temper violent outbursts, whose ultimate outcomes are impossible to predict. Indeed, one could explain the recent wave of apology as a recognition of the long chains of consequence for one's actions. This is the kind of argument Arendt (1958, pp. 233, 237) makes about forgiveness:

> Men ... have known that he who acts never quite knows what he is doing, that he always becomes "guilty" of consequences he never intended or foresaw, that no matter how disastrous and unexpected the consequences of his deed he can never undo it, that the process he starts is never consummated unequivocally in one single deed or event, and that its very meaning never discloses itself to the actor but only to the backward glance of the historian.... The possible redemption from the predicament of irreversibility — of being unable to undo what one has done though one did not, and could not, have known what he was doing — is the faculty of forgiving.... Without being forgiven, released from the consequences of what we have done, our capacity to act would, as it were, be confined to one single deed from which we could never recover....

Elias employs a similar logic, though highlighting the recentness of this condition. For him, the court society, with its complexly stylized ritual, in which a subtle gesture can lead to social, or even real, death, is the paradigm of contemporary civilization. The actors who constitute, and are constituted by, highly complex interaction orders by necessity have highly developed super egos, agencies of self-restraint. Combining Arendt and Elias, then, one can see how apology becomes a necessary part of the modern interaction ritual. This works close up (i.e., personal regret) as well as at a distance (i.e., collective regret) because the same principle governs both, which are, in Elias's terms, merely facets of the same figuration.[15]

Shame Culture versus Guilt Culture Revisited

Perhaps it would be useful, in this context, to revisit what is by now a quite old and much criticized theory of regret: The distinction, originally Benedict's (1989), between a shame culture and a guilt culture. This theory has been rightly criticized for its strong notions of national character and for the suspicion that the argument implies only Westerners are morally developed. Nevertheless, as with many dismissed older theories, there is more there than remains of it in our intellectual collective memory.

According to Benedict (1989) and to others who have followed in this tradition, shame cultures are characterized by high and connected degrees of visibility and conformity. In such societies, the most dangerous transgression is to draw attention to oneself; one avoids doing so through strict conformity to complex social rituals. The most important quality, in such a society, is a reputation for correct social performance. Everything depends on protecting appearances, and failure to do so produces a feeling of shame analogous to the feeling of shame produced by nakedness in public. Such societies require a high degree of self-discipline and frequently demand priority of the group over the individual. The reward for conformity in such a society is security and predictability. Behavioral norms in such societies, moreover, are quite group and context specific, unique cultural forms that are rarely transposable.

In contrast, guilt cultures are characterized by the private judgment of individual consciences, heard as internal voices rather than felt as external gazes. Individuals in such cultures are individually responsible to generalized norms. Guilt, in this account, does not destroy the individual; rather, it forms the foundation of the moral person. Internalizing social norms, as Sigmund Freud emphasized, is part of the process of individuation, not the elimination of the individual.

This distinction is obviously quite overdrawn. We find instances of both guilt and shame in most societies; characterizing a society as fundamentally one or the other is clearly a distortion.[16] Nevertheless, the theory does provide some important insights into the history of regret: Although Benedict's argument is based primarily on a psychological reading of a national character, she contextualizes her reading within a historical and structural frame. In Japan, for example, a feeling of indebtedness, known as *on* — pervasive in Japanese political and social structure, according to Benedict — serves as a support mechanism for a thoroughly hierarchical political system. Each individual is under obligation to someone above them, culminating in the emperor, or the Shogun or feudal lord in premodern history. *On*, more akin to debt than guilt, is therefore depicted by Benedict as the glue of a social system dependent on the primacy of the homogenous group. In contrast, we may recall Nietzsche's argument in *The Genealogy of Morals* that the history of Western morality is the transformation of debt into guilt. Guilt, extrapolating from Benedict's account, is inherently more universalistic because it is founded on, and founds, structural heterogeneity.

For all its ethnocentrism, the attempt to articulate different historical paths to, and structural conditions of, guilt and shame is a clear advance over the ethical universalism and transhistoricism of the universal human rights paradigm. Made more supple by refining its concept of national character with Elias's less essentialist notion of national habitus — an inherently historical phenomenon — revives some of this theory's usefulness in explaining the wave of regret. Moreover, it is not necessary to assume that the politics of regret involves all guilt and no shame. We are reminded, though, how much questions of political ethics are rooted in the duality of emotion and social structure. The politics of regret is a feature of high social–structural and cultural capacities for both shame and guilt. One advantage of revising this approach by reading it through Elias is that doing so shows us how both guilt and shame are products of highly developed social structures[17] and that both can result in a politics of regret but that the politics of regret takes different forms in different places.[18] Most importantly, however, this approach shows the central relationship between guilt and universalism, a connection missing from important sociological accounts of universalization, discussed in the next two sections.

The Rationalized World and the Ethic of Responsibility

To understand the relation just discussed between political ethics and social structure, there is no more useful place to turn than Weber (1946a). Discussions of transition within the philosophical–jurisprudential frame, as we saw, pose a stark choice between retribution and utility, just deserts, and peace at all costs. In the abstract, there are good reasons for defending each of these and long traditions of doing so. But in practice, as discussed in more detail in the next chapter, they often become mere justifications for less admirable positions: on the one hand, the victim's lust for revenge; on the other, the perpetrator's self-serving haste to bury misdeeds. Excluding the victim's lust for revenge and the perpetrator's self-interested amnesia, however, does not solve the problem. According to Weber, then, the absolute terms of the debate — dogma versus opportunism — are not really supple enough to respect the different positions in which equally serious parties advocate different solutions (e.g., purge versus amnesty) as well as see different criteria (e.g. principle versus consequence) as ethical guides. Particularly in his essays on science and politics as vocations, Weber articulates a subtler, and more historical, distinction between what he calls an *"ethic of conviction"* and an *"ethic of responsibility."*

As we will see, this was no mere exercise in political ethics: The distinction, it is often forgotten, rests on a profoundly historical account of the conditions of possibility for the two principles. Indeed, Weber connects his preference for an ethic of responsibility over an ethic of conviction with his wider historical account of the rationalization and disenchantment of the world. For Weber, an ethic of conviction, though perhaps admirably motivated, fails to recognize the contribution of science in the modern rationalized world. In this context, science means acknowledging the inescapability of value conflict and that ends and means are not integrally connected. For a follower of an ethic of conviction, the "ought" does not depend on feasibility, and this kind of a position thus denies the realistic framework of science. In contrast, the ethic of responsibility embraces the ethical irrationality of the world and recognizes that realizing values in politics often involves a so-called "pact with diabolical powers." Weber is careful; this is not dogma versus opportunism, or even ethical policy versus *Realpolitik*. Responsibility is an ethical principle, not the absence of one, but it opts for compromise and small steps in the pursuit of political values. Responsibility lies between conviction and *Realpolitik*.

Though Weber unpacks this argument in general terms, as the next chapter shows, it is important to remember that he developed it immediately following his work on the war guilt question in "negotiations" over the Treaty of Versailles and in reaction to revolutionary parties in Germany in 1918, who were ready to accept the war guilt thesis out of pacifist and other convictions. Weber rejects these positions as blind to necessity, feasibility, and consequence — and exhorted students to understand the ethical obligation of the politician to be "responsible." Again, this is not a call to *Realpolitik*, which would imply no ethical principle, but a call to pursue whatever value one advocates in a manner sensitive to the possibilities of realizing it and to the relativity, rather than absolute hierarchy, of possible outcomes. The ability to recognize this relativity of values and the distinction between means and ends characteristic of the rationalized, scientific world view is possible only at a certain moment in history.

Following Weber, then, regret based on an ethic of conviction seems to be a premodern residue, unless one justifies the regret in terms of its consequences. Weber himself rejected the pacifist voices calling for Germany to accept the war guilt clause — as if Germany had a choice — because he thought this was irresponsible, that is, a rejection of the consequences in favor of the principle. The question remains whether it is ever possible, in Weber's framework, to have a responsible politics of regret. This question is the subject of the chapter that follows, which returns to Weber's framework in much greater detail.

Apology as Universal Norms of Justice

Habermas (1996) provides another argument, generically related to Weber's, potentially useful for explaining the recent wave of regret within a developmental account (The final chapter of this book takes the Habermasian position again in greater detail than outlined here). According to Habermas, modern collective identity has involved a shaky balance between two products of modernization: universalism and particularlism. Universalism refers to the ideas of freedom and democracy that are central features of Enlightenment thinking, but these ideas have been pursued, for the most part, through the particularism of nation-states — structures that have also developed during modernization. For the most part, these two principles have remained in balance to produce what Habermas calls "conventional identity." Fascism, according to Habermas's scheme, finds its organic form of nationalistic identity by embracing particularism at sever cost to universalism.

In contrast, Habermas (1996) would like to see communal identities form on the basis of universalistic principles alone. In the case of Germany, and by extension elsewhere, this should take the form of a "Constitutional Patriotism," in which a "post-conventional" identity is founded on rational principles and embodied in democratic legal structures. For Habermas, universalism is the great achievement of modernity. Habermas's developmental theory analogizes psychological theories of moral development and the social history of legal norms. According to psychologists like Jean Piaget and Lawrence Kohlberg, the younger child seeks direct rewards and avoids punishment and only the older child is able to follow abstract rules; according to Kohlberg, only rational Western men of a particular level of education are able to behave in a universalistic fashion, and only a very few individuals are able to do so consistently. For Habermas, who "reconstructs" historical materialism, the history of society is a learning process, the ultimate achievement of which is a rational — and so, universal — norm of justice. The recent wave of regret, one could infer from this theory, is a result of the triumph of universalistic principles of justice, principles built not only on reciprocity and restitution but also on the horror of past failures.

One problem with Habermas's (1996) account is that it does not provide a good explanation for allegiances based on constitutional patriotism. Emotionally motivating communal feelings on rationalistic principles is difficult. Indeed, for Habermas, the sense of community that requires Germans to accept responsibility for National Socialism is, in important ways, pre- or extrarational. This must be the case, because historical consciousness for Habermas is not, strictly speaking, a rational principle of identification. For Habermas, the reason to remember the Holocaust is that doing so is a promise to the universalistic future, to put it in Arendt's terms.

Attaching a theory of guilt to a Habermasian account of the progress of universal norms may help us see regret as a central indicator of the rationalization process. But the inherent teleology of the account, it seems, does not get us all that much further than the Hegelianism of the Universal Human Rights frame. The process remains rather disembodied. Certainly, Habermas does tie his account of the evolution of norms to more traditionally materialist concerns on the one hand, and to Weberian notions of rationalization on the other. Nevertheless, such approaches seem to us to leave out the most important, and directly relevant, feature of modernity's trajectory: temporality, more specifically the profound transformation in the experience of time that characterizes modernity, the German word for which (*Neuzeit*) again literally means new time. Where the theoretical perspectives enumerated already provide important background considerations, it seems that the rise of historical consciousness crystallizes what is fundamental to the modern regretful experience. The remainder of the book suggests the outlines of this process. This theme of temporalization reappears in, and links together, all four chapters in this part of the book, though the first part, particularly the emphasis on process, clearly sets the framework as well.

Conclusions

The politics of regret, then, is no mere fad, no simple offshoot of more important developments. It appears to be the major characteristic of our age, an age of shattered time and shifting allegiances, indeed of skepticism toward allegiances at all. In a recent paper, the Haitian anthropologist Michel-Rolph Trouillot (2000) asked the same question asked here: Why so many apologies now? In Trouillot's account, the wave of apologies at the political level expresses the triumphant extrapolation of the liberal individual to the collective level: The rhetoric of collective identity, he argues, has copied the integrative tools of the modern individual. Clearly, we disagree with this argument. First, it is certainly less true today than it was a hundred years ago that we anthropomorphize collective identities — or if we do this now, it is more the individual suffering posttraumatic stress or multiple personality syndrome that we extrapolate rather than the sober figure of psychological health. And it is only now that these identities and their spokespersons have become regretful. Second, there is nothing at all triumphant about this grasp by collectivities for human character: Where earlier the king literally embodied the unity of the nation, the problem of memory has emerged at exactly that point when the problem of the collectivity has reached its peak. Memory and regret are not the result of the integration of the collectivity but of the impossibility of this in an age of competing claims, multiple histories, and plural perceptions. Furthermore, to see the state as taking on the character of the individual is to miss the ways the state acts precisely as a surrogate for the individual — what the state commemorates and compensates we do not have to. For us, the rise of regret in all its forms is a sign of the failure of the state to generate adequate psychological defense mechanisms, not of the state's success in doing so. Trouillot has the order of logic reversed: The confessional individual mimics the regretful state, not the other way around — or at the least they are codetermined phenomena. In sum, the appropriate frame for explaining the recent rise of regret is a historical–sociological one that sees regret as part of broad transformations tied up with the decline, rather than the triumph, of the nation-state.

In contrast to the moral philosophers of universal human rights, we thus see the contemporary wave of regret as an embedded social product and not as the coming into self-consciousness of a world historical idea. It may indeed be appropriate and desirable, but like all moral codes and practices, it is socially conditioned. In contrast to the transitologists, we resist seeing transition outcomes as combinatorial solutions to perennial problems. The very meanings of the terms and social identities of the possible players are historical, rather than logical, constructs.

The question is now how to specify or, in more classical social scientific language, to test these accounts of regret. Our considerations here, it should be clear, are a mere prolegomenon to a detailed empirical study of the moments and mechanisms in which regret has developed into this fundamental feature of late modern life. As we have seen, such an account needs to focus on commercial, political, legal, as well as conceptual developments, none of which should be seen as inevitable despite the developmental trajectories outlined here. In addition to determining possible turning points within these developments (e.g., the 1919 Treaty of Versailles, which in many ways introduced the modern notion of war guilt), one must investigate the changing institutional mechanisms for encouraging regret, which include not just the idea of a community of nations and universal human rights but also new ideas for restitution, reparation, apology, redress, and historical inquiry, as well as the trans- and nongovernmental organizations discussed at the beginning of this chapter. Producing this kind of historically situated account hopefully will help us to see present debates as about neither historical necessities nor strategic options but as a form of consciousness particular to our moment.

CHAPTER 7

The Value of Regret?
Lessons from and for Germany

If a guiding motif of the long nineteenth century was that war is the continuation of politics by other means, politics today seems to have become the continuation of war by other means. Power has certainly not disappeared, nor even diminished, but it has often become more subtle: Hegemony has become hegemonic. This cloaking and transformation of violence in symbolic forms, however, has increased the possibility for challenges that do not depend entirely on traditional material resources. "The struggle of man against power," Czech novelist Milan Kundera puts it in *The Book of Laughter and Forgetting*, "is the struggle of memory against forgetting." Victors and victims are now entwined in ongoing struggles of claim and counterclaim, memory and countermemory: Contemporary politics continues past wars as discursive battles over their legacies. The question is whether these discursive struggles tend toward a resolution or generate new cycles of hatred and atrocity.

Mnemonic resistance has become a common strategy in the past few decades, when increasing numbers of individuals and groups have challenged official versions of the past and demanded redress for perceived contemporary and historical wrongs. Perhaps surprisingly, governments and societal elites have become more and more willing to respond to such claims, even when the claimant groups are not particularly powerful in traditional terms. Indeed, a general willingness to acknowledge collective historical misdeeds has disseminated throughout the world, leading to more and more frequent official and unofficial apologies to both internal and external victims. An expectation of acknowledgment has become a decisive factor in processes of "transitional justice" as well as in domestic and international politics more generally. What forms such acknowledgment should take, what acknowledgment means, have thus become central questions where this politics of regret has taken hold.

Of course, there is far from universal agreement that this political regret is a positive development. In the late nineteenth century, the theorist Ernest Renan pointed out that forgetting is at the heart of national self-understanding. Friedrich Nietzsche warned that an excess of history can destroy our humanity: "The past," he wrote, "has to be forgotten if it is not to become the gravedigger of the present." Contemporary theorists of memory are fond of quoting Borges' short story, "Funes the Memorious," about a boy who, after falling on his head, loses the ability to forget. This inability to forget makes his life impossible. In virtually every setting, there are those — and not just former perpetrators — who argue that remembering certain aspects of the past can be toxic to collective identity and political legitimation. How, then, are we to think about this delicate balance between remembering and forgetting? And what modes of memory are least likely to produce the destructive side effects these theorists identify?

Efforts to address these problems of collective memory — how societies deal with the legacies of toxic pasts — almost inevitably begin with the German case, where, as we have seen, the problems of memory have loomed larger and more potently in public discourse than perhaps anywhere else. Whether one views contemporary Germany as illegitimately burdened with a past that will not pass away or as appropriately shaped by difficult memories, politicians and scholars in many other places debating what to do after transitions from regimes of brutality have looked to the German case as something of a canary in the mine of historical consciousness. What have the effects of historical consciousness been there? Have its various forms been beneficial or destructive? Nuremberg was certainly a decisive event in the history of political justice, but it was only the beginning of a longer discourse about guilt and responsibility in Germany and elsewhere. The German case is thus especially instructive for the question of what criteria to employ when deliberating about the best course of action because it provided both a wide palate of arguments as well as a concrete test of various solutions.

How did Germany manage the legacy of its toxic history? As the previous chapters have shown, there is no one answer to this; different solutions vied with each other at the same time, and different ones took precedence in different periods, though always with an awareness of and in reaction to earlier arguments and solutions. It is a commonplace of later commentary, for instance, that the Federal Republic of Germany in its first period "suppressed" the Nazi past. Of course, exactly what we could mean by suppressing the past is rather complicated. Early leaders, we saw, particularly the venerable chancellor Konrad Adenauer, defined the new state as the antithesis of its predecessor. The basic law was self-consciously conceived as a bulwark against the possibility of developments similar to those that had led to the demise of the Weimar Republic. From 1951 to 1953, West Germany negotiated with the State of Israel and Jewish organizations over an unprecedented reparations agreement, at the end of which, though over substantial opposition in his own cabinet and in public opinion, Adenauer agreed to payments and transfers valuing 1.5 billion marks, which climbed to over ten billion marks over the next several decades. West German leaders propagated an official philo-Semitism, participated in commemorative rituals, condemned the so-called uneducable, and claimed to have learned the lessons of the past, which led them then to a rhetoric of "militant" democracy, to a strong commitment to the Western alliance, and to a general posture of "reliability" as a lesson of the past. In what sense, then, did this add up to a "suppression" of the past?

Critiques, as we have seen, focus particularly on the ways both ordinary Germans and their political leaders ranked their own suffering above that of Jews and others who had been persecuted by Nazi Germany, failed to acknowledge varieties of perpetration beyond a narrow clique of political leaders and those directly involved in atrocities (referred to as "Hitler and his henchmen") and refused to discuss the specifics of the crimes, preferring instead a vague passive grammar in public — "the crimes that were committed" or "what happened in those years" — and silence regarding personal experiences. Most important, critics charge, was the failure to undertake a genuine denazification of public life, haste to rehabilitate burdened individuals, calls for a general amnesty — all under the umbrella of vehemently rejecting not only accusations of collective guilt but really also of any guilt at all. Here is what Adenauer said in his first address as chancellor in 1949:

> Through the denazification, much misfortune and much harm was produced. The truly guilty of the crimes that were committed in the National Socialist time and in war should be punished with all severity. But as far as the rest, we can no longer distinguish between two classes of people in Germany: the politically unobjectionable and the objectionable. This distinction must disappear immediately. The war and the disorders of the postwar period have brought such hard trials and such tribulations for so many, that one has to summon understanding for many lapses and misdemeanors. The question of a general amnesty will therefore be examined by the federal government. When the federal government is determined to let the

past be past when it seems defensible, in the conviction that many have already paid for subjectively minor guilt, it is on the other hand also absolutely decided to draw out of the past all the necessary lessons in regard to all those who clamor against the state, may they be attributable to right radicalism or left radicalism.

After only a brief mention of recent anti-Semitic expressions, which he dismissed as bizarre and inexplicable — a mere four years after the liberation of Auschwitz — Adenauer turned to the more pressing problem of German prisoners of war: "The fate of these millions of Germans, who now for years have born the bitter lot of captivity, is so heavy, the suffering of their families in Germany so great, that all peoples must help finally to give back these captives and displaced to their homeland and families." As for the problem of ethnic expellees from the Eastern territories, Adenauer almost threatened, "One must solve it if one does not want to let West Germany become a hotbed of political and economic unrest for a long period."

These last remarks raise the question of Adenauer's motivations. On the one hand, Adenauer's own experiences as a so-called inner emigré who was indeed persecuted by the Nazis and his own long political career before 1933, which included a Catholic Rhinelander's distaste for things Prussian, made accusations of collective guilt nonsensical to him and generated his sympathy for German suffering. On the other hand, as his long-time advisor Herbert Blankenhorn later described it, "Dr. Adenauer said nothing for years on the topic of the Jews, because he wished to win over the German people in its entirety to the cause of democracy. If Mr. Adenauer had said in 1949 what we had done in the past, then the German people would have been against him" (Herf 1997, p. 226). A bit of personal understanding thus combines with what many later critics charged was a debased and complicit *Realpolitik*.

A thorough rejection of this posture, as we saw, was the leading idea of the rebellious new generation coming to maturity in the 1960s. Precisely in the name of "daring more democracy," the so-called sixty-eighters rejected what Adenauer claimed to have done to secure the institutional and popular foundation for that democracy. In contrast to the language of reliability Adenauer and others purveyed in the 1950s, the student movement and the charismatic young chancellor Willy Brandt placed morality over *Realpolitik*. The new generation accused their parents and the system they had built, saw only continuity where their parents had avowed caesura. When Brandt went on his knees in Warsaw, the reversal of posture was complete. Indeed, at times this new regime and its intellectual gurus seemed to claim moral superiority not only over their predecessors but over other nations as well, deriving from their unflinching confrontation with collective responsibility. Of course, one prerequisite for that unflinching acceptance of the burden of history is that it was just that: a historical burden rather than a present accusation.

This epoch of the moral nation, we saw, cleared the way for a new rhetoric of normalization. In a first stage, chancellor Helmut Schmidt (Social Democratic Party) depended on the symbolic work of his predecessor Brandt as a justification for treating the matters as settled and now focused on the "normal" problems West Germany faced as a "normal" state. But with the change of power to Helmut Kohl's Christian Democrats in 1982, a burgeoning neoconservative movement took the lead. Here the concern was to make up for the apparent legitimation deficits of the welfare state in a time of growing demands and declining capabilities. This new intellectual and political trend turned to history as the solution to Germany's legitimation deficit, and Kohl and his advisors pursued a cultural program that sought to accept German history "with all its highs and lows," a favorite trope rung at every opportunity.

Here, the centrality of Nazism in narratives of German history, so often characterized as the telos of the national spirit, stood in the way of the proud identity and healthy patriotism sought by the new cultural politicians. In the process, the moral politics of the sixties was vilified. These Germans, literally and figuratively on their knees, were seen as reveling in national self-flagellation and forcing young Germans to walk around "in hair shirts in perpetuity," as another common trope put it. On numerous occasions, Adenauer's choice for integration and legitimacy over memory and regret was hailed as heroic realism. The vilification of the New Left, however, often encouraged rather overdramatic terms — perhaps partly learned from the left's earlier indiscriminate use of the fascist label — and extravagant claims about the necessity of Adenauer's compromises, namely that not doing so would have led to a civil war, though what form that might have taken in an occupied country is not clear.

Two general competing criteria of how to manage the legacies of the past should be apparent even in this brief account, though clearly emerging more over the course of an historical narrative than as abstract philosophical principles. Classical political ethics, as well as practical politics, pose a stark choice between retribution and utility. In the abstract, there are good reasons for defending each of these, and long traditions of doing so. But in practice, they often become mere justifications for less admirable positions: on the one hand, the victim's lust for revenge; on the other, the perpetrator's haste to bury misdeeds. But we know well the dangers of blood lust, where universal suffering breeds only particularistic sympathy. There is thus a wide moral gulf between quiescence achieved by suppressing the past, and real peace. A past not worked through because it seems to cost too much will indeed create the deficits neoconservatives lament.

The absolute terms of the debate — dogma versus opportunism — are thus not really supple enough to take seriously the different positions apparent in this short narrative from Germany, as well as in the many other cases in which equally serious parties advocate both different solutions (e.g., purge versus amnesty) as well as see different criteria (e.g., principle versus consequence) as ethical guides. For a more versatile framework, I return to the great German sociologist Max Weber (1946a), who, as the previous chapter illustrated, articulates a subtler distinction between what he called an *"ethic of conviction"* and an *"ethic of responsibility."*

As we saw, Weber articulated this distinction in very general terms and sought to connect up his preference for an ethic of responsibility over an ethic of conviction with his wider historical account of the rationalization and disenchantment of the world. To review the discussion in the previous chapter: For Weber, an ethic of conviction, though perhaps admirably motivated, fails to recognize the contribution of science in the modern rationalized world. In this context, science for Weber means acknowledging the inescapability of value conflict and that ends and means are not integrally connected. For a follower of an ethic of conviction, the "ought" does not depend on feasibility, and this kind of a position thus denies the realistic framework of science. In contrast, the ethic of responsibility embraces the ethical irrationality of the world and recognizes that realizing values in politics often involves a so-called "pact with diabolical powers." Again Weber is careful: This is not dogma versus opportunism, or even ethical policy versus *Realpolitik*. Responsibility is an ethical principle, not the absence of one. But it is one that opts for compromise and small steps in the pursuit of political values. The efforts of the German sixty-eighters, on this account, follow an ethic of conviction. It is less clear whether Adenauer's policies and later nostalgia for them follow an ethic of responsibility.

As we also saw, while Weber unpacks this argument in general terms, it is important to remember that he developed it immediately following his work on the war guilt question in negotiations over the Treaty of Versailles and in reaction to revolutionary parties in Germany in 1918 who were ready to accept the war guilt thesis out of pacifist and other convictions. Weber rejects these positions as based on an ethic of conviction — and thus as blind to necessity, feasibility, and consequence — and exhorted students to understand the ethical obligation of the politician to be responsible. Again, this is not a call to *Realpolitik*, which would imply no ethical principle, but a call to pursue whatever value one advocates in a manner sensitive to the possibilities of realizing it and to the relativity, rather than absolute hierarchy, of possible outcomes. Nevertheless, Weber rejects the war guilt clause on the basis of an ethic of responsibility in pursuit of his liberal nationalist values.

The question for the present chapter is whether there can ever be an ethically responsible politics of regret or whether all such calls are ultimately expressions of an irrational moralism, perhaps well motivated but blind to reality. It is certainly easy enough to dismiss Adenauer's compromises as unprincipled *Realpolitik*: Adenauer was expert at exploiting geopolitics to end denazification, to rehabilitate the German soldier, to justify reintegration of Nazi civil servants and personnel continuities at the highest levels. It is, moreover, also easy, though certainly not as easy, to see the New Left as sanctimonious dogmatists, unable to recognize the difference between Hitler and Adenauer, the Third Reich and capitalist West Germany. No matter what the realities of the German case, however, there is still room for debate between those who would hang the associates of criminal regimes in the public square, purge the armies, exclude the complicit right down to the last postman, and those who prefer to let bygones be bygones, whether the victims agree or not. Does an ethic of responsibility always prefer the latter, as Weber's own position against the war guilt clause might suggest?

In the spirit of the ethic of responsibility, which places stock in science not to determine the choice of ultimate values but to help select its most feasible means, our answer has to depend on an analysis of both the different possible ultimate ends and the various means available for pursuing them. Regarding the former, there seems to be a number of competing propositions. For Weber, the choice might have been between peace and the national interest, though Weber saw peace as bogus without vigorously defended national interests. For the present, we have to ask ourselves about both the relationship between peace and national interests as well as what exactly constitutes peace. In the first place, the salience of national identifications in the contemporary world has clearly declined, or at least national principles face, great and increasing competition from other principles of identification. Certainly Weber could reasonably speak in terms of the interests of the nation as paramount. By Adenauer's time, and certainly by the sixties, such values had already begun to appear exhausted, even anachronistic. Today, with national societies divided as much against themselves as against others, national interests cannot as easily justify amnesiac settlements in the name of continuity. It is also clear in many cases — for instance in the debate over the extradition of Chilean dictator Augusto Pinochet — that even the most narrowly domestic disputes never really are. Though borders and allegiances have always been complicated, ever new forms of such complication are arising at ever greater pace, indeed in part as the result of mnemonic battles.

In the second place — the question of what peace means — we can, I believe, responsibly debate, at the level of ultimate values, whether peace means quiescence or requires something more in the way of reconciliation. In the aftermath of the First World War, for instance, Walter Benjamin (1968) worried that the proliferation of memorials and commemorations provided a false consolation, ennobling the "sacrifice" of dead soldiers in the service of ever new programs; real mourning, according to Benjamin, required keeping the wound open, not to motivate new struggles but to prevent the reality of the deaths from being swept up into some future with which they had nothing to do. In a similar vein, Theodor Adorno (1986) argued in 1959 that we must "work through" the past to "break its spell," rather than try to "master" it with silence; only the former will produce enlightenment, whereas the latter lays the foundation for Freud's "return of the repressed."

Along these lines, a good argument can be made that the German quiescence of the 1950s did not serve the long-term interests of peace, with the comparatively great vigor of German protests in the sixties, terrorism in the seventies, and xenophobia in the eighties and nineties as evidence. This is to say nothing of the aggregate and collective psychic burdens on the perpetrators and their children, which have surely produced peculiar symptoms. These are questions all societies seeking some kind of settlement with the legacies of the past must ask: What counts as reconciliation?

The second major kind of question — after we decide the issue of what ultimate value we want to pursue responsibly — is the more technical question of how we do that. As far as I am concerned, far too little thought has been given to the very limited capabilities of both the perpetrators and the victims, and many of the present solutions either demand too much of both or pander to their baser instincts. Simple amnesty, for instance, tramples the feelings of the victim, asking him to live in the house of the hangman without comment. In Talmudic terms, this kind of a failure to do justice for the victims is termed a second guilt: a failure to expiate the injustice after it has occurred, the perpetration of a second harm. On the other hand, lustration, *Berufsverbot*, exclusion from society treat all complicit individuals — regardless of the degree or nature of complicity — as equally guilty. And who among us is not guilty of some prejudice, weakness, callow enthusiasm, and the like? As already mentioned, in 1946, the philosopher Karl Jaspers distinguished four kinds of guilt: criminal, political, moral, and metaphysical. Criminal guilt is quite narrowly defined. Certainly more than the few dozen tried at Nuremberg bore some criminal responsibility for the past, but how much, and what kind, and where do we draw the line? One can draw absolute distinctions only at a distance, for the reality of human complicity is much more complex. And who but the victims would be left after such a cleansing? Moreover, the same process of absolute distinction between perpetrator and bystander leads to a false heroization of the victims as well, one which denies their ordinary humanity through the same logic, now merely reversed, with which they were originally persecuted.

What of apologies, official or individual? Apologies can be either genuine or cynical. Though a cynical apology, particularly if it is accompanied by, or lays the groundwork for, material restitution may help to assuage some of the wounds of persecution, it does not necessarily involve any real learning and must therefore be rejected by the victims to whom it has been addressed — for indeed, an apology is always addressive in one way or another. And this leads me to the case of genuine apology.

On the collective level, an official apology, insofar as it is anything more than instrumental pandering, can effect a turn in the narrative basis of community and can justify new directions. And this is important. But the connection between this collective level and the individual level is not straightforward. Official apologies often alleviate the burden on individuals, doing the work individuals and the institutions of civil society are unwilling to undertake. Such apologies thus stand in for rather than express genuine moral and political regret.

At the individual level, moreover, apology often is misconceived, demanding too much of both perpetrator and victim. In the first place, it presumes that the perpetrator repudiates his earlier self without qualification. There are very few of us, to say nothing of those who have been able to participate in atrocities in one form or another, who are really capable of this. Where an ethic of conviction would tell us to demand nothing else, an ethic of responsibility is more sensitive to human realities and does not base its solutions on wishful thinking or Utopian faith in the human capacity for redemption. In the second place, what can your child's torturer possibly say to you that would make a difference? An apology, after all, always involves some form of exculpation: Times were different, I made a mistake, I did not understand. If it does not, it is not an apology at all. It is repentance or confession and thus is wrongly addressed to the victim, who is not in a position to grant the kind of absolution sought.

Do we really want to build our hope for peace on the abilities of ordinary people to forgive? Sigmund Freud is often quoted as having said that we should always forgive our enemies, but not until after they have been hanged. Where whole societies are complicit, how many of them do we hang? And does doing so really end the cycle? The biblical proclamation that the sins of the fathers shall be delivered to the third and fourth generations seems a moderate prediction in comparison to the historical record.

What, then, can be done in the time of perpetrator and victim? We must do something, but can what we do possibly produce reconciliation in the present? My argument is that such reconciliation is indeed rare. That does not mean that there is nothing to be done. But the question is for whom we are doing it. We certainly owe the victims all possible compensation and help to repair what is really irreparable, though it is in practice often unclear where the limits of victimhood lie. And, at risk of sounding like the sanctimonious Kantian who advocates punishing the criminal to restore the criminal's humanity, we owe it to the perpetrator and to the perpetrator's children to make clear exactly what he or she did wrong, though that effort is most often in vain. But for me, the relevant collectivity, the only one that can be healed and can learn the lessons of history and make something of them, is the next generation. What can we do so that the children of perpetrator and victim can come together in a community in which guilt and suffering alike will not be born as marks of Cain through the generations? Suppressing the past even with the best intentions , it seems to me, mistakes quiescence for peace, burying the problem close to the surface where it will return to haunt later generations.

Whatever material and criminal solutions we pursue in the present, we must engage in testimony as a legacy for the future. This means listening to both victims and perpetrators, and not to judge absolute truth or even to sympathize with either but to learn from their experiences and perspectives. For only through developing realistic images of both sides, which means both interested testimony and disinterested historiography, can we avoid turning ordinary victims into martyrs and ordinary perpetrators into psychopaths, as so many commemorative images and claims do. The excuses of the perpetrators are an important part of their testimony here, not because they lead us to exculpate them but because they provide a record on the basis of which their children can understand their culpability as well as their humanity. For the victims as well, realism is also crucial because only a realistic depiction will aid them in avoiding the well-documented guilt of the second generation, in which children feel their own trials and tribulations are inconsequential because they can never be compared to the suffering of their parents, or in which the legacy of martyred generations keeps the flame of hatred burning.

The closest approximation we have had of such a procedure is the South African Truth and Reconciliation Commission, which has offered amnesty to perpetrators who will testify honestly about their involvement. Sometimes this does indeed seem to have led to reconciliation between perpetrator and victim, though just as often it has not. But it remains to be seen whether perpetrators and victims will be able to produce a civil discourse on the basis of such confrontations. For the moment, perhaps forbearance is all that is possible, or even desirable, though the commission's designers hoped for more.

But the real success of the commission, it seems to me, has been that it has established a record for the future. This works at both a personal and a collective level. The understandable love of children for their complicit parents will not, after such testimony, be able to blind them to the facts of perpetration. The victims have finally received an acknowledgment of their humanity in the opportunity to confront their persecutors, but in such a way that prevents them from denying the humanity of the perpetrators in turn. The children of the victims thereby have the opportunity to see the children of the perpetrators not as the fruits of monsters but as human beings struggling, though from a different perspective, with the legacies — and they are always plural — of the past. This has also been a unique opportunity for whites and blacks to confront each other face to face as citizens in a society in which contact between the races is sharply constrained by geographical, social, and economic distance. Whatever emotional powers were released in this crucible, it was one that required acknowledgment from both sides, thus providing a precedent for future civil discourse and indeed disputation.

At the collective level, the South African process has been remarkable as well, particularly when Nelson Mandela refused to dissent from the final report in which the African National Congress was condemned for various criminal activities. This is the most realistic political justice I have heard of, one where recognizing clear lines of historical perpetration has not led to the canonization of saints, martyrs, and psychopaths but instead to a realistic depiction of a sick society in which lines of admirable and despicable behavior were not as clearly drawn as victor's justice would like.

The South African case is certainly unique, not just for the solutions pursued but for the circumstance that allowed them. The victims there are the majority, the transfer of power was more or less smooth, and many basic institutions continued to operate if with changed personnel. These conditions do not obtain in all cases. They certainly did not in Germany in 1945. But even there, and in similar circumstances, we must ask whether present threats to the collectivity — in the German case, that of the potential spread of Soviet domination — serve as an alibi for past actions and for present solutions. Perhaps confrontation with the past is not always wise in times of emergency. There is a big difference between trying to destroy the truth by burying it and attempting to provide the foundation for a postponed confrontation. Even in the case of East Germany, where opening the files of the secret police revealed often deeply personal violations, it does not seem to me we can really maintain it would have been better — yes, certainly easier — not to know. However much we might empathize with the desire to escape from freedom, as Erich Fromm put it in a different context, we cannot use this as a foundation for political ethics.

An ethic of responsibility in pursuit of genuine peace and reconciliation opens up alternatives to the seemingly intractable choice between imposing retributive convictions and bowing to the pressures of *Realpolitik*. Nowhere was this clearer than in the debate about whether to allow the extradition of Pinochet to Spain. As it was framed, the choice was one between punishing a dictator at all costs or helping secure a new, more peaceful regime and avoiding a Pandora's box of international encroachments on sovereign governments. A third choice, however, would have been consistent with an ethic of responsibility: Do not allow the extradition, but go ahead and try Pinochet in absentia. It certainly would be better if Chile would sponsor its own forum for truth telling — and they have made some gestures in this direction — but there are real impediments to such an endeavor. In lieu of such an effort, however, other countries, or better yet international agencies, could have provided a forum for testimony of all kinds. If Pinochet or his supporters chose not to provide a defense, it would have been at the cost of not preserving their perspective and not engaging in a moral discourse. (That Pinochet has died in the meantime does not make this discussion any more or less of a theoretical exercise.)

This is not a call for a pure historiographical or juridical determination of right and wrong but for the disputational production of collective memories, including some kind of adjudication — legal and scientific — of acceptable and unacceptable versions. The difference here between history and collective memory is crucial, but that difference is only partly epistemological: historical truth versus mnemonic invention. It is more importantly a question of relevance and centrality. When posttransitional societies make the past a matter for historical analysis rather than for political discourse, they treat interest in it as irrelevant and marginal. They thereby allow old subjectivities to remain within their particularistic horizons. One might object that a commission charged with soliciting and reconciling private memories, competing group memories, partial perspectives, and collective mythologies to create a truthful collective memory — perhaps a truths commission rather than a Truth commission — lacks not only legal but also moral jurisdiction. But is it irresponsible to assert moral jurisdiction in the name of humanity where suffering is so universal? Not so long as doing so remains moral and factual rather than juridical or political, and so long as we place our own experiences up to the same measure of disputation and inquiry; this latter fear has provided another argument against extradition — that it would set a precedent allowing American leaders to be extradited, but without the power of extradition and the force of punishment, much of the force of the objection disappears.

Punishment is thus not the only foundation for reconciliation; it is never sufficient and only sometimes necessary for the creation of justice. That is not to say that individual punishment or collective legal responsibility are irrelevant. But such punishment cannot be the ultimate measure of how a society has "dealt" with its past. This is one of the lessons of Nuremberg, the legacy of which has not been unequivocal. Nuremberg certainly was an important early stage in forcing a certain truth to be told, and the moral principles articulated there have been important precedents for much subsequent thought on such matters, if the legal embodiment of those principles has been ambiguous and sometimes even dubious. But it had its costs as well, providing an alibi for an expertly equivocating population eager to lay the blame on a narrow "clique," and providing some basis for accusations of a victor's justice particularly against the Soviet Union, whose moral right to sit in judgment was questionable, not to mention the much less potent accusations against the Western allies for their own failures in the conduct of war.

Nuremberg also enabled some of the false distinctions between two classes of people to which Adenauer had referred, though my observation stems more from a concern that lesser forms of culpability be acknowledged rather than from Adenauer's concern that they not be seen as accountable at all. The latter is indeed what happened to the denazification process, in which early efforts to classify every adult in terms of his or her political involvement produced a vigorous business in so-called "*Persilscheine*," or whitewash certificates. It was perhaps right that this process was abandoned, though probably not for the reasons Adenauer and the German political class in general wanted. The problem was that the goal of the so-called *Spruchkammer* (testimony chamber) was a classification of guilt and certification of innocence rather than truth telling, however partial that can ever be.

These, then, are just some preliminary thoughts on how a politics of regret can be founded on an ethic of responsibility rather than on an ethic of conviction — not retribution for retribution's sake, but that important combination of knowledge and acknowledgment that lays the foundation for reconciliation not between victim and perpetrator but among their children. There is a big difference between delaying confrontation with the past and hindering it in both the present and for the future. The former may serve the present interests of *Realpolitik*; the latter, however, is the only way to meet our responsibility to the future where memory and power have become interchangeable, the hallmark feature of our properly regretful age.

CHAPTER 8

From Theodicy to *Ressentiment*
Trauma and the Ages of Compensation

History tells us that it is by no means a matter of course for the spectacle of misery to move men to pity; even during the long centuries when the Christian religion of mercy determined moral standards of Western civilization, compassion operated outside the political realm and frequently outside the established hierarchy of the Church.... Since then, the passion of compassion has haunted and driven the best men of all revolutions ....

Hannah Arendt (1963, pp. 70–1)

Though non-Western history has had more than its own share of tragedy, of war, murder and devastation; though 1494 and 1789 may even be mere ripples on the surface of history if compared with the abject fate of the Aztecs, the American Indians or the unspeakable horrors that Mongol rule inflicted on Central Asia, it seems that only Western man was capable of a traumatic experience of history.

Frank Ankersmit (2002, p. 76)

It is also true that risks are not an invention of modernity. Anyone who set out to discover new countries and continents — like Columbus — certainly accepted "risks". But these were personal risks, not global dangers like those that arise for all of humanity from nuclear fission or the storage of radioactive waste. In that earlier period, the word "risk" had a note of bravery and adventure, not the threat of self-destruction of all life on Earth.

Ulrich Beck (1992, p. 21)

Introduction

Trauma is of obvious interest to psychologists and human rights advocates, who are concerned, at the individual and aggregate levels respectively, with relieving and preventing suffering. Lately, it has become of great interest to historians as well. In their introduction to an important collection of essays, for instance, two leading historians of trauma argue that "the issue of trauma provides a useful entry into many complex historical questions and uniquely illuminates points of conjuncture in social, cultural, military, and medical history" (Lerner and Micale 2001, p. 6). Key claims of this new historiography include that "[t]here is an exact ratio between the level of the technology with which nature is controlled, and the degree of severity of its accidents" and that "the industrialization process was [thus] reflected in accelerating accident rates and the new institutions such as liability laws and accident insurance policies which grew out of these" (Schivelbusch 1986, p. 134). The historiography of trauma thus goes to the very heart of the theory of modernity, establishing clear connections among industry, transportation, law, science, and social structure. As Wolfgang Schäffner (2001, p. 82) argues, the " ... insurance-technical approach to trauma and accidents is part of a nonrepressive exercise of power, namely through stimulation and regulation. The normalization of nineteenth-century society that derives from extending police decrees and insurance regulations implies increased control of living conditions, a form of control that is an integral part of the social system." As a result, Schäffner (ibid.) points out, "[m]odern society, which the statistician Adolphe Quételet describes in 1848 ... as a probabilistic system, assumed canonical form in the system of accident insurance." Trauma, thus, is not only an unfortunate byproduct of modernity but also is a central feature of it, and insurance, liability, and various forms of risk and compensation are remarkable prisms for theory.

Perhaps it is strange, then, that *trauma* has not been nearly as central a topic for sociologists or scholars of international politics as it has been for historians, psychologists, or even literary critics, for whom it has been such a wellspring of innovative insights. Or perhaps not: In this chapter, I argue that (1) what *trauma* does for cultural history, *ressentiment* does for social and political theory; (2) trauma and *ressentiment* are complimentary processes, the former an inner-directed, the latter an outer-directed mani-festation of the same basic conditions; and (3) taken together, *trauma* and *ressentiment* map major transformations in how we understand history and our responsibility for it. The first section of the chapter reviews the theory of *ressentiment* through readings of its key figures: Friedrich Nietzsche, Max Weber, Max Scheler, and Hannah Arendt. Following this, I discuss a number of theorists writing from the Second World War to the present under the influence of what they see as a new stage in the development of trauma and who, compellingly for my purposes here, discuss whether this latest stage in trauma's biography — in which old remedies no longer give even the appearance of helping — has produced a new stage in the history of *ressentiment* as well.

One question that will emerge from this paired investigation is whether linking *trauma* to *ressentiment* brings our interest in trauma into disre-pute, since *ressentiment* is generally considered an illegitimate reaction. Equally possible, however, is that linking them will raise the reputation of *ressentiment*, since suffering trauma generally evokes sympathy rather than the scorn one heaps on the person of resentment; indeed, *ressenti-ment* might even be a response, more or less legitimate, to the *ressentiment* of others. Given the widespread rise of reparations, restitution, and regret as coins of international politics in the face of epidemic trauma — and the possible association of these practices with a feeling of *ressentiment*, or the possibility that they may be a form of *ressentiment* politics — this kind of inquiry into *ressentiment's* origins, dynamics, and value is clearly a matter of some urgency. Are all demands for reparations and redress borne of *res-sentiment*? And, if so, are they therefore illegitimate?

The Theory of *Ressentiment*

Nietzsche

The modern theory of *ressentiment*, and the widespread adoption of the term's francophone form,[1] begins with Nietzsche (1994). In brief, according to Nietzsche, originally the powerful generalized a distinction between good (i.e., themselves) and bad (i.e., others) into a moral distinc-tion between good and evil. As Weber (1963, p. 107), to whose sociological development of *ressentiment* we turn shortly, puts it, "When a man who is happy compares his position with that of one who is unhappy, he is not content with the fact of his happiness, but desires something more, namely the right to his happiness, the consciousness that he has earned his good fortune, in contrast to the unfortunate one who must equally have earned his misfortune." What Nietzsche calls "the slave revolt in morality" (p.21) began when the Jews — in his view a weak, priestly caste — became jealous of the powerful and inverted the values being imposed on them. Just as the powerful seek legitimation of their privilege, by way of the dynamics identified by Weber, according to Nietzsche, "every sufferer instinctively seeks a cause for his suffering" (ibid.). The early Jewish solution, according to Nietzsche, then developed into the Christian doctrine that the meek shall inherit the earth: The implication is that privilege is attained only through guile and sin and that suffering will be compensated. The weak thus revile the strong for their success and indict all their values: " ... *Ressentiment* defines such creatures who are denied genuine reaction, that of the deed, and who compensate for it through imaginary revenge" (ibid.).

At the heart of the matter is the problem of compensation. In the first place, Nietzsche points out, there is a close connection in German between the words for *guilt* (*Schuld*) and for *debt* (*Schulden*). The sense of guilt that slave morality foists on the world (*"bad conscience"*) developed in relation to the idea that every injury has its equivalent and that it can, in some way, be paid back, an idea rooted in the contractual, material relationship between creditor and debtor. Accordingly, an assumption developed whereby the injured, if not able to exercise immediate power over the perpetrator of his injury, gains a warrant for and title to cruelty. Though the desire for revenge is bad enough since the true noble 'Will' has no interest in others, this production of bad feelings in the perpetrators — and the demand for it when it does not come about automatically — is the fullest realization of slave morality, implicating master and slave alike. Both are caught in a perpetual torment that hinders true action and the liberating character of 'Will.' Memory of injury, in this regard, is the stumbling block to action, for both the noble soul, who is fettered by illegitimate claims, but especially for the victim, who cannot get past his injury: "Willingness liberates; but what is it that puts even the liberator himself in fetters — 'It was' — that is the name of the will's gnashing of teeth and most secret melancholy. Powerless against what has been done, he is an angry spectator of all that is past" (Nietzsche 1954, p. 251). Making the connection between *ressentiment* and what we now know about *trauma*, Nietzsche concludes, "He [the man of *ressentiment*] cannot break time and time's covetousness, that is the will's loneliest melancholy."

In present political circumstances, it thus seems that Nietzschean theory would classify all demands for reparation, redress, or regret as an expression of *Ressentiment* and hence would consider them illegitimate. Such demands seek a compensation that will never be adequate; those who make politics out of pursuing such claims make themselves, and those they charge, slaves to what cannot be changed. Since that demand for compensation is morally charged, moreover, it is a poor imitation to revenge, which would be more noble because more honest. Reparation demands, as sublimated revenge from a position of weakness, are, extrapolated from Nietzsche, the worst of all possible solutions. That it never satisfies is just further evidence against it.

Weber

If Nietzsche single-handedly invented the theory of *ressentiment*, it remained for others to develop and to sociologize it. Almost immediately, Weber (1963) began to do so, drawing out the important connection, to which we return later, to forms of theodicy, the explanation of evil and suffering. Theodicy, according to Weber, is part of every salvation religion that draws its members from disadvantaged classes. In Weber's analysis, *ressentiment* is a "theodicy of disprivilege," an effort by ordinary people to come to terms with their position in a status and class hierarchy: "*Ressentiment* is a concomitant of that particular religious ethic of the disprivileged which, in the sense expounded by Nietzsche and in direct inversion of the ancient belief, teaches that the unequal distribution of mundane goods is caused by sinfulness and the illegality of the privileged, and that sooner or later God's wrath will overtake them" (p. 106). As a result, Weber concludes, "the moralistic quest serves as a device for compensating a conscious or unconscious desire for vengeance" (ibid.). This compensation takes the form of a delayed reward: " ... the sense of honor of disprivileged classes rests in some concealed promise for the future.... What they cannot claim to be, they replace by the worth of that which they will one day become, to which they will be called in some future life here or hereafter ... by their sense of what they signify and achieve in the world as seen from the point of view of providence" (ibid., p. 106). Disprivilege, then, is compensated by righteous indignation at oppressors, though tempered by confidence in redemption of suffering; worthiness of this redemption is thus demonstrated, as Nietzsche made clear in book three of *The Genealogy of Morals*, by asceticism, the intentional exacerbation of one's own suffering and hence the ultimate perversion of Will.

Nevertheless, Weber (1963) points out, it is clear that not every class has the same need for theodicy's compensations, nor will that need be constant over time. For instance, he claims, the urban middle classes, because of their distinctive pattern of economic practices, thought, and distance from nature, incline toward a rational religious understanding, as does, to a slightly lesser degree, the work ethic of the merchant and artisanal classes, who experience a more direct relationship between effort and reward than others (ibid., p. 97). The need for salvation, and for promises of it through theodicy, then, emerges largely among the disprivileged because the need for salvation grows out of some sort of distress; social and economic oppression are powerful sources of salvation beliefs. In contrast, the privileged require legitimation and self-confidence, whereas the need for salvation is more remote to them; again, injury and suffering (i.e., trauma) not only occur more frequently in the lower strata but require the most complex compensations because their victims are without recourse other than theodicical; their only possibility for revenge is imaginary. I reserve for later the question of whether this social structure of theodicical need remains stable under the partially democratizing influence of the railway accident, if the industrial accidents and other sources of trauma characteristic of late modernity, in contrast, are indeed undemocratically distributed. This calls to mind Ulrich Beck's (1992) assertion, quoted at the beginning of this chapter, about the universalization of risk in late modernity as well.

Scheler

Though the theme of *ressentiment* was widespread in German social thought in the first decades of the twentieth century, the most significant development in the theory was that of Max Scheler — an apostate sociological disciple of the phenomenological philosopher Edmund Husserl — who published an extended essay titled *Ressentiment* in 1912, and expanded it in 1914 (Scheler 1998). As opposed to Weber's effort to connect *ressentiment* and theodicy in his sociology of religion, Scheler's approach is that of a sociologist of emotions concerned with the destructive effects of *ressentiment* on contemporary man's psychic life. Scheler largely accepts and elaborates Nietzsche's ideas about *ressentiment* through his own socio-psychological observations, relating it to the concepts of revenge and envy. As a sociologist, however, and this time broadly in line with Weber, Scheler places the powerful emotions of revenge and envy, and their tendency to become *ressentiment*, in a social structural context, emphasizing the importance of social distance and mobility.

First, Scheler expostulates, the impulse for revenge leads to *ressentiment* the more it changes into actual vindictiveness, the more its direction shifts toward indeterminate groups of objects that need only share one common characteristic and the less it is satisfied by vengeance taken on a specific object. Hence, the tendency of *ressentiment* is to become principled yet impersonal. In a later test of Scheler's theory, the Danish sociologist Svend Ranulf (1964, p. 1) thus equates *ressentiment* with "moral indignation" and with the "disinterested disposition … to assist in the punishment of criminals," which is embodied in law — such a disposition is far from universal; indeed, in many cultures it is incomprehensible why one who was not himself injured has any stake in the conflict. Interestingly, when it is groups that hold *ressentiment*, what is decisive is the discrepancy between the political, constitutional, or traditional status of the group and its factual power. Thus social *ressentiment* will be slight both in a democracy that features equality and in an extremely stratified yet legitimate system, such as India's caste system; conversely, social *ressentiment* is strongest in a system like liberal democracy, which proclaims but does not meet equal rights. Moreover, revenge tends to become *ressentiment* the more it is directed against lasting situations that are felt to be injurious but beyond one's control. Thus, Jewish *ressentiment* exemplifies both of these points: On the one hand there is a discrepancy between the pride of being the "chosen people" and the experienced contempt and discrimination, whereas on the other hand the contempt and discrimination appear to be a lasting situation, a destiny (Scheler 1998).

Second, according to Scheler, envy develops when a desire for an object that remains unfulfilled becomes hatred against the object's owner. Envy thus leads to "*ressentiment* when the coveted values are such as cannot be acquired and lie in the sphere in which we compare ourselves to others. The more powerless envy is also the most terrible. Therefore *existential envy*, which is directed against the other person's very *nature*, is the strongest source of *ressentiment*" (Scheler 1998, pp. 29–33, italics in original). Nevertheless, a psychological law comes into play amid the tension between desire and impotence and, up to a point, interferes with the development of *ressentiment*. It is the law, Scheler (ibid.) argues, that underpins the story of the fox and the sour grapes, that is a law of the release of tension through illusory valuation. Here, then, we do not have a falsification of values but rather a new opinion about the qualities of the desired object; it is not that sweetness is bad, just that the grapes are sour. The values as such are acknowledged as before. Theodicy motives thus operate at the level of emotion as well as of politics, though they can be revolutionary or conservative.

Scheler's (1998) major point of dissent from Nietzsche, however, concerns the blame the latter assigned to Christian love, Nietzsche's identification of Christianity with humanitarianism (i.e., the doctrine of charity for the weak), and resultant condemnation of it as slave morality par excellence. A highly complex personality struggling with temptation and his own sense of sin, Scheler was a convert to Catholicism and thus believed that Nietzsche was wrong to implicate Christianity per se in *ressentiment*. Though Nietzsche is correct, Scheler argues, in his condemnation of humanitarianism he was wrong to equate it with Christian love. Humanitarianism, Scheler follows Nietzsche in arguing, is the idea and movement of modern universal love of man, which means that its interest is on the sum total of human individuals — to such an extent, in fact, that it renders the love for any part of mankind, such as family or nation, an unjust deprivation to what we consider to belong to humanity. But nowhere in

Christianity's vocabulary, Scheler inveighs, is the concept of mankind to be found; to the contrary, Christianity's primary concept, he claims, is "Love your neighbor." Besides having different objects of love, moreover, primitive Christian love and humanitarian love differ on the subjective side of the process of loving. "Christian love," Scheler (ibid., p. 93, italics in original) claims, "is primarily a spiritual *action* and *movement*, as independent of our body and senses as the acts and laws of thinking. Humanitarian love is a *feeling*, and a passive one, which arises primarily by means of psychical contagion when we perceive the outward expression of pain and joy." Finally, the two differ also in the foundation of their valuation. Whereas what gives value to Christian love is the salvation of the lover's soul, the justification of humanitarian love is the advancement of "general welfare." Despite Scheler's analysis, however, this disjunction between some originary Christian love and modern humanitarianism is fairly clearly elided in the present, where religious organizations are often at the forefront of humanitarian efforts. I return to this critique of humanitarianism shortly, when I analyze Arendt's theory, in which the critique of humanitarianism is a centerpiece.

Despite his imputed misreading of the two kinds of love, however, Nietzsche was right, Scheler believed, to argue that *ressentiment* was the root of the humanitarian idea. For the force in the development of this idea in modern times was not an affirmation of positive values but a "protest, a counter-impulse against ruling minorities that are known to possess positive values" (ibid., p. 99). And along with that, humanitarianism is born out of *ressentiment* also vis-à-vis the idea of God: "Bitterness against the idea of the highest lord, inability to bear the 'all-seeing eye,' impulses of revolt against 'God' as the symbolic unity and concentration of all positive values and their rightful domination" (ibid.) Moreover, humanitarian love was the "manifestation of the inner protest and aversion against the immediate *circle* of the community and its inherent values — against the "community" that has physically and mentally formed a man" (ibid., italics in original). The latest form of this manifestation, Scheler argues, is the protest against patriotism and any organized community, clearly a protest at the heart of contemporary tendencies to replace proximate identity forms — namely nations — with humanity in general. Humanitarianism, in this light the antithesis of sovereignty, is hostile to the very carriers of Will, to any genuinely creative impulse at all. Like a physician who gives up medicine for fear of malpractice claims or companies that stop making a product because of the liabilities involved, humanitarianism, one might say, drives the carriers of Will right out of business.

Arendt

Scheler's interpolation of Nietzsche has had a number of interesting after-lives. One of the most remarkable is in Hannah Arendt's 1963 essay *On Revolution* (Arendt 1991), the writing of which obviously drew heavily on Scheler's book, though Arendt does not explicitly acknowledge it.[2] There Arendt reworks Scheler's critique of humanitarianism into a theory of revolution's violent worldview. In the first place, as demonstrated by the quote at the beginning of this chapter, though Arendt does not use the language of *ressentiment* she believed it is a uniquely modern principle that in turn underlies uniquely modern politics: "The social question," she also writes, " … began to play a revolutionary role only when, in the modern age and not before, men began to doubt that poverty is inherent in the human condition, to doubt that the distinction between the few, who through circumstances of strength or fraud had succeeded in liberating themselves from the shackles of poverty, and the laboring poverty-stricken multitudes, was inevitable and eternal" (ibid., p. 22). The central distinction Arendt draws, then, is between the sense of compassion and that of pity — clearly related to Nietzsche's and Scheler's contrast between the noble morality that abjures reference to others and the slave morality caught in endless comparison. Compassion, for Arendt, is a genuine emotion that is specific and limited, inspired only by real individuals rather than expressed toward entire classes; its strength comes from the strength of emotion rather than from reason and thus remains ungeneralizable and unprincipled — being principled, in this context, would be a bad thing. Compassion, she concludes, is mute, or at least awkward with words. Because compassion abolishes distance, the public space in which politics matters, it remains without larger consequence or motive: "If virtue will always be ready to assert that it is better to suffer than to do wrong, compassion will transcend this by stating in complete and even naïve sincerity that it is easier to suffer than to see others suffer" (p. 86).

In contrast to compassion, what Arendt (1991) calls *pity* is loquacious, even eloquent. Pity, which Arendt alternately claims has nothing whatsoever to do with compassion or is merely a perversion of it, works where compassion does not: "Pity, because it is not stricken in the flesh and keeps its sentimental distance, can succeed where compassion will always fail; it can reach out to the multitude and therefore, like solidarity, enter the marketplace" (ibid., p. 88). Nevertheless, this does not speak for pity's virtues: "Pity, in contrast to solidarity, does not look upon both fortune and misfortune … and it therefore has just as much vested interest in the existence of the unhappy as thirst for power has a vested interest in the existence of the weak" (ibid.). For Arendt, the politics of pity, the desire to ameliorate, to use suffering as an excuse to seize power, underlies the revolutionary impulse as well as underwrites its violent, principled extremism. Where Nietzsche's (1994, p. 45) revolt seems against moral philosophy and where he writes that "the sphere of legal obligations ... has really never quite lost a certain odor of blood and torture" and that "the categorical imperative smells of cruelty" (ibid.), Arendt writes that "pity, taken as the spring of virtue, has proved to possess a greater capacity for cruelty than cruelty itself' (ibid., p. 89).

Legacies of *Ressentiment*

We take the politics of pity so much for granted today — we are all now humanitarians, are we not? — that it is easy to forget this powerful alternative tradition of critique. Arendt (1991) certainly appreciates the achievements of the French Revolution and values the public discourse at which pity is so adept but is not willingly content with the costs. Whether we call it the *politics of pity, moral indignation,* or *ressentiment,* it seems to motivate us to unimaginable horrors. From Nietzsche to Arendt, then, the central modern principle of legitimation — humanitarianism — seems ironically to be at the heart of our downfall; in the name of eliminating suffering and bettering ourselves, we have unleashed suffering on an unprecedented scale. Later, I inquire into the difference implied here among the suffering inflicted in the name of revolution, the stochastic trauma of the railway accident, and the *"useless suffering"* — to borrow a term from Emmanuel Levinas (2001), whose contribution I will examine shortly — caused when revolutionary ideology combines with technology to reorder the world through industrial and scientific violence and even threatens human self-abnegation.[3] Here it is enough to point out this strange inversion in the heart of our philosophical tradition, an inversion at odds with the dominant contemporary discourse of reparation and regret— pity — through which we seek to make up for the misdeeds of Will.

Brown

It is interesting to note, then, that the kind of humanitarianism' in the dock here is neither merely the extremism of the French revolutionary *"Terror"* nor the total domination of National Socialism but, some would argue, affects liberalism as well, even particularly. Humanitarianism, after all, sees itself as a liberal ideology, as liberalism sees itself as part of a humanitarian project. Indeed, this is the position of the American political theorist Wendy Brown (1995) who is concerned that contemporary identity politics, with its emphasis on injustice and disadvantage, operates largely through accusation and the demand for redress. "Identity politics," Brown thus writes, "may be partly configured by a peculiarly shaped and peculiarly distinguished form of class resentment that is displaced onto discourses of injustice other than class, but a resentment, like all resentments, that retains the real or imagined holdings of its reviled subject as objects of desire" (ibid., p. 66-67). The liberal solution to disenfranchisement, in other words, is inclusion in power. To achieve it, however, there must be a redistribution of power downward, which means that the claim for equal freedom can be achieved only by violating the principle of freedom for the strong: The welfare state's progressive tax structure, some argue, penalizes the successful, thus not treating all equally; indeed, not only is this idea in some respects illiberal, but it is often also motivated by *ressentiment* against the powerful. Enfranchisement for the weak comes at the cost of freedom for the strong. The contradiction, thus, is not soluble within liberalism itself because, Brown argues, "liberalism contains from its very inception a generalized incitement to what Nietzsche terms *ressentiment*, the moralizing vengeance of the powerless, 'the triumph of the weak as weak'" (ibid.). Nietzschean thought, thus, does not only incline toward the right; in many ways, the theory of *ressentiment* raises much larger challenges to a theorist of the left, like Brown, though through all of these transformations, the left–right categorization is no longer so clear. Whether or not one agrees with Brown's diagnosis of liberalism or its strategies of compensation and redress, the combined weight of the tradition she brings to bear on the critique of liberalism should serve as a warning to our easy approval of redress as a strategy of humanitarian politics.[4] After all, it was not just Nietzsche, nor only guilty parties, who believe that too much memory can be the gravedigger of the present. Even Paul Ricoeur (2004), the suspicious hermeneutician, has recently asserted the value of forgetting.

Améry

Brown (1995) also offers some intriguing sociological suggestions for explaining the rise of *ressentiment* in contemporary politics, to which we return in the conclusion. Nevertheless, there remains one major moment in the literature on *ressentiment* of decisive importance: the argument of Jean Améry (1986). Améry, who changed his name from Hans Maier when he felt his freedom of identity choice was being robbed by the Nuremberg racial laws, is important for two reasons. First, his essays make clear the connection between the socio- and psychodynamics of *ressentiment* and those of trauma, and second, and for the present purposes even more significant, because he makes a compelling case for the positive value of *ressentiment* in certain circumstances.

As a Holocaust survivor and torture victim, Améry (1986, p. 68-9) makes the point that "anyone who has been tortured remains tortured."

Indeed, this kind of removal from progressive temporality is the very heart of trauma. For Améry, it is the heart of *ressentiment* as well. In an intentionally provocative turn of phrase, he argues that *ressentiment* "nails every one of us onto the cross of his ruined past. Absurdly, it demands that the irreversible be turned around, that the event be undone" (ibid., p. 69). As a result, for Améry, "resentment blocks the exit to the genuine human condition, the future" (ibid.). In this, then, Améry clearly agrees with Nietzsche's diagnosis, the burden of the "it was." In contrast to Nietzsche, Scheler, and Arendt, however, the connection between *ressentiment* and humanitarianism is perhaps not so clear in Améry: "I know that the time-sense of the person trapped in resentment is twisted around, dis-ordered, if you wish, for it desires two impossible things: regression into the past and nullification of what happened … For this reason the man of resentment cannot join in the unisonous peace chorus all around him, which cheerfully proposes: Not backward let us look but forward, to a better, common future!" (ibid.). Humanitarianism, it seems, leans in two directions: too progressive, and too concerned with the past. Améry can abide neither.

Améry's (1986) putative *ressentiment*, and hence rejection of forward-looking humanitarianism, thus has two sources: In the first place, it is the illegitimate ease with which the Germans, in whose midst he wanders, reject the obligations of their own past that angers him. His inability to move forward, he argues, is matched equally by his persecutors' excessive ease. Indeed, one can well imagine the sense Améry had, twenty years after his traumatic experience, that he was out of synch with the world around him and that the perpetrators were exacerbating his discomfort by moving more quickly, by relieving themselves of their burdens, more than they had a right.

Second, however, Améry (1986) is also arguing with those fellow victims who claim they do not have the same resentments he does: Not all of the desire to move forward came from perpetrators. In this regard, Améry was arguing particularly with Primo Levi (1989, p. 136), who believed more fully, perhaps, in the critique of *ressentiment*. Levi thus argues in his memoir of Améry that Améry's choice to fight against what he saw as premature forgetting "led him to positions of such severity and intransigence as to make him incapable of finding joy in life, indeed of living." In a classic condemnation of revenge and the *ressentiment* that motivates it, Levi writes, "those who trade blows with the entire world achieve dignity but pay a very high price for it because they are sure to be defeated" (ibid.). Levi's attitude, one might say, is closer to the Sermon on the Mount — "Turn the other cheek" — than it is to full-blown *ressentiment*, a distinction possible only in Scheler rather than in Nietzsche, though Levi does not express it in those terms. Nevertheless, as a result of this diagnosis, Levi claims, he was not at all surprised by Améry's suicide in 1978. By the same token, few commentators seemed surprised when Levi took his own life, too.

What kind of *ressentiment*, then, did Améry (1986) suffer? Surely, in Nietzsche's and Scheler's account, there is something similar to Marx's description of reification, the process whereby we suffer under systems of objective-seeming domination that nevertheless we ourselves created; in a way, it is possible that for *ressentiment* to have its full effect, one must remain unaware of it — and this Améry certainly was not. As such, he sought to take control of the idea, both theoretically and politically. "My personal task," he thus writes, "is to justify a psychic condition that has been condemned by moralists and psychologists alike. The former regard it [*ressentiment*] as a taint, the latter as a kind of sickness. I must acknowledge it, bear the social taint, and first accept the sickness as an integrating part of my personality and then legitimize it" (ibid., p. 69). Améry thus remains a vigilant observer and understands well why he wants what he wants: "Self-confessed man of resentments that I am, I supposedly live in the bloody illusion that I can be compensated for my suffering through the freedom granted me by society to inflict injury" (ibid.). Despite an episode of having exchanged blows with a Polish guard in the concentration camp, and feeling empowered by this futile act of defiance, the blows Améry now exchanges are metaphorical, intellectual, and institutional: "The horsewhip lacerated me; for that reason, even I do not dare demand that the now defenseless thug be surrendered up to my own whip-swinging hand. [But] I want at least the vile satisfaction of knowing that my enemy is behind bars" (ibid., p. 81). This is the only way, he believes, for his trauma to heal: "Thereupon I would fancy that the contradiction of my madly twisted time-sense were resolved" (ibid., p. 69).

Améry's (1986, p. 81) *ressentiment*, then, was a "special kind ... of which neither Nietzsche nor Max Scheler was able to have any notion." In reaction, Améry argues that lazy or cheap forgiveness is a form of self-subjugation and is amoral at its core. Subjugation to what? For previous theorists of *ressentiment*, and of trauma as well, the special nature of traumatic suffering is its disjuncture from natural time, which is "actually rooted in the physiological process of wound-healing." For Améry, submission to natural time under his special circumstances is immoral: "Man has the right and privilege" (ibid., p. 33), meaning Améry has the right and privilege, "to declare himself to be in disagreement with every natural occurrence, including the biological healing that time brings about. What happened, happened. This sentence is just as true as it is hostile to morality and intellect" (p. 70). In these unusual circumstances, "the moral person demands annulment of time — in the particular case under question, by nailing the criminal to his deed" (ibid., p. 72). The message here, it is important to note, is both therapeutic and political: This moral refusal to submit to time is essential for healing the victim's trauma; by the same token, Améry argues, this kind of refusal also performs a historical function.

Levinas

Améry (1986) clearly takes a highly complex position, not necessarily consistent with the tradition of critique or internally with itself. One might even doubt that it is *ressentiment* exactly that he is suffering, since his demand for justice is not disinterested. Or perhaps his case is so bad that he is unable to see it as clearly as he claims. The major difference between the conditions of Améry's theory and that of his predecessors, however, is the nature of his injury, not just the injuries to his body and soul but also to his ability to hope for a tolerable social existence. However horrible the French revolutionary terror or the anonymous death of the railway accident were, something important has changed in the possible meaning of the suffering represented by the Holocaust. Though *uselessness* or *senselessness* have always been a feature of suffering, the difference now is that there are no longer any compensations, even illusory, for useless suffering, which reached its apotheosis in the gas chamber. Perhaps this is why *ressentiment* is not just a syndrome or weakness for Améry; it is his only recourse. This, at any rate, is the position implied by the theories of Emmanuel Levinas, a Lithuanian-born Jewish philosopher, also a student of Husserl and later of Martin Heidegger, who lost most of his family in the Holocaust.

Following Nietzsche, Levinas (2001) argues that people want to believe evil has some intention and direction behind it, that injury is somehow connected to malice. But as Améry (1986, p. 70) points out, "The atrocity as atrocity has no objective character. Mass murder, torture, injury of every kind are objectively nothing but chains of physical events.... They are facts within a physical system, not deeds within a moral system." In Levinas's language, this means that our capacity to cope with suffering has been dramatically altered. According to Levinas, theodicy, the desire to save morality in the name of faith or to make suffering bearable, still existed "in a watered down form at the core of atheist progressivism which was confident, nonetheless, in the efficacy of the Good which is immanent to being, called to visible triumph by the simple play of natural and historical laws of injustice, war, misery, and illness" (ibid., p. 376). Nevertheless, Levinas argues, "Perhaps the most revolutionary fact of our twentieth century consciousness ... is that of the destruction of all balance between explicit and implicit theodicy in Western thought and the forms suffering and its evil take in the very unfolding of this century" (ibid.). If Nietzsche preferred to say God is dead, Levinas points out that we tried but failed to save him:

"This is the century that has known two world wars, the totalitarianisms of right and left, Hitlerism and Stalinism, Hiroshima, the Gulag, and the genocides of Auschwitz and Cambodia. This is the century which is drawing to a close in the haunting memory of the return of everything signified by these barbaric names: suffering and evil are deliberately imposed, yet no reason sets limits to the exasperation of a reason become political and detached from all ethics." For Levinas, "the disproportion between suffering and every theodicy was shown at Auschwitz with a glaring, obvious clarity" (ibid., 376–77). The fundamental philosophical problem for Levinas is thus whether there can be any morality and faith after this end of theodicy. Levinas's project, then, is to rescue theodicy from history and sociology — a difficult task indeed.

Ressentiment and the Account of Modernity

The conceptual history undertaken in the foregoing pages has been motivated by the sense that *ressentiment* and trauma are related aspects of a single discursive universe. This became particularly clear in Améry (1986), though also in the other authors, who emphasized both the origins of *ressentiment* in suffering and the temporal disruptions that characterize its operation. Nevertheless, it is important to point out that the differences among the authors are not just disputes over how to define an ideal type but also are differences of history and context, which shape the conditions both for the operation and epidemiology of *ressentiment* as well as for theorizing about it — the same applies to trauma as well.

Is it really appropriate to parse the definitional peculiarities of Nietzsche versus Améry? Or is something more sociological and historical required? In conclusion I explore some of the resources at our disposal to answer this question, and sketch an as yet highly speculative theoretical account as a first gesture to redeeming the promise identified by the historians of trauma quoted at the beginning: the unique potential of the history of the concept of trauma — and by the implication we hope we redeemed, in the foregoing, of *ressentiment* as well — for the sociological account of modernity. Such an account, it must be added, is squarely apropos of our Westphalian order and its unfolding contradictions. Is it not the case, after all, that legitimation in modern times oscillates irresolutely between humanist and nationalist claims, between recourse to the rights of man and to the rights of states? Modern world order has not yet provided a global system to appease collective national insecurities, despite some regional progress.

Indeed, some scholarly accounts link the processes of modern internationalism to *ressentiment* and trauma explicitly. According to Brown (1995), for instance, a number of related processes have brought us to our contemporary interest in reparations and redress and have suffused them with the odor of *ressentiment*. In her view, these include first, "increased global contingency" combined with "the expanding pervasiveness and complexity of domination by capital and bureaucratic state and social networks" that have intensified the senses of "impotence, dependence, and gratitude inherent in liberal capitalist orders and constitutive of *ressentiment*" (ibid., p. 68). Second, she points to the impact of secularization and desacralization, which undermine the ability of Nietzsche's ascetic priests to cause guilt and depravity not only in the disprivileged but in the powerful as well. And third, redolent of Weber, Alexis de Tocqueville, and Arendt, she highlights the destruction of intermediate associations as protectors of the isolated individual from the inability of liberalism to follow through on its promise to protect individuals (ibid.).

Each of these explanations certainly contributes to the overall picture of the rise of *ressentiment* in and with modernity, particularly within liberalism, though a number of other contributory processes come to mind as well, including dynamics not addressed within the universe of this Weberian scheme of rationalization, secularization, and atomization. As mentioned in chapter six, Emile Durkheim's account of the rise of individualism, for instance, provides a still-convincing account of the noncontractual elements of contractual obligation necessary for a complex commercial system. As the division of labor in European societies increased, according to Durkheim, these societies saw the progressive disappearance of segmentary organization — according to Scheler the kind of social organization least conducive to *ressentiment*. The increasing efficiencies of industrial production also required vast new supplies of labor, which meant that people migrated into cities, leaving behind their taken-for-granted social solidarities (Durkheim 1984). With large numbers of different people with different traditions, different languages, different stories, and different jobs living next to each other, individualism became the predominant ideology and common sense, requiring new forms of exchange, standardization, and commensuration.[5] In commerce as well, a new moral universe was necessary, because contractual relationships multiply as the division of labor increases and segmentation declines. But for contracts to be binding, there needs to be an agency of enforcement. This agency is both institutional — the law and its agent, the state — as well as cultural, what Durkheim (1984) calls the *noncontractual elements of contractual obligation,* which involve such intangibles as trust and an expectation of recourse. In this way, new commercial arrangements give rise not only to the statistical gaze described by Quetelet, discussed in the first paragraph, but also to the institutions of compensation. According to Durkheim (ibid.), restitutory law, in contrast to penal law, is the hallmark of complex society. This kind of an explanation goes a long way to explicating the relations between institutions of compensation and the rising experience of trauma, which authors like Wolfgang Schivelbusch (1986, p. 159) in turn explain in terms of the denaturalization of temporal experience with the advent of mechanized travel: "In the railroad journey, the traditional experience of time and space was demolished the way the individual experience of battle of the Middle Ages is abolished in the modern army (and the individual craft activity is abolished in manufacturing and industrial production)."

Durkheim's (1984) and Schivelbusch's (1986) accounts contribute a great deal to the sociology of trauma rather than merely to the descriptions and diagnoses outlined already. But clearly they do best with a particular point in time — the late nineteenth century — just as Levinas and Ulrich Beck whose theory of risk was mentioned at the beginning of the chapter, do better with the twentieth century. Yet other theories, not least Arendt's account of the rise of ideology in the French revolution, do better for earlier periods, though it seems useful to treat these theories as explaining different moments in an overall process. Other theories, moreover, date the seminal stages of this process even earlier than Arendt. Nietzsche's theory is vaguely ancient in reference, though neither historical nor sociological. Discussions of theodicy often go back to the Book of Job and then spend a great deal of time and attention, for the obvious reason that this is the source of the term, with Leibniz's 1710 treatise, *Theodicy*, and then with Voltaire's scathing satire *Candide* after the Lisbon earthquake of 1755, in which Voltaire's Leibniz — defender of God at all costs, in face of all reason, by explaining evil as the best of all possible worlds — earns the name Pangloss, which subsequently becomes an adjective (*panglossian*) for excessive, even stupendous, optimism. Something clearly happened between the world for which Leibniz was really too late, and the one Voltaire helped articulate.

One further set of theories deserves at least brief mention here — namely those that address the decline of religious eschatology that prepared the rise of rationalism and the birth of modernity — because they describe clear preparations a century earlier for the ideas Arendt identified as operative in the French Revolution and Weber and Scheler, among others, found operative at the end of the nineteenth century. Reinhardt Kosellek (1985, pp. 8–9), for instance, writes that before the modern era "the future as the possible end of the World is absorbed within time by the Church as a constituting element, and thus does not exist in a linear sense at the end point of time. Rather, the end of time can be experienced only because it is always-already sublimated in the Church." In contrast, "the experience in a century of bloody struggles was, above all, that the religious wars did not herald the Final Judgment ... this disclosed a new and unorthodox future" (ibid.). There is thus a stark contrast between a world of prophecy, in which "events are merely symbols of that which is already known" (ibid.), where "apocalyptic prophecy destroys time through its fixation on the End" (ibid.), and one of prognosis, which "produces the time within which and out of which it weaves" (ibid.).

Combining this attention to the crisis of eschatology with a consideration of technological factors, Lutz Niethammer (1992, pp. 135–36) describes a similar decline of existential security with the invention of the prognosticative chronotype:

> It eventually became apparent that there were worldly reasons to change the basic conditions of existence and to detach them from the cyclicity of nature. Once new discoveries burst the limits of the world, and trade, technology, and institutionalized relations of power freed part of society from direct ties with the sequences of nature, elements of total explanation of the world could be transferred from the jurisdiction of salvationist history to the scientific processing of experience.... Out of the various histories through which men and women reached agreement over the origins and institutions of their group ... a new universal history had to come into being, with a perspective that would provide an understanding of the cosmos to replace the religious world-view.

This account, which forms the core of the next chapter, thus synthesizes the religious explanation with technological factors and the increased capacity for abstract thought due to the spread of print culture, which theorists like Benedict Anderson (1991) describe. It offers a powerful explanation for the rise of philosophies of history in the nineteenth century, as well as for the more mundane institutionalization of empirical historical discourse.

Interestingly, the philosopher of history Frank Ankersmit (2002) reverses the causal logic of this account, though in the process reinforcing the association. According to Ankersmit, quoted at the beginning of the chapter, the susceptibility to collective trauma cannot be explained by the objective qualities or amounts of pain and suffering. In this regard, Ankersmit must disagree with Levinas, who seems to place a great deal of explanatory weight on the nature of the injuries — or accumulation of injuries — in the twentieth century. Ankersmit suggests that "in the West a shift may be observed from collective pain to an awareness of this pain and ... this is how this peculiar Western capacity for suffering collective trauma originated." As such, Ankersmit reinforces Niethammer's (1992) and others' attribution of causal power to the rise of abstract thought. In this sense, Améry's positive existential valuation of resentment is part of thinking made possible by the modern capacity to translate suffering into trauma. In Ankersmit's (2002, p. 79) sketch, moreover, "the historian's language originates in the 'logical space' between traumatic experience and a language that still had a primordial immediacy and directness in its relationship to the world — and that pushes this language aside." Here, however, one can note the limits of the entailed logical links in providing moral history. Améry's hold on resentment reminds us just that, as it renders both progressive temporality and modernity's downplaying of primoridalism to be inefficient contexts for rehabilitating the trauma of the Holocaust.

It is unclear whether Ankersmit (2002) thinks traumatic consciousness gives rise to history or whether he is implying that both are caused by a wider set of transformations. It also seems plausible to make the case that historical consciousness preceded traumatic consciousness and that the linear, progressive temporality of history — and its individual corollary, biography — are part of the conditions that increase the likelihood of trauma and traumatic interpretations of suffering; this is certainly clear in Arendt's account of the politics of pity. This discussion of the rise of progressive temporality, which instructs individuals as well as collectivities how to understand their experience, is obviously one of the conditions for the experience of trauma because it is precisely this capacity that is disrupted by the kinds of experiences one has in industrial civilization.

Here, then, is yet further support for the belief that trauma is a novel modern disease, though two caveats must be stressed. One, the argument here is that the interpretive category, progressive temporality, gives rise to the syndrome rather than that the syndrome, trauma, gives rise to a new framework of interpretation. Two, being far from uniform, the process of modernity presents limits, even contradictions, to the moral repercussions of trauma. Given that the discovery of equivalence is still expanding conceptually and geographically — statutory law, described by Durkheim (1994) as national law, has only partially turned into international law, whereas the latter has hardly included with any efficacy broader moral claims, at least until very recently — trauma became politically relevant in world politics without as yet having become a strong norm.

Finally, I take no small inspiration from the account of German philosopher Odo Marquard (1998), who, in a similar way to Giambattisto Vico, traces the history of compensatory culture as follows: "First, in the age of religion, God sat in judgment over humankind; then, in the age of theodicy, humankind sat in judgment over God; finally, in the age of critique, humankind sat in judgment over itself" (ibid., p. 31). This latest stage, according to Marquard, following Nietzsche, involves what he calls an *overtribunalization* of history, not a positive condition. In Marquard's account, three new philosophies — the philosophy of history, philosophical anthropology, and philosophical aesthetics — which all emerged in the period after about 1750, are efforts "to compensate for a human loss of "life-world" (ibid., p. 41). They are, he says, "attempts to compensate for this overtribunalization by an 'escape into unindictability'" (ibid., p. 41). Nevertheless, it is clear from the conceptual history undertaken in this chapter that this escape has been temporary and that judgment day has arrived, if it is now a self-judgment — and indeed condemnation — of man by man. Following Marquard, the older compensatory systems no longer suffice. Insurance and reparation are rather thin shoulders on which to carry the burdens of theodicy, though it is interesting that in the wake of the January 2005 South Asian tsunami, it was governments and industry in the dock, not God.

Conclusions

In conclusion, I offer a somewhat more differentiated historical typology before flagging the implications of this body of thought for contemporary politics, domestic as well as international. To wit:

1. The end of eschatology gave rise to linear temporality and history, thus placing man at the center of the moral universe. As a result, and because of the concomitant decline of supernatural beliefs (matched by what Weber has to say about the social location of Salvationism, which does not attract the new middle class), theodicy lost its efficacy; witness again Voltaire's response to Leibniz.
2. This centering of man in history gave rise to the revolutionary ethos sketched by Arendt in which humanitarianism provides powerful tools with which to vent *ressentiment*. Here redemption comes through a vision of the future, which provides *ressentiment* with a constructive goal.[6]
3. The rise of industry and speed generated a new kind of randomness to injury coupled with a denaturalization of temporal experience in travel and electronic communications (i.e., telegraphy). The stochastic nature of these injuries gave rise to a new form of outrage — why me! — because of the obvious amoral quality to the injury; it is no longer possible to believe, in any but the most illusory or metaphorical fashion, in just desserts. Combined with the statistical worldview that arises to confront and control this randomness, insurance, psychiatry, and law collude to generate a new moral universe of compensation. This connection between modern injury and rational compensation is also expressed in the

dehumanizing experience of mechanical death in World War One and in the social welfare programs that states developed — first and foremost to care for veterans — in its wake.

4. Finally, useless suffering reaches its apotheosis in the middle of the twentieth century, with the stunning combination of genocide in the heart of Europe and the capacity for the nuclear self-abnegation of humankind. What possible compensations could there be left to the cowering individual, who has learned to internalize risk as a basic feature of personality?

In sum, we have moved through a developmental trajectory characterized by the progression (decline?) from eschatology and theodicy, to revolution, to accident — which used to mean coincidence — and insurance, through therapy to reparation. In this light, it seems as if ours is the proper age, as implied by Améry, for *ressentiment*. What kind of money is there left that is not blood money? *Ressentiment* is only a delusion and weakness if we do not embrace and understand it, as Améry seems to have done. As a result, we worry less than Brown and others that the demand for reparations as part of identity politics and international relations is an undesirable, even sordid attitude.

CHAPTER 9

Collective Memory and Chronic Differentiation

Historicity and the Public Sphere

1995 was a banner year for commemoration. A half century earlier, according to dominant Western narratives, justice had vanquished two tyrannies, bringing forth a new paradigm of world history. But it was not just the "roundness" of the number fifty that gave cause for commemoration. The flurry of fifty-year markings of World War Two events was only an instance of our epoch's wider preoccupation with memory. Everywhere we turn, it seems, memory is at the center of local and national agendas. As the previous chapters have shown, the mass media and entertainment industries find nostalgia an endless attraction to consumers; governments commemorate failures as well as triumphs; and social movements and other identity groups turn to "repressed" histories as sources of their cohesion and as justification for their programs. Whether through the marketing of idealized pasts, a general politics of regret, or historical identitarianism, ours is an era in which the presence of the past — real or imagined — is potent and problematic. Indeed, many commentators have seen this pervasive historical consciousness as emblematic of our contemporary condition. Across many disciplines, and in the wider public too, collective memory we have seen has become a favorite term.

Strangely, many commentators have characterized the end of the last century in remarkably similar terms, seeing the late nineteenth century as undergoing a profound memory crisis. Intellectuals in that period paid serious attention to memory, be it individual or social, just as the political world around them was seeking to harness and exploit it. Writers like Marcel Proust, Henri Bergson, and Sigmund Freud contributed to the veritable obsession with memory that they saw in their societies. They excavated, theorized, diagnosed, indeed propagated, their age's pervasive nostalgia — a medical condition — responding to it with a simultaneous fascination, engagement, and terror (Bergson 1990; Freud 1966–74; Proust 1961). The scholar Ernst Renan (1947–61) identified forgetting as the core of his era's nationalisms. States invented traditions to shore up their legitimacy. Bourgeois families became fascinated with their genealogies. Autobiography became a common genre.

How are the memory crises of the nineteenth and twentieth *fins-de-siecle* related? Are they fundamentally distinct problems? Are they identical? Or are they imbricated, successive phases in a longer, more general developmental process? One problem with answering this question is that most theories of memory have treated forms of memory as a symptom or indicator of other, more fundamental processes. But as chapter five showed, memory is not a result of social forms; it is their very medium. Some historical perspective on memory can help, but more important, I have hinted, are developmental accounts that have placed temporalities at the heart of their theories, though often without doing so in terms of memory as the medium of existence in time. In this final chapter, I argue that we need to bring memory more into the center of our epochal accounts because different forms of remembering not only characterize different epochs but also are fundamental features of existence in them. Like all general processes, of course, the one described here exists only through its many and various parts. A theory of memory and modernity, therefore, needs to be a theory of modernity's many institutional forms of remembering. Placing memory at the center of epochal theories, however, requires us to rethink the very category of memory itself.

The History of Memory

"*Memoria*," writes Mary Carruthers (1990, p. 260), "can be considered as one of the modalities of medieval culture (chivalry might be another)." What a strange observation, how foreign to our contemporary understanding of memory. We tend to think of memory as a faculty rather than as a modality, and we view it as a symptom rather than as a core constituent. Of course, Carruthers was referring not to memory per se but to *Memoria*, the art of memory. From as early as Greek antiquity to the Renaissance, mnemonics was a rhetorical art whereby orators employed elaborate conceptual architectures to remember long passages and complex details. Each element to be remembered was located in an imaginary palace of memory so that it could be easily rediscovered in its proper place by conceptually touring that palace. The art of memory, moreover, was an elite practice associated with the high status of orators and later of scholars. How, then, can *Memoria* have been a modality of medieval culture? More importantly, what does this observation tell us about our contemporary understanding of memory?

Most generally, comparing earlier conceptions of memory and their places in society demonstrates that memory has a history. "'Memory,'" Matt Matsuda (1996, p. 4) writes, "is not merely a theme to search out in literary texts, nor a convenient trope to impose generically upon recollections, rituals, or remembrances." We can study classical, Renaissance, and modern memory, Matsuda argues, as distinct social forms; there is not one memory, but many memories.[1] Recognizing that memory has a history prevents us from reading earlier societies' use of memory through the lens of our own and from seeing our own approach as universal or "natural."

In the second place, looking at the differences between Renaissance and later memory concepts calls into question the ways we use the memory concept in contemporary discourses. As Ian Hacking (1995) argues, a crucial distinction between the memory of *ars memoria* and that of the nineteenth-century *"sciences of memory"* is that where the former is concerned with knowledge how, the latter are concerned with knowledge that. In other words, as Hacking puts it, a new presumption of the nineteenth century is that "there is a body of facts about memory to be known" (ibid., p. 200). This is the case whether we are talking about personal or collective memory. Where the personal memory was seen by Freud and others as the wellspring of the soul, the collective memory conceived by the Durkheimian tradition was a social fact that conferred identity on individuals and groups. Since the late nineteenth century, the sciences of both personal memory (i.e., psychology) and collective memory (i.e., sociology) have treated memory as an entity (i.e., the memory) with properties that can be enumerated, tested, and ultimately manipulated. Where such naming may be an essential phase in constituting a process as an object for scientific observation, it appears in later moments as a costly reduction of a process, or processes, to a thing. This conception of memory as a thing, institutionalized in the nineteenth century, continues to shape our understanding.

A third interesting implication of Carruthers's (1990) claim that *Memoria* is a modality of medieval culture is that memory could possibly be so central to an epoch's character. This is in rather stark contrast to the best-known macrohistorical theories, which treat memory as a result of social forms rather than as a central medium. Macrohistorical theory, insofar as it speaks about memory at all, has favored either teleological accounts of memory's disappearance in modernity or technologically determinist explanations of mnemonic form. The "classical" sociological theorists, for instance, hardly mention memory, despite the nearly pervasive discussion of it in *fin-de-siecle* culture.[2] Edward Shils (1981) explains this shared neglect of tradition and memory by demonstrating how Max Weber and his contemporaries were the victims of their own overdrawn dichotomies. The classical theorists, Shils writes, "oversubscribed to the naive view that modern society was on the road to traditionlessness...." (ibid., p. 9). From such a perspective, an interest in how the past works on the present was antiquarian, or at least useful only as a contrast to the ways that modern societies function. Memory was a feature of primitive societies, they supposed, and its last residues should disappear in modernity.

Later theorists have pursued a rather different historical approach to memory, seeing it as the byproduct of the stage of technological development. Epochal generalizations about the developing relations between memory and technologies of communication describe a broad shift from orality to literacy over millennia. Founding this tradition, Marshall McLuhan (1962) theorizes the effects of electronic communications on "typographic" culture within a history that included the move from manuscript to print culture two centuries earlier and from orality to literacy a millennium before that. McLuhan's student, Walter Ong (1982), traced a long-range pattern from orality to manuscript literacy to print culture to media culture, drawing out implications for memory: The invention of writing in antiquity was the seed for the rise of more abstract thinking. Because this capability resided in the hands of a small elite, it was not until the vast expansion of literacy in the seventeenth and eighteenth centuries occurred that the profound possibilities of print communication became a dominant cultural form. In the process, memory became a public affair, an object of contemplation and concern, as the result of vastly expanded mnemonic capabilities.

Writers like André Leroi-Gourhan (1993) and Jacques Le Goff (1992) carry forward the argument for memory by distinguishing five periods in the history of memory, each characterized by the different fundamental technological capacities: oral transmission, written transmission using tables or an index, simple index cards, mechanography or print, and electronic serial transmission. But even as these authors attend directly to the developmental history of memory — even as they consider these mnemonic forms central features of their periods — memory still appears as a separable feature of societies (sometimes the result of technological form, sometimes as the technological form itself) rather than as their existential mode: Memory, in other words, is still a special topic. Given this common way of treating memory even by those who attend to it directly, it is not surprising that more general theorists of modernity have not included it in their accounts.

Memory and Modernity

This is not to say that no contemporary theories of modernity and postmodernity confront the issues raised by memory; indeed, as hinted in previous chapters, a rising interest in the history of temporality can serve as an important resource for thinking about memory. A key point in many histories of temporality is that a significant transformation in the experience of time occurred at some debatable point between the Middle Ages and the nineteenth century. Many authors describe an existential crisis arising out of the increased possibility for abstract thought previously discussed, out of accelerating change resulting from increased industrialization and urbanization as well as out of the resultant decline of religious world views and of traditional forms of political authority. Reinhardt Koselleck (1985), for instance, describes a shift in the balance between a "space of experience" and a "horizon of expectation." Through the seventeenth and eighteenth centuries, a wide variety of new experiences and events produced an awareness of the "noncontemporaneity of the contemporaneous" which led, in turn, to a sense of a human future and of the distinctness of history.

Eric Hobsbawm (1972, p. 11) describes the rise of linear historical consciousness as a necessary solution to the existential problems of rapid transformation: "Paradoxically, the past remains the most useful analytical tool for coping with constant change." John Thompson (1995) attributes a similar dynamic largely to transformations in media technology, which extended individuals' experiences beyond the sphere of day-to-day encounters: "The process of self-formation [thus] became more reflexive and open-ended." Russell Jacoby (1977) and Marshall Berman (1988) attribute to late modernity a condition — at least partly related to rampant commodification — that makes it harder and harder to relate to the past, producing what Jacoby calls *social amnesia*. Others have pointed out that the prosaic condition of migration from rural to urban environments generated the kind of pathological nostalgia that previously resulted only from foreign adventuring (Vromen 1993).

The connection between nationalism and temporality appears to have been especially important. David Cressy (1994), for instance, traces a new kind of temporality in England to the seventeenth century, one that gave expression to a mythic and patriotic sense of identity: "The calendar became an important instrument for declaring and disseminating a distinctively Protestant national culture...binding the nation to the ruling dynasty and securing it through an inspiring providential interpretation of English history." Benedict Anderson (1991) combines insights into the spread of print literacy, capitalist commerce, and the decline of religious world views to explain the rise of historicizing national identities as a pervasive modern principle. In his account, the transformation of temporality and the associated rise of interest in the past made it possible "to think the Nation" (ibid., p. 22). Print capitalism, according to Anderson, was the principle agent of this transformation toward what Walter Benjamin (1968, p. 265) calls the "empty, homogeneous time" of the nation-state. Felt communities of fate were secured across wide territories by newspapers and novels, which produced shared culture among people who would never meet. As a result, in Anthony Smith's (1986) words, "ethnic nationalism has become a 'surrogate' religion which aims to overcome the sense of futility engendered by the removal of any vision of an existence after death, by linking individuals to persisting communities whose generations form indissoluble links in a chain of memories and identities."

Others have given similar insights a more critical turn. Jonathan Boyarin (1994, p. 15-16), for instance, points out that statist ideologies "involve a particularly potent manipulation of dimensionalities of space and time, invoking rhetorically fixed national identities to legitimate their monopoly on administrative control." Prasenjith Duara (1995, p. 4) writes that the relationship between linear historicity and the nation-state is repressive: "National History secures for the contested and contingent nation the false unity of a self-same, national subject evolving through time," enabling "conquest of Historical awareness over other, 'nonprogressive' modes of time." Hobsbawm (1983b) notes the proliferation of state-led efforts to "invent" useful traditions to shore up their facing legitimacy in the mid to late nineteenth century. Particularly after 1870, in conjunction with the emergence of mass politics, political leaders "rediscovered the importance of 'irrational' elements in the maintenance of the social fabric and the social order" (ibid). Many thinkers thus advocated the construction of a new "civil religion"; successful leaders sought to imbue educational institutions with nationalist content, to expand public ceremony, and to mass produce public monuments.

Moving to a slightly later period, theorists have emphasized the importance of the First World War for perceptions of temporality. Walter Benjamin (1968, p. 87), in particular, portrayed the war experience as a decisive moment in a longer-term trend, typified by a decline of storytelling, a process which he sees, however, as "only a concomitant symptom of the secular productive forces of history...." The conditions for storytelling, "woven thousands of years ago in the ambiance of the oldest forms of craftsmanship," have lost their most basic support "because there is no more weaving and spinning to go on while … [stories] are being listened to." "Boredom," Benjamin writes, "is the dream bird that hatches the egg of experience. A rustling in the leaves drives him away …. With this, the gift for listening is lost and the community of listeners disappears" (p.). For Benjamin, the First World War brought this process into a new phase: " … never has experience been contradicted more thoroughly than strategic experience by tactical warfare, economic experience by inflation, bodily experience by mechanical warfare, moral experience by those in power" (p. 91). This cataclysm left people not only without the conditions for telling stories but also without communicable experiences to tell. And theories about the impossibility of representation in our worlds of contemporary horror only proliferated and appear more realistic after the Holocaust.

Postmodern theorists often place memory in the center of their accounts, but it is often the unhistorical concept critiqued already, drawing sharp discontinuities between the modern and postmodern conditions of memory. Many such authors address the ruptured sense of continuity that they see as characterizing our highly mediated society in contrast to earlier epochs. Though writing in an earlier period — the interwar twenties and thirties — Maurice Halbwachs (1992) presaged this kind of an account of memory. Fundamental to Halbwachs's seminal work on social memory is, as we saw, his sharp distinction between history and memory. History, according to Halbwachs, is "dead memory," a way of preserving pasts to which we no longer have an "organic" experiential relation. To some degree, this is a universal process: Memory inevitably gives way to history as we lose touch with our pasts. But it is also a special condition of modernity, in which the historical mode of apprehending the past more and more pushes memory out as the appropriate way of relating to what has gone before. Halbwachs is here advancing an early and subtle version of what has recently been called the *"detraditionalization"* thesis regarding memory, but, as we have seen, that thesis was already well accepted more generally by the classical theorists of the late nineteenth century.[3]

This image fits well with the presumptions of the theorists previously discussed. Many contemporary scholars of memory work with an image of oral culture as richly expressive and of literate culture as detached and introspective. "Memory," as Patrick Hutton (1993, p. 7) puts it, "first conceived as a repetition, is eventually reconceived as a recollection." Hobsbawm and Ranger (1983) distinguish sharply between custom and tradition: The former is the unproblematic sense of continuity that undergirds the gradual, living changes of "traditional" societies; tradition, in contrast, aims at invariance and is the product of explicit ideologies.

A rather straightforward detraditionalization thesis seems to pervade even the most sophisticated of the postmodernist efforts to document the contemporary condition of memory, despite postmodernism's purported distrust of grand narratives elsewhere. Pierre Nora (1984–86), for instance, begins by observing the paradoxes of memory in postmodernity. "We speak so much of memory," he writes, "because there is so little of it left." Nora can in this way be seen as the true heir to Halbwachs, though Nora sees this process as even more dramatic and irreversible, and as more clearly political, than Halbwachs did. Where premodern societies live within the continuous past, contemporary societies have separated memory from the continuity of social reproduction; memory has become a matter of explicit signs, not of implicit meanings. We now compartmentalize memory as a mode of discourse; our only recourse is to represent and invent what we can no long spontaneously experience. Nora thus contrasts contemporary "*lieux*" or places of memory to earlier lived "milieux." The former are impoverished versions of the latter: "If we were able to live within memory, we would not have needed to consecrate *lieux de mémoire* in its name."

Nora's project is to catalog all of these places of memory in French society. He organizes the analyses in his massive seven-volume collection on French "*Lieux de Memoire*" around three principles he sees as layered on top of each other in telling ways: the Republic, the Nation, and "Les Frances." For Nora, this ordering represents an historical progression from unity, though uncertainty, to multiplicity. The peculiar status of the second, the memory nation, is the linchpin. In its ascendancy, the memory-nation relied on national historical narratives to provide continuity through identity. In the nineteenth century, change was still slow enough that states could control it through historiography. But, Nora argues, the nation as a foundation of identity has eroded as the state has ceded power to society. The nation itself, earlier shored up by memory, now appears as a mere trace. In contrast to theories of the nation discussed already, Nora thus sees the nation-state as declining in salience, the last incarnation of the unification of memory and history, a form in which history could provide the social cohesion that memory no longer could. History too has now lost its temporary ability to transmit values with pedagogical authority. All that is left, as Hutton (1993) characterizes Nora's project, is to autopsy the past, at best to celebrate its celebrations.

Many writers, however, note that older styles of memory persist — not merely as ruins but as pockets of meaningful practice — in the interstices of modern historical consciousness and see in this coexistence an indictment of the clear dichotomy between memory and history, whereas others worry that such dichotomous accounts are inappropriately teleological. Still others, moreover, charge that the dichotomy between oral and written modes of memory serves a colonialist mentality that devalues non-Western forms of remembering (Rappaport 1990; Zonabend 1995). These critiques notwithstanding, it is clear that the situation of memory has changed rather dramatically both over the centuries and especially in the last few decades. Nora's approach raises as many questions as it answers: given the scope of the cataloging project, what is not a *lieu de mémoire*? Is not the attempt to catalog even what one recognizes as impoverished memory traces itself a political act of recuperation (Englund 1992)? Nonetheless, Nora's theory remains the most comprehensive empirical effort to confront the contemporary situation of memory and to place memory at the center of a theory of the epoch. But it is still a unilinear story of decline and discontinuity, the twin mantras of the nostalgic late modernism it purports to critique.

Not all postmodern writers, however, are quite so unequivocal. In *Twilight Memories*, Andreas Huyssen (1995) characterizes the situation of memory in postmodernity as paradoxical as well. He notes, for instance, the simultaneous popularity of museums and the resurgence of the monument and the memorial at the same time as there is an "undisputed waning of history and historical consciousness" (ibid., p. 9). Novelty, he says, is now associated with new versions of the past rather than with visions of the future. This memory boom, however, is not to be confused with the historical fever to legitimatize nation-states, which Nietzsche derided at the end of the nineteenth century: "In comparison, the mnemonic convulsions of our culture seem chaotic, fragmentary, and free-floating." (ibid., p. 9).

Huyssen suggests developmental continuities between modernity and the present, and does not judge them completely in terms of loss: "The current obsession with memory" he writes, "is not simply a function of the *fin de siecle* syndrome, another symptom of postmodern pastiche. Instead, it is a sign of the crisis of that structure of temporality that marked the age of modernity with its celebration of the new as Utopian, as radically and irreducibly other" (ibid.). Where Benjamin and Adorno ascribe the contemporary crisis of memory to the forgetting at the center of the commodity,[4] Huyssen (1995, p. 9) relates the further development of media technologies since their time to "the evident crisis of the ideology of progress and modernization and to the fading of a whole tradition of teleological philosophies of history." As a result, the postmodern condition of memory is not necessarily worse than the modern: Rather than being simply antihistorical, relativistic, or subjective, the shift from history to memory represents a welcome critique of compromised teleological notions of history. The contemporary crisis of memory, Huyssen (ibid.) argues, "represents the attempt to slow down information processing, to resist the dissolution of time in the synchronicity of the archive, to recover a mode of contemplation outside the universe of simulation and fast-speed information and cable networks, to claim some anchoring space in a world of puzzling and often threatening heterogeneity, non-synchronicity, and information overload." Where postmodern anti-epistemology derides any easy correspondence between experience and memory, Huyssen characterizes that fissure as "a powerful stimulant for cultural and artistic creativity."

Temporality Transformed

Though agreeing with much in the foregoing accounts, I offer a somewhat different reading of the history of memory in modernity and postmodernity — one based on accumulation of temporalities rather than on the displacement of one by another — that places memory at the center of our epochal theories. Such a reading is necessarily highly speculative but can be grounded by relating its grand narrative to the concrete realities of institutional practices, whose homologies nevertheless become fully visible only within the more speculative account.

The first step in the speculative theory is to note the different developmental schemes offered by sociological theory, the differences depending on the frame of reference. In the first place, many of the theorists cited here place special emphasis on the decline of religious world views in the transformation of temporality. As we saw in the previous chapters, for instance, Koselleck (1985, p. 8-9) writes that "the future as the possible end of the World is absorbed within time by the Church as a constituting element, and thus does not exist in a linear sense at the end point of time. Rather, the end of time can be experienced only because it is always already sublimated in the Church." In contrast, "the experience in a century of bloody struggles was, above all, that the religious wars did not herald the Final Judgment...this disclosed a new and unorthodox future" (ibid., p. 9). There is thus a stark contrast between a world of prophecy, in which "events are merely symbols of that which is already known," where "apocalyptic prophecy destroys time through its fixation on the End," and one of prognosis, which "produces the time within which and out of which it weaves" (ibid., p. 14).

Combining this attention to the crisis of eschatology with a consideration of technological factors, Lutz Niethammer (1992, p. 135), as we also saw, describes a similar decline of existential security with the invention of the prognosticative chronotype:

> It eventually became apparent that there were worldly reasons to change the basic conditions of existence and to detach them from the cyclicity of nature. Once new discoveries burst the limits of the world, and trade, technology, and institutionalised relations of power

freed part of society from direct ties with the sequences of nature, elements of total explanation of the world could be transferred from the jurisdiction of salvationist history to the scientific processing of experience.... Out of the various histories through which men and women reached agreement over the origins and institutions of their group... a new universal history had to come into being, with a perspective that would provide an understanding of the cosmos to replace the religious world-view.

This account thus synthesizes the religious explanation with technological factors and the increased capacity for abstract thought due to the spread of print culture as described above. It offers a powerful explanation for the rise of philosophies of history in the nineteenth century, as well as for the more mundane institutionalization of empirical historical discourse.

Other theorists, as we have seen, place more control in the hands of the state. According to Friedland and Boden (1994, pp. 9–10), "Bureaucracies enabled as they constrained, and the controlling centers were to assume that expanding and rather singular rationality that characterizes modernity." Koselleck (1985, p. 10-11) writes that "the genesis of the absolutist state is accompanied by a sporadic struggle against all manner of religious and political predictions. The state enforced a monopoly on the control of the future by suppressing apocalyptic and astrological readings of the future. In doing so, it assumed a function of the old Church for anti-Church objectives." Anderson (1991), as we have seen, shows how the nation requires a historicist form in its effort to replace the existential promises of salvationism. History and the nation, as both positive and negative observers note, go hand in hand.

The literature thus provides us with a fairly clear account of the rise of linear historicity out of the cyclicity of rural living and Church eschatology. In contrast to more conventional accounts, these readings provide a framework in which temporality and memory are not incidental but rather the constitutive media of modernity: The related crises of temporality and of memory are what modernity is. In German, for instance, the word for *modernity* (*Neuzeit*) translates literally as "new time." And, as Richard Terdiman (1993, p. 24) puts it, "The nineteenth century's preoccupation with the developmental character of time cannot be divorced from the disruptions of memory which underlay its theoretical concerns and determined their urgency.... A myth of historical progress makes the loss of memory less troubling." But this modern temporality is not a disembodied demiurge; it is a set of institutional forms and practices that respond to concrete existential circumstances as well as to their place in a developmental order.

From the official side, states developed neotraditional liturgies and offered new narratives to unify their vast territories and to ground a sense of belonging in their diverse populations. Nation-building went hand in hand with state building and was accomplished through public commemorative rituals, museums, monuments, holidays, festivals, architecture, and the like. At a slightly less official level, publics became quite interested in the present vestiges of the past. From the Renaissance on, there was a profound transformation in the relation that populations had to the ruins of older societies in their midst. Archaeology took root as an important enterprise, ruins were converted into relics, and a classical revival gripped the arts and sciences. By the eighteenth century, neoclassicism was the prevalent model not just for public architecture but also for public thinking.

Crucial to the character of the eighteenth and nineteenth centuries — the so-called age of ideology — was also the development of grand historical schemes, be they evolutionary (e.g., Social Darwinism, modernization theory), revolutionary (e.g., Marxism, Utopianism), or devolutionary (e.g., Weber's theory of the iron cage). The philosophy of history was the secular attempt to satisfy the providential yearnings formerly calmed by religious eschatology, and it also served the expansionist political programs and legitimation strategies of the administrative state. Within the universities, the philosophy of history was also connected to the development of historiography (Breisbach 1994; Iggers 1983). The latter, first conceived as a way of revealing how the grand program manifested itself in the world, eventually became a basis for rejecting not only particular grand schemes but also the very idea of grand schemes at all. Historicism, which is based on belief in teleological accounts of the stages of history, begat historism, which is based on belief in the uniqueness of every historical culture, in the incommensurability of worldviews, and in the randomness of history. It is not by chance that so many of the recent debates about postmodernism, multiculturalism, and identity have invoked the practice of historiography.

More deeply into civil society, collecting and genealogy became important endeavors. The very ideas of the museum and of collecting were reconceived from about the late eighteenth century, only partly the result of colonialism (Bennett 1995). Regarding private life, Philip Ariés's (1974) work on attitudes toward death and dying in Western culture attributes the rising importance and frequency of commemorative funerary practices in the nineteenth century to an increased sense of change: The past — even the personal past — was no longer felt to be immediately present but was something that required preservation and recovery. Rather suddenly, the cemetery became an important place for the articulation of the lost past. Literary theorists, as well, note the spread of the novel and of autobiography as expressions of the rising sense of individuality, itself possible only because of the now more varied — both within themselves and in comparison to others — life courses many people now experienced. Mikhail Bakhtin, for instance, argued that the nineteenth-century novel's prosaic sense of time made it the first literary genre to convey the world truly historically (Morson and Emerson 1990). Psychoanalysis, with its focus on repressed memory, was one more practice marked through with the insecurities of accelerating experience (Hutton 1993; Kern 1983).

Memory and the Public Sphere

Chief among the institutional forms in which the role of memory in modernity, and vice versa, can be made more visible is that of the so-called public sphere. According to Jürgen Habermas (1989), the preeminent theorist of the public sphere, beginning in about the sixteenth century on an important new space opened up between the authority of the state and the privacy of civil society — both of these themselves new forms — in which private individuals were able to debate the proper relations between the state and civil society. This arena of debate constituted not just a new kind of publicity but also the very idea of publicity itself. A crucial feature of this new form of discourse was the popular periodical press, which helped transform the nature of political authority: The kind of public scrutiny carried out in the press and in the public sphere at large forced the state into a posture of responsiveness previously unimaginable and unpractical.

Though theorists of the public sphere have not discussed it in terms of memory, it is not difficult to see how important memory is for the public sphere and vice versa. One of the conditions for the possibility of a public sphere, following theorists like Emile Durkheim (1984) and Norbert Elias (1994), is, as we have seen, a sufficient degree of differentiation so that public discourse is necessary.Where the varieties of experience in localities and across short life spans were more limited and uniform, the foundations of cohesion were assumed rather than hypothetical; where experiences are largely identical among people both in a given time and place as well as across generations, identity is manifest in the rhythms of everyday life and in the ritualism of cyclical communion. But where people from different milieux congregate together in urban settings, leaving behind both their earlier contexts and to some degree their earlier selves, where the labors of life are more highly differentiated than in rural households, where classes and guilds and interest groups form, the basis of agreement, the bonds of commonality, are much less obvious, requiring vast new efforts and conceptual frameworks.

Memory thus becomes a public affair; that is, we are able to conceptualize a collective memory — a public with a memory — only in the context of the interaction of multifarious interests and world views. For there to be a collective memory, there have to be different memories to collect; the stories of traditional societies are not collective (collected) memories in this sense because they are always present to all. The problem of collective memory is thus synonymous with the problem of collective identity in complex society, and in democratic societies at least, the space where such collection occurs is the public sphere, where private and official come together in new ways and where contestation is the rule.

In important senses, the high modernity of the eighteenth and nineteenth centuries constitutes a radical departure from the absolutist claims that went before. The kind of discourse that occurs in "public" makes sense only because people are able to conceive of futures that they believe they can control. From this perspective, it is hardly surprising how many new mnemonic activities arose both simultaneously and within the public space and were integral to its functioning. Yet all of these efforts more or less fit within a coherent linear temporality, one grand story of descent and progress. The state was the dominant purveyor of such temporality, but even nonstate versions were ordered in this way. This was an age that both formulated time's arrow and believed that it could still be one.

But this search for agreement, this hope for man-made foundations that could support the weight of existential insecurity in an ever more complexifying society — a feature of societies that exist in time rather than outside of it — was part of a developmental process already under way, a slippery slope entered on with the first real challenge to the inviolability of natural law. Western society became too complex from the Middle Ages on to support one monolithic principle of legitimation. The age of ideology can be seen as the attempt to replace that one monolithic principle with a number of new monolithic principles. As Nora argued, the nation state of the nineteenth century was a last incarnation of the unity of memory and the nation. But though it may be possible to be the only articulated monolith available, the very existence of more than one such candidate begins to undermine the monolithic principle itself. Fissiparous difference, which characterizes the modern secular state, makes the appeal to a unified national identity inherently contradictory. The hope for a unitary collective memory of the nation state in the nineteenth century was thus a task doomed from the start, indeed from much earlier. The hysterical fever with which that memory was pursued in the late nineteenth century merely testifies to the profound insecurity out of which the attempt grew.

Chronic Differentiation

Nora is correct to describe the nation-state's loss of salience but is wrong to attribute it to a unilinear decline of memory in favour of history. It is not a shift from one to the other but is the proliferation of alternatives along-side the original that in fact diminishes its dominance. The nation-state is not the last union of memory and history but is the last that can claim to be the only such unity without being successfully challenged. The rise of alternate histories and alternate historicities, which do not require the disappearance of national history per se, chips away at its dominance: The nation-state now has to compete with alternative claimants. In contrast to the unilinear accounts from traditionalism to detraditionalization, from the organic presence of memory to its dead remains, therefore, the account that I am advancing emphasizes multiplicity: not Nora's multiplicity of histories but a multiplicity of historicities. New technologies and new social forms have undermined the absolutism of the nation just as others did the old absolutism of the Church, but now we have a multiplicity of contenders for partial allegiance and we are drawn to various and often conflicting temporal frames of reference.

I offer the term *"chronic differentiation"* to characterize the developmental unity of this process in all of its stages. The term is intended as a pun based on its dual reference. In one sense, *chronic* means ongoing and is often associated with a negative, as in permanent pain or some other "chronic" condition, like unemployment. In a second sense, *chronic* refers to time, as in chronometer (i.e., clock) or chronicle (i.e., a continuous historical account). Chronic differentiation thus indicates the connection between the ongoing differentiation of society that has accelerated markedly since the Middle Ages and the differentiation of temporalities associated with it. We experience chronic differentiation not just in the sense that social differentiation is ongoing and linear but also in the sense that it is time itself that is being differentiated. As we have seen already, the differentiation of society and the differentiation of temporalities are part of the same process.

Though chronic differentiation describes a general process, it is no disembodied telos; chronic differentiation merely summarizes the variety of technical, institutional, and existential developments that have been occurring over the last 150 or so years. As already mentioned, the late nineteenth century experienced a proliferation of inquiries into memory and obsessions with the lost past: the rise of the archive and institutional record keeping, professional historiography, political commemoration, interest in ordinary genealogy, the middle-class cemetery, and psychoanalysis. Each of these developments in its own way makes sense within the social structures of the time, in which nation-states were expanding their control over vaster territories and further into the lives of their citizens; rampant industrialization was transporting entire segments of populations off the land and into factories; commerce and government were becoming more international; and ethnicity-based nation-building was ever more an endeavor of retrenchment in the face of migratory and political complexities.

In other words, by the late nineteenth century, the commemorative project of nation-state legitimation had been made even more untenable by the increasing technological, institutional, and existential complexifaction of Western societies, by their continued social differentiation.[5] Many historians have placed great weight on the invention of photography and other recording technologies in creating a revolution of memory, though it is important to note that photography was at first restricted to portraiture and only later picked up the wide variety of new themes that painting had already begun addressing (Kern 1983). Nonetheless, by the late nineteenth century ordinary people found themselves stretched in different ways by multiple chronic frames: factory time, calendrical time, local time, national time, official time, leisure time, lifetime, public time, private time, family time. By the end of the nineteenth century, the failure of nation-states to provide existential security and identitarian unity in face of these multiplications seemed to have reached a crisis level.

Many commentators have described the rise of fascism and communism in terms assimilable to this account. Fascism in particular was a "reactionary modernism," one that sought the benefits of technological efficiency and rational administration without the loss of automatic collective allegiance (Herf 1984). Fascist states attempted to resacralize the world by bringing back the aura of tradition, which they did by manipulating exactly those technical means that had led to the problematic desacralization in the first place. Fascism's aesthetic politics thus repossessed the rituals and cults that the modern era had promised to crush (Falasca-Zamponi 1997). The Nazi German notion of *Gleichschaltung* — the elimination of intermediate associations that could diminish direct allegiance to the all-encompassing state — can also be seen in this light: As the crisis of legitimacy in complex society became ever greater, attempts to recapture it became ever more extreme; the attempt to eliminate alternative associations reveals how much the struggle was one over the authority to monopolize and to control identity and destiny. Central to totalitarianism is the effort to eliminate nonstate frameworks for nonsanctioned remembering.

What has happened since then to the mnemonic public sphere, now that it has reasserted itself against the totalitarian effort to eliminate it? Though the national state and capitalist industry have tried to hang onto uniform time and homogeneous history, they have produced the conditions that undermine the very effort: Nations are more fissiparous than ever; capitalism fetishizes the new to extreme degrees; mass media technologies offer individualized control. A process that began with the decline of church eschatology and that reached crisis proportions in the late nineteenth century has now brought us to a new level of fragmentation. But it is a peculiar kind of fragmentation, in a sense more schizophrenic than democratic: At times we flit among multiple identities and contradictory realities, with ever greater capacities for cognitive and existential dissonance. Indeed, the musical analogy can be extended: from the homophony of Church eschatology to the polyphony of national-statism to the polytonality of multiculturalism. Note that this last stage is polytonal rather than atonal; we are still capable of commitment and conflict, and the mix includes pockets of partial tonality and polyphony.[6]

This is the state of our contemporary public sphere, where absolutism — often in the form of religious or political fundamentalism — old-fashioned liberalism, and multiculturalism mix it up side by side. Of course, these are not free-floating conceptual possibilities but are the results of concrete and conceptual developments. As Jonathan Boyarin (1994, p. 13) writes, "While we continue imagining ourselves in a reliably Newtonian world, new technologies of transportation and communication have changed the very conditions of our possible experiences of 'proximity' and 'simultaneity.'" At the same time, we can trace the path-dependent logic of ideology from the dominance of the nation-state, through the eliminationism of National Socialism to contemporary multiculturalism, which, again, I emphasize is not the straightforward infinity of equally incommensurable identities but a hodgepodge of identities that claim incommensurability with others that claim the right to eliminationist domination with others that pursue individualizing universalism.

Yet within this hodgepodge — which, as Huyssen (1995) points out, can be a situation of creative potential as well as one of loss — Boyarin (1994, p. 15) asserts, "There remains a powerful tendency for collective identities to be cast as national histories in support of claims to independent statehood. Living historically implies that the creation of nationness, and conversely the elaboration of the construct, nation, is necessarily historical." The contemporary public sphere is filled with groups competing over history and competing in terms of history. But that competition goes on and even increases as other historicities old and new proliferate side by side. Indeed, some of the most radical mnemonic identitarianisms are fostered where the distances of historical origin and geographical dispersion are overcome in the simultaneity of cyberspace. We exist with, indeed move rather fluidly among, the multiple temporalities of face-to-face community, global village, archival history — all sorts of records are available in the prodigious real and virtual libraries, government archives — national history (especially through the media), and various not necessarily coherently integrated identities (e.g., male, father, husband, American, sociologist, white) that take place in locations more widely dispersed than ever before.[7] Even more surprising than the diversity of temporalities and spatialities in which we exist is the comfort with which we do so. As these multiplicities have expanded, so have our abilities to move among them. As Friedland and Boden (1994, p. 9) remark, "As the centres reached out to control the periphery and the future, their subjects also achieved increasing control over the space and time of their lives as distinctions between work time and family time grew."

In this sense, the current proliferation of historical identitarianism, commodified nostalgia, museification, record keeping, *lieux de mémoire*, separation, and regret are part of one process: not that they are the same things — indeed, each of these practices and institutional forms has its own logic, and there are often conflicts among them and with less past-oriented frameworks — but that their differences result from the same process of chronic differentiation. Though the use of the past is a hallmark of multiculturalism, multiculturalism also implies a diversity of chronic frames, some traditionally historical, some involving new temporalities, and some not historical at all. Of course, even the most pluralistic states in the most multicultural societies are concerned about their cohesion; they continue to offer unitary narratives to integrate the many alternatives available, and they worry about the authority they have ceded to the public sphere over such matters as history standards and public storytelling. But holdouts seeking to revive the kind of grand narratives that the nation-states of the nineteenth century developed to secure their populations and to solidify their legitimacy have become rarer and sound more extreme than ever. Our contemporary reality is that even though states continue to offer such narratives, they do so with an awareness of — and indeed defer-ence to — the alternative frameworks available; often, contemporary states seem to recognize that they produce the very conditions that undermine the very possibility of such unitary national communities.

Endnotes

Chapter One

1. Indeed, over the last decades, organizational theory has turned to narrative and culture as both constitutive and instrumental features of even the most bureaucratized organizations; see, for instance, Czarniawska (1997), Martin (1991), and, more generally, Powell and DiMaggio (1991).
2. For overviews, see Berezin (1994, 1997) and Brint (1994).
3. See for instance, Edelman (1977).
4. Here, though not only here, Barry Schwartz's work has been signal.
5. See the introductory essay by Goudsblom and Mennell in Elias, Mennell, and Goudsblom (1998), Bakhtin (1993), and Bourdieu (1984).
6. I explain these ideas in more detail in chapters four and five. For a general introduction, see Morson and Emerson (1990).
7. This theme also frames the analysis in *In the House of the Hangman* (Olick 2005).
8. Bakhtin is certainly not the only one to look at *"great time"* in political discourse. I have also drawn much inspiration, as several of the essays in part two make clear, from the practice of *"conceptual history,"* particularly as I have found it contributing to the general theory of temporalization in modernity by Reinhardt Koselleck, among others. For a general overview, see Richter (1995).
9. Among the most important entries in this literature is *Transitional Justice* (Teitel 2000).
10. See, especially, Le Goff (1992), Matsuda (1996), and Olick and Robbins (1998).
11. See chapter two of *On Revolution* (Arendt 1991) in particular.
12. For a more thorough discussion of Weber's implications for the politics of regret, see also chapter 12 and 13 of *In the House of the Hangman* (Olick 2005).

Chapter Two

1. This article was presented at the meeting of the International Institute of sociology, Tel Aviv, Israel, July 1999, and at the meeting of the American Sociological Association, Chicago, Illinois, August 1999. I thank Jan-Werner Mueller, Ina Mueller-Mack, Howard Schuman, Barry Schwartz, Charles Tilly, Robin Wagner-Pacifici, and Harrison White for help of various kinds. I particularly appreciate Howard Schuman's generosity in response to my analysis of his work. A version of this chapter appeared in *Sociological Theory* 17, 3 (November 1999): 333–348.

2. I use this term to refer to a historically specific constellation of ideas about collective justice. It seems that a general willingness to acknowledge historical misdeeds has disseminated throughout the world recently, leading to more and more official and unofficial apologies to both internal and, perhaps even more surprisingly, external victims. An expectation of acknowledgment has become a decisive factor in processes of "transitional justice" as well as in domestic and international politics more generally.

3. This distinction between operational and sensitizing concepts comes from Herbert Blumer (1969, pp. 153–82). Blumer saw *"operational"* concepts as delimiting fixed and measurable phenomena and *"sensitizing"* concepts as evolving fields of purview and modes of perceiving general areas of social process.

4. Halbwachs's Strasbourg colleague, Marc Bloch (1925, 1974), also used the term *collective memory* in 1925 as well as in his later book on feudal society.

5. This statement can be taken as a powerful suggestion that we need to inquire into those technologies of memory — such as the archive, museum, or library — that are purely social. I take up this point in detail later.

6. From our present perspective, of course, notions of public availability are usually much more complex, allowing for differential access and subversive readings. See Johnson et al. (1982).

7. Later research (e.g., Schuman and Corning 2000) points out the different ways to experience contemporary events — such as by participating in them directly or observing them through mass media — and the different ways such experiences enter into memory, either individual or collective.

8. There are now several reviews of the collective memory literature. See, especially, Olick and Robbins (1998), Thelen (1989), Kammen (1995), and Zelizer (1995b).

9. These issues go back at least as far as Jean-Jacques Rousseau, who attempted to distinguish between the *"will of all"* (the unanimity of individual preferences) and the *"general will"* (the best interests of the collectivity). Emile Durkheim, of course, was powerfully influenced by Rousseau's communitarianism. In more contemporary discussions, work on public opinion also conceptualizes an ontological distinction between the aggregation of individual opinions and public opinion per se. See Blumer (1969, p. 195–200), Herbst (1993), and Noelle-Neumann (1984).

10. The most significant sociological examples of this kind of work come from Howard Schuman and various colleagues, who employ survey research to measure generational effects and knowledge of historical events across

different national populations. See Schuman and Scott (1989), Schuman and Rieger (1992), Schuman and Corning (2000), and Schuman, Belli, and Bischoping (1997), as well as the other essays in Pennebaker, Paez, and Rimé (1997). See also Vinitzky-Seroussi (1998), who approaches collective memory through "autobiographical occasions," high school reunions in particular. Historians Roy Rosenzweig and David Thelen (1998) also use survey research as well as depth interviewing to produce an aggregate picture of what I am calling American "collected" memory. The individualist orientation of this work is clear when they quote Carl Becker's famous essay, "Everyman his Own Historian" (cited in Rosenzweig and Thelen 1998, p. 178).

11. Both survey researchers and oral historians, of course, can partition their samples, and often focus on the differences between elite and popular attitudes (Converse 1964).

12. Similarities between this account and that of phenomenological sociology, which emphasizes the use of typifications and ad hocing strategies, are fairly clear.

13. To treat language, and by extension collective memory, as transcendental in this way does not necessarily imply treating it as having crossed into another ontological realm, from phenomenon to noumenon. As Norbert Elias (1991) argues, there is a difference between being transcendent and transcendental. If language is a system with an independent logical reality, it is because we construct it as such. An analogous argument can be found in Berger and Luckmann (1967).

14. It appears as if the collectivist approach is the most common in sociological work using the term *collective memory,* but that appearance can be deceptive. A residual individualism is sometimes hidden, for instance, by a substantive focus on, for example, ideological products, symbols, and monuments, which are public goods: The dependent variable in such studies is collective, but focusing on such a dependent variable — rather, say, than on individual memories of collective events — does not mean that the independent variable or indeed that the overall ontology is collectivist. Many sociologists — particularly Barry Schwartz (1991, 1996), Edward Shils (1981), Eviatar Zerubavel (1996), myself (Olick 1999b; Olick and Levy 1997), and others both within and outside of sociology — do employ a genuinely collectivist approach. But we often use the collective nature of the object of analysis to stand in for an argument about the collectivist nature of our approach.

Chapter Three

1. An early version of this paper was presented at the 1995 annual meeting of the American Sociological Association held in Washington, D.C. I am grateful for helpful comments from Karen Barkey, Wendell Bell, Priscilla Ferguson, Kelly Moore, Francesca Polletta, Joyce Robbins, Guenther Roth, Barry Schwartz, Allan Silver, Paula England, Charles Tilly, and two anonymous reviewers. A version of this chapter appeared in *American Sociological Review* 62, 6 (Dec. 1997): 921–936.

2. Both political culture and collective memory are overgeneralizing concepts: Political cultures and collective memories are always multiple, diverse, and fluid, with different institutional fields (Bourdieu 1993) operating according to different rules and interacting with each other in different and shifting ways. This chapter refers mainly to elite public discourse, although that discourse is situated within others as much as possible. No assumption is made that elite versions are the political culture or collective memory per se, only that they are dominant versions of each.

3. Although public opinion can be an important element in political cultures, it is not the same thing as political culture. In the first place, public opinion is subjective, whereas political culture is intersubjective; they thus belong to different ontological orders and require different analytical strategies. Second, elite-produced symbols do respond to their reception in public opinion, but no one-to-one correspondence exists between political culture and its reception, no matter how much politicians try to improve their "numbers." Numerous examples of official symbolism, for instance, contradict public opinion. Moreover, public opinion is not a straightforward measure of popularity (i.e., of nonelite beliefs). Public opinion concerns public political issues, as does political culture, but surveys of attitudes (or at least our interpretations of those surveys) often conflate the public and the private: One's attitude about an issue is not necessarily what one expects the government's attitude to be. Though I refer to some survey data and to some extrapolitical issues as illustrations, the chapter focuses primarily on political culture, which differs from public opinion, popular culture, and the private sphere.

4. The gap between the upper and the lower parts of Figure 1 indicates that contravention is not strictly a type of cultural constraint; rather, it is a response to, or transformation of, cultural constraint. Thus, contravention is of a different order from but is related to proscription and prescription.

5. The following account is based on a systematic survey and analysis of all major issues for, and statements by, government incumbents and agencies concerning the Nazi past over forty years of West German history (Olick forthcoming). The chapter's examples are chosen from that more systematic study for their value in illustrating the conceptual argument about different kinds of cultural constraint.

6. Many Germans regarded the entire process as capricious. "Big fish" often escaped punishment because the requirements for prosecution were stricter and the political pressures greater, whereas "small fish" were more easily given a "bad" classification. On the other hand, the system was widely corrupt, and many managed to arrange dubious exculpations. Furthermore, the Allied attitude toward German guilt changed dramatically as the cold war began; they saw a shift away from guilt as essential to winning Germans over to the West, and earlier policies of blame and punishment thereby became inexpedient. See Olick (2005, ch. 6).

7. The description of the Nazi years as a "catastrophe" — first popularized in an important essay by the renowned German historian Friedrich Meinecke (1950) — implies a natural disaster beyond human control that sweeps over a landscape. As such, it evokes inevitability rather than culpability.

8. Although many historians and commentators (mostly detractors) argue that the Allies forced the Germans into this move, Wolffsohn (1988), among others, provides convincing evidence that this was not the case. Nonetheless, the power of the gesture is still tangible for a state wishing to reestablish its place among "civilized" nations. The majority of the population, however, disapproved of the plan, as did a substantial portion of Adenauer's cabinet.

9. Indeed, such an acknowledgment had been a major discussion point in negotiations over the *Wiedergutmachung* (reparations). Israeli leader David Ben-Gurion insisted on it as essential. Adenauer steadfastly refused (Deutschkron 1991).

10. In response to attacks on the synagogue in Cologne and the general wave of anti-Semitic vandalism in the winter of 1959–1960, Adenauer spoke as follows in a special radio address delivered on January 16, 1960: "To all of my German fellow citizens I say: If you catch a hoodlum anywhere, punish him on the spot and give him a sound thrashing. That is the punishment he has earned." Adenauer's point was that these attacks were the work of children and provided no insight into, or evidence of, genuine anti-Semitism. He went on to dismiss concerns abroad about the state of German society: "To our opponents abroad and doubters abroad I say, the unanimity of the entire German people in the condemnation of anti-Semitism and of National socialism has shown itself in the most complete and strongest way imaginable…." One assumes he is referring to solid rejection of extremist parties in elections. " … The German people has shown that these thoughts and tendencies have no foundation in it." In light of the events that spurred this statement, Adenauer's claims appear to be at least somewhat overconfident.

11. In recent years, some scholars have disagreed with this judgment. From the center, Weber and Steinbach (1984) argue that West Germany did an admirable job of prosecuting Nazi criminals within the rule of law and its strictures. From farther right, Lübbe (1983) states that a certain degree of collective amnesia was essential for the legitimacy of the new state in the 1950s. Even more polemically, Kittel (1993) argues, contrary to the common view, that early West German leaders were overwhelmingly preoccupied with confronting the past, although he equates mentioning the past (even to deny it) with "mastering" it. Also see Moeller (1996).

12. A 1947 survey in West Germany included the statement that national socialism was a good idea badly realized; 55 percent of the respondents agreed. In 1955, 48 percent of respondents agreed that without the war, Hitler would have been one of Germany's greatest statesmen (Klessmann 1987). As recently as 1995, when respondents to a poll were asked, "Was the expulsion of the Germans from the East just as great a crime against humanity as the Holocaust against the Jews?" 36 percent of all Germans (40 percent of those over age 65) answered yes (Moeller 1996, p. 1009).

13. German Jewish expatriate philosopher Hannah Arendt (1950, p. 345) documents this phenomenon in the American Jewish magazine *Commentary*. She described the self-absorbed and defensive reactions she encountered when she revealed on a 1950 trip to Germany that she was a German Jew:

    This is usually followed by a little embarrassed pause; and then comes — not a personal question, such as "Where did you go after you left Germany?"; no sign of sympathy, such as "What happened to your family?" — but a deluge of stories about how Germans have suffered (true enough, of course, but beside the point): and if the object of this little experiment happens to be educated and intelligent, he will proceed to draw up a balance between German suffering and the suffering of others.

14. The differences and the competition between official and vernacular memory form a central theme in social memory studies (see, e.g., Bodnar 1992; Kammen 1991; Wagner-Pacifici and Schwartz 1991). On the problems of ordinary people confronting (i.e., not confronting) the past, see Mitscherlich and Mitscherlich's (1967) famous argument that Germans after the war suffered a pathological "inability to mourn."

15. In a 1951 survey, only 32 percent of the population answered that they thought Germany carried the guilt for the war; in 1962, it was 53 percent and in 1967 62 percent (Klessmann 1987). For a detailed historical discussion, see Olick (2005).

16. An analogous observation that the scholarly literature on Nazism pays insufficient attention to anti-Semitism has been at the heart of the controversy over Daniel Goldhagen's (1996) book. Whatever the merits of the positions in the "Goldhagen controversy" (Schoeps 1996), this lack of reference in political discourse is even clearer and certainly more important than its absence in scholarly discourse.

17. Bude (1992) discusses the differences between Germany and other Western nations undergoing similar social transformations in this regard. In Germany, he argues that antifascism — the accusation that present political and social organizations were continuous with earlier fascist forms — was decisive for the student movement; elsewhere it was only derivative or not even an issue.

18. The language frequently used by Chancellor Kohl illustrates this refusal to acknowledge the realities of international migration. Kohl intoned repeatedly in the context of these debates that "Germany is no immigration country," though of course it has in fact always been such a country. In addition, Kohl often distinguished between *Bürger* (citizens) and *Mitbürger* (approximately co-citizens).

19. For a more extensive analysis of this "grammar of exculpation," see Olick (2005) and Schirmer (1988).

20. For texts of the debate, see Baldwin (1990) and *"Historikerstreit"* (Piper 1987). See Maier (1988) and Evans (1989) for intellectual histories.

Chapter Four

1. Early versions of this paper were presented at the annual meeting of the German Studies Association, Chicago, Illinois, October 1996, and at the annual meeting of the American Sociological Association, Toronto, Canada, August 1997. I gratefully acknowledge the help of generous colleagues who commented on drafts of this paper, including Nicki Beisel, Courtney Bender, Daniel Levy, Dirk Moses, Francesca Polletta, Joyce Robbins, Guenther Roth, Oliver Zimmer, anonymous reviewers for *American Sociological Review*, and an *American Sociological Review* deputy editor. I owe an extraordinary debt to Barry Schwartz and Priscilla Ferguson. A version of this chapter appeared in *American Sociological Review* 64 (June 1999): 381–402.

2. There is, of course, a long-standing and important debate about the authorship of the so-called Bakhtin texts (see Morson and Emerson 1990). I refer to Bakhtin alone here out of convenience rather than to take a position in that debate.

3. Bakhtin is responding to the choice between a formalism that treats genres as ideal, transcendental grammars instantiated in speech acts, and a Marxist "stylistics" that reduces speech to conditions outside of language. The former, according to Bakhtin, removes the temporal dimension because what matters are variations of a permanent form rather than the historical accretion of the form itself; the latter, equally unacceptable, sees utterances as formally random, wholly determined "materially." Bakhtin calls his method, intended to reject rather than to combine these options, *"sociological poetics."*

4. Looking at official speech (i.e., statements made by government leaders in their official capacities) does not mean that official speech is the only or most important kind of commemoration or collective memory. Genres of unofficial commemoration exist as well. The relation between official and unofficial genres is always an empirical question for the history of memory.

5. At the time, the Allied authorities declared that Germany was not being occupied for the purpose of freeing it but rather as a conquered enemy country. This attitude, however, did not last long in the face of the emerging cold war: The West wanted their part of Germany as a bulwark against the Soviet Union, and a politics of collective guilt did not serve this purpose. Opinion polls in the early 1950s show approximately two thirds of West Germans strongly denying any collective guilt (Merritt 1995, p. 143). The sufferings of the postwar period, moreover, were decisive for shaping these attitudes. The last months of the war brought massive material destruction, terror from bombings, and loss of family members; many German women suffered brutal rapes at the hands of the advancing Soviet army; the ethnic cleansing of Germans from Eastern territories following the Potsdam accords was unprecedented, with estimates of ten million refugees and upward of one million dead on the marches. Research into these experiences of ordinary people has led some oral and social historians to challenge the traditional periodization in which May 8, 1945, marks a decisive rupture in German history. Instead, they identify a distinct period running from the defeat at Stalingrad in 1943 to the currency reform of 1948 (Broszat, Henke, and Woller 1988).

6. Data are drawn from a systematic survey and analysis of all major issues for and statements by government incumbents and offices concerning the Nazi past over fifty years of West German history (Olick forthcoming). Unless otherwise indicated, texts of speeches are drawn from the *Bulletin des Presse-und-Informationsamtes der Bundesregierung* (*Bulletin of the Federal Press and Information Agency*), a newsletter published almost every business day since 1951 containing most major speeches, statements, and announcements by the federal government, or from the *Stenographischer Bericht des deutschen Bundestages* (*Stenographic Report of the German Bundestag*). Unless otherwise noted, translations are my own.

7. Little remarked in public discourse or in academic commentary is the fact that the Nazis used the same term to refer to their success in stemming the great inflation and in reviving the devastated German economy in the 1930s.

8. The German public, both after the war and to some degree until today, has denied any connection between their own suffering, expulsion, and division after the war and Germany's vicious behavior during the war. As recently as 1989, 72 percent of respondents to a West German opinion poll disagreed with the statement that division of the country was a deserved punishment for the crimes of the Third Reich (Noelle-Neumann 1991, p. 68). At the official level, early leaders avoided the implication that Germany's division was in any way related to the war, although later speakers increasingly drew a connection between 1933 and 1945. These were considered separate injustices, as were the expulsions of Germans from the Eastern territories. Moreover, many Germans have seen the Holocaust and the expulsions as equivalent, though unrelated, crimes. In a 1995 poll, when asked, "Was the expulsion of the Germans from the East just as great a crime against humanity as the Holocaust against the Jews?" 36 percent of all Germans (40 percent of those over 65) answered "yes" (Moeller 1996). Presumably, this number was much higher in the 1950s.

9. Part of the debate concerning the June 17 occasion concerned whether to call the event a national celebration ("*Nationalfeiertag*") or a national commemoration day ("*Nationalgedenktag*"). Social Democrats advocated the former because they were proud of the uprising's provenance as a workers' revolt; Christian Democrats resisted the more celebratory label, arguing that it was improper to celebrate the nation while it was still divided. The compromise solution was to call June 17 the Day of National Unity ("*Tag der deutschen Einheit*") (Hattenhauer 1990).

10. Indeed, Social Democratic leaders were opposed to celebrating even the return of sovereignty. Given the continued division of the nation, they saw no occasion for expressions of joy.

11. Brandt and Kiesinger, moreover, bore different relations to the Nazi past. Kiesinger had been a member of the Nazi party as early as 1933. Brandt, on the other hand, was a member of the early Social Democratic opposition and emigrated to Scandinavia when his situation became untenable. Though conservatives, including Adenauer, attacked Brandt as a traitor to the nation, others have commented that Brandt was a necessary symbolic counterweight to Kiesinger's historical burdens (Grosser 1985).

12. There is a well-developed sociological literature pointing out the connections between collective memory and generations. Mannheim (1952) founded this tradition with his argument that generations form when cohorts share powerful social and political experiences during their adolescence (also see Schuman and Scott 1989). Shils (1981) points out that new generations define themselves against their elders and thus bear different relations to the past than do previous generations. For an investigation of the role of generational structures in German memory, see Bude (1992).

13. The expression "*difficult fatherland*" (*schwieriges Vaterland*) had already appeared in Heinemann's inaugural address; it indicates a more direct confrontation with the costs as well as benefits of nationhood.

14. The oil crisis of 1973, combined with worldwide recession and an increased threat of terrorism, called into question not only the current state of affairs but the entire hopeful narrative of progressivism. Schmidt's administration governed under the banner of reduced possibilities and the normal problems of an overextended welfare state.

15. Schmidt's desire to avoid the politics of commemoration stems from his overwhelmingly pragmatic understanding of politics and not from a neo-conservative interest in reviving lost traditions.

16. Compare this to Scheel's rebuke to critics who assert that *Vergangenheitsbewältigung* (mastering the past) is the goal: Scheel asserts that being interested in and responsible for the past is not to engage in self-flagellation but that it is morally necessary.

17. Prominent SPD intellectual Günter Gaus (not to be confused with the writer Günter Grass) charged that Kohl had stolen the term from him, perverting its meaning to exculpate young to middle-aged Germans. Kohl defended the expression, which he claimed he had used as early as 1982, as a basis for reconciliation between younger Germans and Israelis. The statement could have been taken to mean that without the grace of a late birth and anti-Nazi parents Kohl would have been a Nazi supporter. Interestingly, Schmidt's statement was closer to the meaning that Kohl was accused by left-wing critics of having intended. In his 1998 campaign, SPD chancellor candidate Gerhard Schröder referred to himself as a *Spätgeborener* (one who was born late).

18. As we saw at the beginning of the previous chapter, several years later in 1981 Schmidt stirred international controversy when, on his return from a much-criticized trip to Saudi Arabia during which he negotiated the sale of West German Leopard 2 tanks to Israel's sworn enemy, he reportedly proclaimed that West German foreign policy should no longer be "held hostage" to Auschwitz (Wolffsohn 1988, p. 42).

19. Main statements relating to the Bitburg affair are taken from Hartmann (1986).

20. The *Waffen-SS* was an elite commando unit of the *SS* (*Schutzstaffel*) under *Wehrmacht* (army) command. The Nuremberg tribunal declared the *SS* an illegal organization, the primary repressive arm of the Nazi state, and members were guilty by association. Defenders of the *Waffen-SS* claim it was just an elite military unit and not part of the Nazi repressive apparatus. Critics charge that *Waffen-SS* troops were used for especially difficult "cleansing" operations.

21. These positions are somewhat ironic in light of von Weizsäcker's personal history. Von Weizsäcker served as part of the legal team that defended his father, Ernst, at Nuremberg. The elder von Weizsäcker was a high-ranking figure in the Nazi Foreign Ministry under Joachim von Ribbentrop. The defense was that he thought he could do more good from within the system than from outside. He was convicted.

22. Indeed, Grosser (1985, p. 340) argues that Scheel's speech ten years earlier was " … even clearer, even more forceful."

23. To avoid displacing the commemoration of *Kristallnacht* on November 9, for instance, the new Germany chose to mark unification on October 3, the official day of unification, rather than on November 9, the day the Berlin Wall fell. In addition, when presidential candidate Stefan Heitmann commented

that he thought it was time to draw a line under the German past — to move out from under its shadow — the Christian Democratic Union summarily withdrew its support.

Chapter Five

1. See Gillis (1994), Middleton and Edwards (1990), Butler (1989), Darian-Smith and Hamilton (1994), and Pennebaker, Paez, and Rimé (1997), as well as special issues of *Communication, Representations, Qualitative Sociology,* and *Social Science History,* among many others. For a comprehensive review of the field, see Olick and Robbins (1998).

2. Identity, of course, is another neologism requiring just as much explanation. See Handler (1994).

3. In this way, the concept of collective memory shares with cultural sociology at large the dichotomy between implicit (i.e., so-called deep structural) and explicit (i.e., material) locations. See Wuthnow and Witten (1988).

4. Major works on the history of memory's material means include Goody (1986), Ong (1982), Thompson (1995), Hutton (1993), Le Goff (1992), and Leroi-Gourhan (1993).

5. Relevant texts here include Ariés (1974), Benjamin (1968), Berman (1982), Hobsbawm (1972), Anderson (1991), Kern (1983), Kosellek (1985), and Nora (1992).

6. These forms have been referred to by theorists of temporality as *"chrono-types."* See the essays in Bender and Ellerby (1991).

7. Indeed, processualism and relationalism as labels represent somewhat different emphases. For relationalists, the irreducibility of structures to an arrangement of preconstituted units is objectionable, in *"substantialist"* approaches the assumption that there are substances that exist outside of relations. In this sense, Levi-Strauss's synchronic structuralism in which every term gains its meaning only from its place in a system of meanings is an acceptably relational ontology, as are static forms of network structuralism in American sociology. For processualists, the Heraclitan assumption of permanent change is central, which implies that relational structures are never fixed — hence, Elias's analogy to the dance (see following). Many of the authors on whom I draw (e.g., Bourdieu, Elias, White, Abbott) combine both of these elements into what I call *"process-relationalism"* to emphasize both elements and to distinguish it on the one hand from Levi-Strauss's (1963) synchronic relationalism and static network sociology and on the other hand from dialectical theories of change.

8. In a very different language, and for somewhat different purposes, Foucault (1977) articulates a concept of *"counter-memory,"* though that idea in turn overtotalizes the variety of mnemonic resistance and dissent.

9. This difference in the postures of history and memory, of course, underlies a long discourse about relations between the two. Historians distinguish their enterprise from memory as vastly superior because of their epistemological orientation. In contrast, writers like Maurice Halbwachs have argued that history is "dead memory," the past to which we no longer have any organic relation. Writers like Pierre Nora have argued that the transition to modernity has entailed a troublesome loss of meaning and identity as the

social foundations for memory have eroded. Many others, however, have attacked the very philosophical foundation of the distinction in such a way that the differences between history and memory blur. Perhaps more usefully, writers like Yosef Yerushalmi (1982) have argued that history must also strive to be memorable, lest it become "a rampant growth."

10. Indeed, as Patrick Hutton (1993) observes, there are strong logical and intellectual-historical links between questioning the event, the history of mentalities, and the recent interest of historiography in memory.

11. A museum, for instance, is not a thing but a social relationship among producer, text, and viewer, nor is *"museum"* a permanent and unchanging essence nor *"museification"* always the same process.

12. Of course, these genres were — and continue to be — historical accretions. They drew — and draw — in part on older traditions but became more clearly demarcated and stringent as time went on, as one might expect across periods of relative institutional stability.

Chapter Six

1. Earlier versions of this paper were presented at "Utopia, Violence, Resistance," Center for Historical Analysis, Rutgers University, April 2000; Department of Sociology, University of Washington, April 2001; and Department of Sociology, Rutgers University, September 2001. Thanks go to John Torpey, Charambolos Demetriou, Omer Bartov, Matt Matsuda, Charles Tilly, Deb Minkoff, Kurt Lang, Steve Pfaff, and Karen Cerulo for these opportunities or for advice. A version of this chapter appeared in *The Politics of the Past: On Repairing Historical Injustices*, edited by John Torpey. Rowman and Littelfield, 2003: 37–62.

2. Norbert Elias (1994), one of this chapter's central inspirations, carefully distinguishes between evolutionary and developmental theory. For Elias, the physical world changes mostly very slowly, the biological somewhat faster through *"evolution,"* and the social much more quickly through *"development."* This distinction between evolution and development is the foundation on which Elias refutes charges that his account of "the civilizing process" partakes of the sins of nineteenth-century evolutionism: Development has none of the connotations of necessity inherent in evolutionist accounts. By extension, the desire in this chapter is to avoid the frequently overt teleological tone of accounts in which the politics of regret reflects the supposed moral maturation of Western societies (and, by extension, their superiority over other less-developed societies). See the following discussion of the so-called "Asian values" debate.

3. Though the literature is vast, a selection of these ideas can be found in Belgrade Circle (1999), Donnelly (1998), Ishay (1997), Lauren (1998), Perry (1998), Robertson (2000), and Steiner and Alston (1996).

4. The Nuremburg Tribunals do indeed form a central frame of reference for most subsequent efforts. Nevertheless, as Macguire (2001) and Bass (2000), among others, demonstrate, the road to Nuremburg was long and varied.

5. For a discussion of the numerous parliamentary debates in the Federal Republic of Germany on this issue, see Jaspers (1966) and Dubiel (1999).

6. For the German case, see, especially, Adorno (1986), Mitscherlich and Mitscherlich (1967), Lübbe (1993), and Schwan (1997).

7. The following section outlines some of these.

8. On the one hand, Habermas (2001, p. 124) argues, "...Asiatic societies... deploy positive law as a steering medium in the framework of a global-ized system of market relations. They do so for the same functional reasons that once allowed this form of law to prevail in the Occident over the older guild-based forms of social integration...Asiatic societies cannot participate in capitalistic modernization without taking advantage of the achievements of an individualistic legal order." On the other hand, he suggests, "...the [Western] understanding of human rights must jettison the metaphysical assumption of an individual who exists prior to all socialization and, as it were, comes into the world already equipped with innate rights." As a result, "the choice between 'individualist' and 'collectivist' approaches disappears once we approach fundamental legal concepts with an eye toward the dia-lectical unity of individuation and socialization processes" (ibid., 126).

9. Mamdani (1996) similarly highlights the historical development of what he calls *"rights talk"* in the case of Africa. He traces the present-day opposition of *"culture"* and *"rights"* to forms of accepted rule adopted during the late colonial period and the transformation of these forms after independence. He thus argues that South Africa apartheid was not an exceptional form of rule but rather a generic one in Africa, parallel to the indirect rule of the colonial state.

10. Arendt's writings have served more as a source for the human rights discourse than she herself did as a participant in the accompanying movement.

11. Major works in this tradition, some of which are discussed following, include Ash (1998), Borneman (1997), Elster (1998), Hayner (2001), Hesse and Post (1999), Huntington (1991), Kritz (1995), McAdams (1997), Minow (1998), O'Donnell and Schmitter (1986), O'Donnell Schmitter, and White-head (1986), Offe (1997), Rosenberg (1995), and Teitel (2000), among others. Some of these works participate in both the universal human rights litera-ture and the transitional justice literature, which are often inextricable in practice.

12. The relationship between political contests and religious crusades is a prob-lematic one. In one sense, religious and political matters were indistinguish-able in earlier periods. But in another sense, political disputes — involving land and sovereignty — were often seen as rather mundane contests between kings and were thus devoid of the moral overlay of religious crusades. In the modern period, religion and politics are separated by secular states at least in the letter of the law. Yet political contests now often take on the moral vocabulary and righteous tone of religious crusades, whereas religious con-tests employ the instruments of politics.

13. In identifying "the *politics of regret,*" this chapter makes both a quantitative and a qualitative claim, though the former is perhaps more difficult to sub-stantiate than the latter. Do people apologize more frequently now than in earlier epochs? This is not exactly the concern here. In the first place, I argue that the nature of apology as an act differs greatly in the modern world. In the second place, I claim that apology has entered the political realm where it was not previously present. My assertion that this is the case is, at this

point, anecdotal based on reading of discourse surrounding postconflict settlements from different eras, but I believe it would bear up to a rigorous quantitative analysis. Though there are cases of political apology before the modern era and before the last twenty years, moreover, they were, I hypothesize, comparatively rare and of a qualitatively different sort (see Brooks 1999).

14. See, especially, Hobsbawm and Ranger (1983), Huyssen (1995), Le Goff (1992), Nora (1992), Samuel (1996), Terdiman (1993), and Yerushalmi (1982), and see Olick and Robbins (1998) for reviews.

15. Later on, I discuss an argument that the apologetic state mimics the apologetic individual. In contrast, I argue in a similar way to the statement here that the two are codetermined.

16. Just to complicate matters, a book by a major figure in the universal human rights literature is called *The Mobilization of Shame* (Drinan 2001).

17. In perhaps surprising ways, the Benedict account reinforces Habermas's (2001, p. 124) position in the Asian values debate that "Asiatic societies ... cannot participate in capitalistic modernization without taking advantage of the achievements of an individualistic legal order."

18. It should be noted here that despite Benedict's argument that Germany is a guilt culture and Japan is a shame culture, apology pervades everyday discourse in Japanese culture. See Tavuchis (1991), however, for a typology of apology.

Chapter Seven

A version of this chapter appeared in *Religion and Public Life* 33 (Spring 2003): 21–32.

Chapter Eight

A version of this chapter appeared in *Memory, Trauma, and World Politics: Reflections on the Relationship between Past and Present.* Duncan Bell, editor. Palgrave, 2006.

1. In this context, it is important to point out both that the Francophone "*ressentiment*" is a relatively more common expression in German and that it carries overtones of bitterness that exceeds that of resentment in English, which sometimes seems fleeting and petty.

2. In all likelihood, Scheler's essay was so well known in Arendt's circle that the connections were obvious. Because Arendt's reputation today far outweighs Scheler's, that connection is no longer so obvious even to close readers.

3. Here one thinks again of the work of Ulrich Beck.

4. For a trenchant critique of Brown, see Balfour (2005).

5. On the sociology of commensuration, see Espeland and Stevens (1998).

6. In this regard, John Torpey's (2006) important book on reparations, which attributes the rise of reparations to the decline of effective faith in the future, is clearly within the Arendtian paradigm, though he applies it to the present in novel and perspicuous ways.

Chapter Nine

A version of this chapter appeared in *Ayer* 32, 1998: 119–145.

1. As I argue here, however, understanding the distinct memories of distinct ages does not necessarily imply a discontinuist history; even the most archaeological historiography does not hold the layers to be randomly piled.

2. Durkheim (1961), is certainly insightful about temporality, but he addresses memory directly only in his discussion of commemorative rituals at the end of *The Elementary Forms of Religious Life* and there only as a feature of primitive societies. Social reproduction is perhaps the central category of Marx's thought, but the Marxist tradition emphasizes the automatic and unconscious quality of the process; conscious attention to the past is characterized as an irrational residue of earlier social forms. "The tradition of the dead generations," Marx (1992) writes, "weighs like a nightmare on the minds of the living." Simmel (1959) writes that "all the uncertainties of change in time and the tragedy of loss associated with the past find in the ruin a coherent and unified expression." This remark is prescient of later theories that characterize postmodernity as a culture of loss, but Simmel did not develop it more than aphoristically. Weber too, had little to say about memory, despite his interest in traditional legitimation: "By its very 'progressiveness' [civilized society]...gives death the imprint of meaninglessness." Meaningful death is elusive because memory is inadequate to hold together the diversity of our life experiences. But this is an intriguing aside rather than the beginnings of a theory of memory.

3. For a more thorough discussion from a variety of viewpoints, see the important volume of essays on the detraditionalization thesis by Heelas, Lash, and Morris (1996).

4. Richard Terdiman (1993) argues against the tendency in these thinkers to reduce problems of memory to problems of capitalism: commodification and memory are parallel processes of reification rather than cause and effect. Each, Terdiman claims, underwent epochal reconfigurations in the nineteenth century and together became linked parts of modernity's operating system.

5. One result of this social differentiation in terms of social roles and social structures was the increased homogenization within and across societies as local cultures were assimilated to the increasingly institutionalized structures of high politics and life in the administrative state (cf. Weber 1979).

6. In this sense, Nora's theory of contemporary memory asserts atonality.

7. It is now possible, for instance, to obtain images of our children in kindergarten over the Internet while we sit in our offices or in the library.

References

Abenheim, Donald. *Reforging the Iron Cross: The Search for Tradition in the West German Armed Forces.* Princeton, NJ: Princeton University Press, 1988.

Abbott, Andrew. "Things of Boundaries." Social Research 62 (1996): 857–82.

_____. "Transcending General Linear Reality." *Sociological Theory* 6 (1988): 169–86.

_____. "What Do Cases Do? Some Notes on Activity in Sociological Analysis." Pp. 53–82 in *What Is a Case? Exploring the Foundations of Social Inquiry,* edited by Charles C. Ragin and Howard S. Becker. Cambridge, UK: Cambridge University Press, 1992.

Abrams, Philip. *Historical Sociology.* Ithaca, NY: Cornell University Press, 1982.

Adenauer, Konrad. *Erinnerungen, 1953-1955 [Memoirs, 1953-1955].* Stuttgart, Germany: Deutsche Verlags-Anstalt, 1966.

Adorno, Theodor W. "What Does Coming to Terms With the Past Mean?" Pp. 114–29 in *Bitburg in Moral and Political Perspective,* edited by Geoffrey Hartman. Bloomington: Indiana University Press, 1986.

Adorno, Theodor W., Else Frenkel-Brunswik, Daniel J. Levinson, and R. Nevitt Sanford. *The Authoritarian Personality.* New York: W.W. Norton, 1950.

Alexander, Jeffrey C. "Analytical Debates: Understanding the Relative Autonomy of Culture." Pp. 1–27 in *Culture and Society: Contemporary Debates,* edited by J. C. Alexander and S. Seidman. New York: Cambridge University Press, 1990.

Almond, Gabriel, and Sidney Verba. *The Civic Culture: Political Attitudes and Democracy in Five Nations.* Boston: Little, Brown, 1963.

_____, eds. *The Civic Culture Revisited.* Newbury Park, CA: Sage, 1980.

Alonso, Ana Maria. "The Effects of Truth: Representation of the Past and the Imagining of Community." *Journal of Historical Sociology* 1 (1988): 33–57.

Amery, Jean. *At the Mind's Limits.* New York: Schocken, 1986.

Anderson, Benedict. *Imagined Communities: Reflections on the Origin and Spread of Nationalism,* rev. ed. New York: Verso, 1991.

Ankersmit, Frank R. "Trauma and Suffering: A Forgotten Source of Western Historical Consciousness." Pp. 72–84 in *Western Historical Thinking: An Intercultural Debate,* edited by Jörn Rüsen. New York: Berghahn, 2002.

Apter, David. "The New Mytho/logics and the Specter of Superfluous Man." *Social Research* 52 (1985): 269–307.

Arendt, Hannah. *Between Past and Future: Eight Exercises in Political Thought.* New York: Penguin Books, 1978.

_____. *On Revolution.* New York: Penguin Books, 1991.

_____. "The Aftermath of Nazi Rule: Report from Germany." *Commentary* 10 (1950): 342–53.

_____. *The Human Condition.* Chicago: University of Chicago Press, 1958.

Ariés, Philippe. *The Hour of Our Death.* New York: Oxford University Press, 1981.

_____. *Western Attitudes towards Death from the Middle Ages to the Present.* Baltimore: Johns Hopkins University Press, 1974.

Ash, Timothy Garton. "The Truth about Dictatorship." *New York Review of Books* 45, #3, February 19, 1998.

Assmann, Jan. *Das kulturelle Gedächtnis: Schrift, Erinnerung und politische Identität in frühen Hochkulturen.* Munich: C.H. Beck, 1992.

Baker, Keith Michael. *Inventing the French Revolution: Essays on French Political Culture in the Eighteenth Century.* New York: Cambridge University Press, 1990.

Bakhtin, Mikhail. *The Dialogic Imagination: Four Essays.* Translated by C. Emerson and M. Holquist. Austin: University of Texas Press, 1985.

_____. *Problems of Dostoevsky's Poetics.* Edited and translated by C. Emerson. Minneapolis: University of Minnesota Press, 1963.

_____. *Speech Genres and Other Essays.* Translated by W. McGee. Austin: University of Texas Press, 1986.

_____. *Toward a Philosophy of the Act.* Edited by Vadim Liapunov and Michael Holquist. Translated by Vadim Liapunov. Austin: University of Texas Press, 1993.

Bakhtin, Mikhail, and Pavel N. Medvedev. *The Formal Method in Literary Scholarship: A Critical Introduction to Sociological Poetics.* Translated by A. J. Wehrle. Baltimore: Johns Hopkins University Press, 1978.

Baldwin, Peter, ed. *Reworking the Past: Hitler, the Holocaust, and the Historians' Debate.* Boston: Beacon, 1990.

Balfour, Lawrie. "Reparations after Identity Politics." *Political Theory* 33 (2005): 786–811.

Barkan, Elazar. *The Guilt of Nations: Restitution and Negotiating Historical Injustices.* New York: Norton. 2000.

Bass, Gary Jonathan. *Stay the Hand of Vengeance: The Politics of War Crimes Tribunals.* Princeton, NJ: Princeton University Press, 2000.

Bauman, Zygmunt. *Modernity and the Holocaust.* Ithaca, NY: Cornell University Press, 1989.

Belgrade Circle, ed. *The Politics of Human Rights.* London: Verso, 1999.

Beck, Ulrich. *Risk Society: Toward a New Modernity.* Newbury Park, CA: Sage, 1992.

Bell, Lynda S., Andrew J. Nathan, and Ilan Peleg, eds. *Negotiating Culture and Human Rights.* New York: Columbia University Press, 2001.

Bellah, Robert N., Richard Madsen, William Sullivan, Ann Swidler, and Steven M. Tipton. *Habits of the Heart: Commitment and Individualism in American Life.* New York: Harper and Row, 1985.

Bender, John, and David E. Ellerby. *Chronotypes: The Construction of Time.* Stanford: Stanford University Press, 1991.

Benedict, Ruth. *The Chrysanthemum and the Sword: Patterns of Japanese Culture.* Boston: Houghton Mifflin, 1989.

Benjamin, Walter. "The Storyteller." In *Illuminations.* Translated by H. Zohn. New York: Schoken, 1968.

Bennett, Tony. *The Birth of the Museum: History, Theory, Politics.* London: Routledge, 1995.

Berezin, Mabel. "Fissured Terrain: Methodological Approaches and Research Styles." Pp. 91–116 in *The Sociology of Culture: Emerging Theoretical Perspectives.* Edited by D. Crane. Cambridge, UK: Basil Blackwell, 1994.

_____. "Politics and Culture: A Less Fissured Terrain." *Annual Review of Sociology* 23 (1997): 361–383.

Berger, Stefan. *The Search for Normality: National Identity and Historical Consciousness in Germany since 1800.* Oxford: Berghahn Books, 1997.

Berger, Peter, and Thomas Luckmann. *The Social Construction of Reality.* Garden City, NY: Doubleday Anchor, 1967.

Bergson, Henri. *Matter and Memory.* Translated by N. M. Paul and W. S. Palmer. New York: Zone Books, 1990.

Berman, Marshall. *All That Is Solid Melts into Air: The Experience of Modernity.* New York: Penguin, 1982.

Bloch, Marc. *Feudal Society.* Chicago: University of Chicago Press, 1974.

_____. "Mémoire collective, tradition, et coutume: a propos d'un livre." *Revue Synthese* 40 (1925): 73–83.

Blumer, Herbert. *Symbolic Interactionism: Perspective and Method.* Berkeley: University of California Press, 1969.

Bodnar, John. *Remaking America: Public Memory, Commemoration, and Patriotism in the Twentieth Century.* Princeton, NJ: Princeton University Press, 1992.

Boltanski, Luc. *Distant Suffering: Morality, Media and Politics.* Cambridge, UK: Cambridge University Press, 1999.

Borneman, John. *Settling Accounts: Violence, Justice, and Accountability in Postsocialist Europe.* Princeton, NJ: Princeton University Press, 1997.

Bourdieu, Pierre. *Distinction: A Social Critique of the Judgement of Taste.* Boston: Harvard University Press, 1984.

_____. *The Field of Cultural Production.* New York: Columbia University Press, 1993.

_____. *The Logic of Practice.* Translated by Richard Nice. Stanford: Stanford University Press, 1990.

_____. *The Rules of Art: Genesis and Structure of the Literary Field.* Translated by Susan Emanuel. Stanford: Stanford University Press, 1996.

Bourdieu, Pierre, and Loïc J. D. Wacquant. *An Invitation to Reflexive Sociology.* Chicago: University of Chicago Press, 1992.

Boyarin, Jonathan, ed. *Remapping Memory: The Politics of TimeSpace.* Minneapolis: University of Minnesota Press, 1994.

Brandt, Willy. *My Life in Politics.* New York: Viking, 1992.

Breisbach, Ernst. *Historiography: Ancient, Medieval, and Modern.* 2d ed. Chicago: University of Chicago Press, 1994.

Brint, Steven. "Sociological Analysis of Political Culture: An Introduction and Assessment." Pp. 3–41 in *Political Culture and Political Structure: Theoretical and Empirical Studies.* Vol. 2 of *Research on Democracy and Society.* Edited by Frederick D. Weil and Mary Gautier. Greenwich, CT: JAI, 1994.

Brochhagen, Ulrich. *Nach Nürnberg: Vergangenheitsbewältigung und Westintegration in der Ära Adenauer* (*After Nuremberg: Mastering the Past and Western Integration in the Adenauer Era*). Hamburg: Junius, 1994.

Brooks, Peter. *Troubling Confessions: Speaking Guilt in Law and Literature.* Chicago: University of Chicago Press, 2000.

Brooks, Roy L. *When Sorry Isn't Enough: The Controversy over Apologies and Reparations for Human Injustice.* New York: New York University Press, 1999.

Broszat, Martin, Klaus-Dietmar Henke, and Hans Woller, eds. *Von Stalingrad zur Währungsreform: Zur Sozialgeschichte des Umbruchs in Deutschland* (*From Stalingrad to the Currency Reform: On the Social History of the Transformation in Germany*). Munich: R. Oldenbourg, 1988.

Brown, Wendy. *States of Injury: Power and Freedom in Late Modernity.* Princeton, NJ: Princeton University Press, 1995.

Brubaker, Rogers. *Citizenship and Nationhood in France and Germany.* Cambridge, MA: Harvard University Press, 1992.

Bude, Heinz. *Bilanz der Nachfolge: Die Bundesrepublik und der Nationalsozialismus* (*The Summation of the Consequences: The Federal Republic and National Socialism*). Frankfurt, Germany: Suhrkamp, 1992.

Burke, Peter. "History as Social Memory." Pp. 97–113 in *Memory: History, Culture, Mind,* edited by Thomas Butler. New York: Blackwell, 1989.

Buruma, Ian. *The Wages of Guilt: Memories of War in Germany and Japan.* New York: Farrar, Straus, Giroux, 1994.

Butler, Thomas, ed. *Memory: History, Culture and the Mind.* New York: Blackwell, 1989.

Carr, David. *Time, Narrative, and History.* Bloomington: Indiana University Press, 1991.

Carruthers, Bruce G., and Wendy Nelson Espeland. "Accounting for Rationality: Double-Entry Bookkeeping and the Rhetoric of Economic Rationality." *American Journal of Sociology* 97 (1991): 31–69.

Carruthers, Mary. *The Book of Memory: A Study of Memory in Medieval Culture.* Cambridge, UK: Cambridge University Press, 1990.

Cassirer, Ernst. *Substance and Function.* Translated by William Curtis Swabey and Marie Collins Swabey. New York: Dover, 1953.

Converse, Philip. "The Nature of Belief Systems in Mass Publics." Pp. 206–61 in *Ideology and Discontent,* edited by David E. Apter. New York: Free Press, 1964.

Coles, Robert. *The Call of Stories: Teaching and the Moral Imagination.* New York: Houghton Mifflin, 1990.

Coser, Lewis. "Introduction." Pp. 1–34 in *On Collective Memory,* edited and translated by Lewis Coser. Chicago: University of Chicago Press, 1992.

Cressy, David. "National Memory in Early Modern England." Pp. 51–73 in *Commemorations: The Politics of National Identity,* edited by John R. Gillis. Princeton, NJ: Princeton University Press, 1994.

Czarniawska, Barbara. *The Organization: Dramas of Institutional Identity.* Chicago: University of Chicago Press, 1997.

Dahrendorf, Ralf. *Reflections on the Revolution in Europe.* New York: Random House, 1990.

Darian-Smith, Katherine, and Paul Hamilton, eds. *Memory and History in Twentieth Century Australia.* Melbourne, Australia: Oxford University Press, 1994.

Dayan, Daniel and Elihu Katz. *Media Events: The Live Broadcasting of History.* Cambridge, MA: Harvard University Press, 1992.

Deak, Istvan, Jan Tomasz Gross, and Tony Judt. *The Politics of Retribution in Europe: World War II and Its Aftermath.* Princeton, NJ: Princeton University Press, 2000.

Deutsch, Karl. *Nationalism and Social Communication.* Cambridge, MA: MIT Press, 1966.

Deutschkron, Inge. *Israel und die Deutschen: Das schwierige Verhältnis. (Israel and the Germans: The Difficult Relationship).* Cologne, Germany: Wissenschaft und Politik, 1991.

Dienstag, Joshua Foa. *Dancing in Chains: Narrative and Memory in Political Theory.* Stanford: Stanford University Press, 1997.

DiMaggio, Paul. "Culture and Cognition." *Annual Review of Sociology* 23 (1997): 263–87.

Dittmer, Lowell. "Political Culture and Political Symbolism: Toward a Theoretical Synthesis." *World Politics* 29 (1977): 552–83.

Donnelly, Jack. *International Human Rights.* Boulder, CO: Westview Press, 1998.

Dohrn-van Rossum, Gerhard. *History of the Hour: Clocks and Modern Temporal Orders.* Translated by Thomas Dunlap. Chicago: University of Chicago Press, 1996.

Douglas, Mary. *Purity and Danger: An Analysis of Concepts of Pollution and Taboo.* New York: Praeger, 1966.

Drinan, Robert F. *The Mobilization of Shame.* New Haven, CT: Yale University Press, 2001.

Duara, Prasenjith. *Rescuing History from the Nation: Questioning Narratives of Modern China.* Chicago: University of Chicago Press, 1995.

Dubiel, Helmut. *Niemand ist frei von der Geschichte: Die nationalsozialistiche Herrschaft in den Debatten des Deutschen Bundestages (No one is free from History: National Socialist Domination in the Debates of the German Bundestag).* Munich: Carl Hanser Verlag, 1999.

Durkheim, Emile. *The Division of Labor in Society.* Translated by W. D. Halls. New York: Free Press, 1984.

———. *The Elementary Forms of the Religious Life.* Translated by Jay Swain. New York: Collier Books, 1961.

Edelman, Murray J. *Political Language: Words that Succeed and Policies that Fail.* New York: Academic Press, 1977.

———. *The Symbolic Uses of Politics.* Urbana: University of Illinois Press, 1967.

Elias, Norbert. *The Civilizing Process.* Translated by Edmund Jephcott. Oxford: Blackwell, 1994.

———. *What Is Sociology?* Translated by Stephen Mennell and Grace Morrissey. New York: Columbia University Press, 1978.

———. *The Symbol Theory.* London: Sage, 1991.

Elias, Norbert, Stephen Mennell, ed., and Johan Goudsblom, ed. *On Civilization, Power, and Knowledge: Selected Writings.* Chicago: University of Chicago Press, 1998.

Elkins, David J. and Richard Simeon. "A Cause in Search of Its Effect, or What Does Political Culture Explain?" *Comparative Politics* 11 (1979): 127–45.

Elster, Jon. "Coming to Terms with the Past." *European Journal of Sociology* 39 (1998): 7–48.

Emirbayer, Mustafa. "Manifesto for a Relational Sociology." *American Journal of Sociology* 103 (1997): 281–317.

Englund, Steven. "The Ghost of Nation Past." *Journal of Modern History* 64 (1992): 299–320.

Espeland, Wendy N., and Mitchell C. Stevens. "Commensuration as a Social Process." *Annual Review of Sociology* 24 (1998): 313–43.

Etzioni, Amitai, and David Carney. *Repentance: A Comparative Perspective*. Lanham, MD: Rowman & Littlefield, 1997.

Evans, Richard J. *In Hitler's Shadow: West German Historians and the Attempt to Escape from the Nazi Past*. New York: Pantheon, 1989.

Falasca-Zamponi, Simonetta. *Fascist Spectacle: The Aesthetics of Power in Mussolini's Italy*. Berkeley: University of California Press, 1997.

Feldman, Lily Gardner. *The Special Relationship between West-Germany and Israel*. Boston: Allen and Unwin, 1984.

Fentress, James, and Chris Wickham. *Social Memory*. Oxford: Blackwell, 1992.

Foucault, Michel. *Language, Counter-Memory, and Practice*. Translated by Donald F. Boucahrd and Sherry Simon. Ithaca, NY: Cornell University Press, 1977.

Frei, Norbert. *Vergangenheitspolitik: Die Anfänge der Bundesrepublik und die NS-Vergangenheit*. Munich: C.H. Beck, 1966.

Friedland, Roger, and Diedre Boden. "NowHere: An Introduction to Space, Time and Modernity." Pp. 1–60 in *NowHere: Space, Time and Modernity*, edited by Roger Friedland and Deidre Boden. Berkeley: University of California Press, 1994.

Friedlander, Saul. *Probing the Limits of Representation: Nazism and the "Final Solution."* Cambridge, MA: Harvard University Press., 1992

Friedrich, Jörg. *Die kalte Amnestie: NS-Täter in der Bundesrepublik (The Cold Amnesty: Nazi Perpetrators in the Federal Republic)*, 2d ed. Munich: Piper, 1994.

Freud, Sigmund. *The Standard Edition of the Complete Psychological Works of Sigmund Freud*. Edited by James Strachey. 24 vols. London: Hogarth Press, 1966–74.

————. *Totem and Taboo: Resemblances between the Psychic Lives of Savages and Neurotics*. New York: Vintage Books, 1946.

Gans, Herbert. *Popular Culture and High Culture: An Analysis and Evaluation of Taste*. New York: Basic Books, 1974.

Gedi, N., and Y. Elam. "Collective Memory — What Is It?" *History and Memory* 8, no. 2 (1996) :30–50.

Geertz, Clifford. *The Interpretation of Cultures*. New York: Basic Books, 1973.

Giddens, Anthony. *The Constitution of Society: Outline of the Theory of Structuration*. Cambridge: Polity, 1984.

Gillis, John, ed. *Commemorations: The Politics of National Identity*. Princeton, NJ: Princeton University Press, 1994.

Giordano, Ralph. *Die zweite Schuld oder von der Last, ein Deutscher zu sein*. Hamburg: Rasch und Roehring, 1987.

Goffman, Erving. *Interaction Ritual: Essays on Face-to-Face Behavior*. New York: Pantheon, 1967.

Goldhagen, Daniel Jonah. *Hitler's Willing Executioners: Ordinary Germans and the Holocaust*. New York: Knopf, 1996.

Goody, Jack. *The Logic of Writing and the Organization of Society*. New York: Cambridge University Press, 1986.

Greiffenhagen, Martin, and Sylvia Greiffenhagen. *Ein schwieriges Vaterland: Zur politischen Kultur im vereinigten Deutschland* (*A Difficult Fatherland: On Political Culture in United Germany*). Munich: List, 1993.

Grosser, Alfred. *Das Deutschland im Westen: Eine Bilanz nach 40 Jahren* (*Germany in the West: An Assessment after 40 Years*). Munich: DTV, 1985.

Habermas, Jürgen. *Between Facts and Norms: Contributions To a Discourse Theory of Law and Democracy.* Cambridge, MA: MIT Press, 1996.

———. "Eine Art Schadensabwicklung." Pp. 62–83 in *"Historikerstreit." Die Dokumentation der Kontroverse um die Einzigartigkeit der nationalsozialistischen Judenvernichtung,* edited by Ernst Piper. Munich: Piper, 1987.

———. "Remarks on Legitimation through Human Rights." Pp. 113–29 in *The Postnational Constellation: Political Essays,* edited, translated, and introduced by Max Pensky. Cambridge, MA: MIT Press, 2001.

———. *The Structural Transformation of the Public Sphere: An Inquiry into a Category of Bourgeois Society.* Cambridge, MA: MIT Press, 1989.

Hacking, Ian. *Rewriting the Soul: Multiple Personality and the Sciences of Memory.* Princeton, NJ: Princeton University Press, 1995.

Halbwachs, Maurice. *On Collective Memory.* Edited by Lewis Coser. Chicago: University of Chicago Press, 1992.

———. *The Collective Memory.* Edited by Mary Douglas. New York: Harper & Row, 1966.

Handler, Richard. "Is Identity a Useful Cross-Cultural Concept?" Pp. 27–40 in *Commemorations: the Politics of National Identity,* edited by John Gillis. Princeton, NJ: Princeton University Press, 1994.

Hartman, Geoffrey, ed. *Bitburg in Moral and Political Perspective.* Bloomington: Indiana University Press, 1986.

Hattenhauer, Hans. *Geschichte der deutschen Nationalsymbole: Zeichen und Bedeutung* (*History of German National Symbols: Symbol and Meaning*). Munich: Olzog, 1990.

Hayner, Priscilla B. *Unspeakable Truths: Confronting State Terror and Atrocity.* New York: Routledge, 2001.

Heelas, Paul, Scott Lash, and Paul Morris, eds. *Detraditionalization: Critical Reflections on Authority and Identity.* Oxford: Blackwell, 1996.

Hegel, G. W. F. *The Philosophy of History.* New York: Dover Publications, 1956.

Herbst, Susan. "The Meaning of Public Opinion: Citizen's Constructions of Political Reality." *Media, Culture, and Society* 15 (1993): 437–54.

Herf, Jeffrey. *Divided Memory: The Nazi Past in the Two Germanys.* Cambridge, MA: Harvard University Press, 1997.

———. *Reactionary Modernism: Technology, Culture and Politics in Weimar and the Third Reich.* Cambridge, UK: Cambridge University Press, 1984.

Hesse, Carla Alison, and Robert Post. *Human Rights in Political Transitions: Gettysburg to Bosnia.* New York: Zone Books, 1999.

Hillgruber, Andreas. *Zweierlei Untergang: Die Zerschlagung des deutschen Reiches und das Ende der europäischen Judentums.* Berlin: Siedler, 1986.

"Historikerstreit:" Die Dokumentation der Kontroverse um die Einzigartigkeit der nationalsozialistischen Judenvernichtung (*"Historians' Dispute." The Documentation of the Controversy over the Uniqueness of the National Socialist Destruction of the Jews*). *German Studies Review,* Vol. 11, No. 3, pp. 543–544. Munich: Piper, 1987.

Hobsbawm, Eric. "Introduction: Inventing traditions." Pp. 1–14 in *The Invention of Tradition*, edited by Eric Hobsbawm and Terence Ranger. New York: Cambridge University Press, 1983a.

———. 1983b. "Mass Producing Traditions: Europe, 1870–1914." Pp. 263–307 in *The Invention of Tradition*, edited by E. Hobsbawm and T. Ranger, New York: Cambridge University Press, 1983b.

———. *Nations and Nationalism since 1780: Programme, Myth, Reality.* Cambridge, UK: Cambridge University Press, 1990.

———. "The Social Function of the Past: Some Questions." *Past and Present* 55 (1972): 3–17.

Hobsbawm, Eric, and Terence Ranger, eds. *The Invention of Tradition.* New York: Cambridge University Press, 1983.

Hunt, Lynn. *Politics, Culture, and Class in the French Revolution.* Berkeley: University of California Press, 1984.

———. *The New Cultural History.* Berkeley: University of California Press, 1989.

Huntington, Samuel P. *The Third Wave: Democratization in the Late Twentieth Century.* Norman: University of Oklahoma Press, 1991.

Hutton, Patrick. *History as an Art of Memory.* Hanover, NH: University Press of New England, 1993.

Huyssen, Andreas. *Twilight Memories: Marking Time in a Culture of Amnesia.* New York: Routledge, 1995.

Iggers, Georg G. *The German Conception of History: The National Tradition of Historical Thought from Herder to the Present,* rev. ed. Middletown, CT: Wesleyan University Press, 1983.

Ignatieff, Michael. *The Warrior's Honor: Ethnic War and the Modern Conscience.* New York: Metropolitan Books, 1998.

Ikenberry, G. John. *After Victory: Institutions, Strategic Restraint, and the Rebuilding of Order after Major Wars.* Princeton, NJ: Princeton University Press, 2001.

Ishay, Micheline. *The Human Rights Reader: Major Political Writings, Essays, Speeches, and Documents from the Bible to the Present.* New York: Routledge, 1997.

Jacoby, Russell. *Social Amnesia: A Critique of Conformist Pychology from Adler to Laing.* Hassocks, UK: Harvester Press, 1977.

James, William. *The Principles of Psychology.* (1890), with Introduction by G.A. Miller, paperback, Cambridge, MA: Harvard University Press, 1983.

Jaspers, Karl. *Die Schuldfrage: Zur politischen Haftung Deutschlands.* Munich: Piper, 1965.

———. *Wohin treibt die Bundesrepublik? Tatsachen, Gefahren, Chancen.* Munich: Piper, 1966.

Johnson, R., G. McLennan, B. Schwarz, and D. Sutton, eds. *Making Histories: Studies in History-Writing and Politics.* Minneapolis: University of Minnesota Press, 1982.

Kammen, Michael. *Mystic Chords of Memory: The Transformation of Tradition in American Culture.* New York: Random House, 1991.

———. "Review of Frames of Remembrance: The Dynamics of Collective Memory, by Iwona Irwin-Zarecka." *History and Theory* 34, no. 3 (1995): 245–61.

Kern, Stephen. *The Culture of Time and Space, 1880–1918.* Cambridge, MA: Harvard University Press, 1983.

Kittel, Manfred. Die *Legende von der "Zweiten Schuld": Vergangenheitsbewältigung in der Ära Adenauer (The Legend of "The Second Guilt": Mastering the Past in the Adenauer Era)*. Berlin: Ullstein, 1993.

Klessmann, Christoph. "Geschichtsbewusstsein nach 1945: Ein neuer Anfang?" ("Historical Consciousness after 1945: A New Beginning?"). Pp. 111–29 in *Geschichtsbewusstsein der Deutschen: materialien zur Spurensuche einer Nation,* edited by W. Weidenfeld. Cologne, Germany: Verlag Wissenschaft und Politik, 1987.

Koselleck, Reinhardt. *Futures Past: On the Semantics of Historical Time.* Translated by Keith Tribe. Cambridge, MA: MIT Press, 1985.

Kritz, Neil J.. ed. *Transitional Justice: How Emerging Democracies Reckon with Former Regimes.* Washington, DC: United States Institute of Peace Press, 1995.

Landsberg, Alison. *Prosthetic Memory: The Transformation of American Remembrance in the Age of Mass Culture.* New York: Columbia University Press, 2004.

Lauren, Paul Gordon. *The Evolution of International Human Rights: Visions Seen.* Philadelphia: University of Pennsylvania Press, 1998.

Le Goff, Jacques. *History and Memory.* Translated by S. Randall and E. Claman. New York: Columbia University Press, 1992.

Lerner, Paul, and Mark S. Micale. "Trauma, Psychiatry and History: A Conceptual and Historiographical Introduction." Pp. 1–30 in *Traumatic Pasts: History, Psychiatry, and Trauma in the Modern Age, 1870–1930,* edited by Mark S. Micale and Paul Lerner. Cambridge, UK: Cambridge University Press, 2001.

Leroi-Gourhan, Andre. *Gesture and Speech.* Translated by Arthur Berger. Cambridge, MA: MIT University Press, 1993.

Levi, Primo. *The Drowned and the Saved.* New York: Vintage, 1989.

Levi-Strauss, Claude. *Structural Anthropology.* Translated by Claire Jacobson and Brooke Grundfest Schoepf. New York: Basic Books, 1963.

Levinas, Emmanuel. "Useless Suffering." Pp. 371–380 in *The Problem of Evil: a Reader,* edited by Mark Larrimore. Oxford: Blackwell, 2001.

Levkov, Ilya, ed. *Bitburg and Beyond: Encounters in American, German and Jewish History.* New York: Shapolsky, 1987.

Lübbe, Hermann. "Der Nationalsozialismus im deutschen Nachkriegsbewusstsein" ("National Socialism in German Postwar Consciousness"). *Historische Zeitschrift* 236 (1983): 579–99.

MacIntyre, Alisdair. *After Virtue: A Study in Moral Theory.* Notre Dame: University of Notre Dame Press, 1984.

Maier, Charles. *The Unmasterable Past; History, Holocaust, and German National Identity.* Cambridge, MA: Harvard University Press, 1988.

Mamdani, Mahmood. *Citizen and Subject: Contemporary Africa and the Legacy of Late Colonialism.* Princeton, NJ: Princeton University Press, 1996.

Mann, Michael. *The Sources of Social Power: The Rise of Classes and Nation-States, 1760–1914,* vol. 2. New York: Cambridge University Press, 1993.

Mannheim, Karl. "The Problem of Generations." Pp. 276–322 in *Essays on the Sociology of Culture.* London: Routledge and Kegan Paul, 1952.

Marquard, Odo. *Farewell to Matters of Principle: Philosophical Studies.* New York: Oxford University Press, 1998.

Martin, Joanne. *Cultures in Organizations: Three Perspectives.* New York: Oxford University Press, 1991.

Marx, Karl. "The Eighteenth Brumaire of Louis Bonaparte." in *Surveys from Exile: Political Writings*, vol. 2. London: Penguin, 1992.

Matsuda, Matt K. *The Memory of the Modern*. New York: Oxford University Press, 1996.

McAdams, A. James. *Transitional Justice and the Rule of Law in New Democracies*. Notre Dame: University of Notre Dame Press, 1997.

McDonald, Terence, ed. *The Historic Turn in the Human Sciences*. Ann Arbor: University of Michigan Press, 1996.

McLuhan, Marshall. *The Gutenberg Galaxy: The Making of Typographic Man*. Toronto: University of Toronto Press, 1962.

Meinecke, Friedrich. *The German Catastrophe: Reflections and Recollections*. Translated by S. B. Fay. Cambridge, MA: Harvard University Press, 1950.

Merritt, Richard L. *Democracy Imposed: U.S. Occupation Policy and the German Public, 1945–1949*. New Haven, CT: Yale University Press, 1995.

Merritt, Anna J., and Richard L. Merritt. *Public Opinion in Semisovereign Germany: The HICOG Surveys, 1949–1955*. Urbana: University of Illinois Press, 1980.

Middleton, David, and Derek Edwards, eds. *Collective Remembering*. Newbury Park, CA: Sage, 1990.

Minow, Martha. *Between Vengeance and Forgiveness: Facing History after Genocide and Mass Violence*. Boston: Beacon Press, 1998.

Mitscherlich, Alexander, and Margaret Mitscherlich. *Die Unfähigkeit zu trauern: Grundlagen kollektiven Verhaltens (The Inability to Mourn: Principles of Collective Behavior)*. Munich: Piper, 1967.

Moeller, Robert G. "War Stories: The Search for a Usable Past in the Federal Republic of Germany." *American Historical Review* 101 (1996): 1008–48.

Morson, Gary Saul, and Caryl Emerson. *Mikhail Bakhtin: Creation of a Prosaics*. Stanford: Stanford University Press, 1990.

Mosse, George L. *Fallen Soldiers: Reshaping the Memory of the World Wars*. New York: Oxford University Press, 1990.

Neier, Aryeh. *War Crimes: Brutality, Genocide, Terror, and the Struggle for Justice*. New York: Times Books, 1998.

Neisser, Ulrich, ed. *Memory Observed: Remembering in Natural Contexts*. New York: W.H. Freeman, 1982.

Niethammer, Lutz. *Posthistoire: Has History Come to an End?* London: Verso, 1992.

Nietzsche, Friedrich. 1994. *On the Genealogy of Morality*. Edited by Keith Ansell-Pearson and Carol Diethe. Cambridge, UK: Cambridge University Press, 1994.

———. "On the Uses and Disadvantages of History for Life." Pp. 57–124 in *Untimely Meditations*, edited by D. Breazeale and translated by R. J. Hollingdale. New York: Cambridge University Press, 1997.

———.Thus Spoke Zarathustra. *The Portable Nietzsche*, edited by Walter Kaufman. New York: Viking, 1954.

Nino, Carlos Santiago. *Radical Evil on Trial*. New Haven, CT: Yale University Press, 1996.

Noelle-Neumann, Elisabeth. *Demoskopische Geschichtsstunde: Vom Wartesaal der Geschichte zur Deutschen Einheit (Demoscopic History Lesson: From the Waiting Room of History to German Unity)*. Zürich: A. Fromm, 1991.

———. *The Spiral of Silence: Public Opinion — Our Social Skin*. Chicago: University of Chicago Press, 1984.

Noelle, Elizabeth, and Peter Erich Neumann, eds. *Jahrbuch der Öffentlichen Meinung, 1965–1967.* Allensbach, Germany: Allensbacher Institut, 1967.

Nolte, Ernst. "Vergangenheit, die nicht vergehen will" ("The Past that Will Not Pass Away"). Pp. 39–42 in *"Historikerstreit:" Die Dokumentation der Kontroverse um die Einzigartigkeit der nationalsozialistischen Judenvernichtung.* Munich: Piper, 1987.

Nora, Pierre. "Between Memory and History: Les Lieux de Memoire." *Representations* 26 (Spring 1989): 1–21.

_____, ed. *Les Lieux de mémoire,* 7 vols. Paris: Gallimard, 1992.

_____, ed. *Les Lieux de mémoire: Les Frances, La Republique, Le Nation,* 7 vols. Paris: Gallimard, 1984–86.

Novick, Peter. *That Noble Dream: The "Objectivity Question" and the American Historical Profession.* New York: Cambridge University Press, 1988.

O'Donnell, Guillermo A., and Philippe C. Schmitter. *Transitions from Authoritarian Rule: Tentative Conclusions about Uncertain Democracies.* Baltimore: Johns Hopkins University Press, 1986.

O'Donnell, Guillermo, Philippe A. Schmitter, and Laurence Whitehead. *Transitions from Authoritarian Rule: Comparative Perspectives.* Baltimore: Johns Hopkins University Press, 1986.

Offe, Claus. *Varieties of Transition: The East European and East German experience.* Cambridge, MA: MIT Press, 1997.

_____. "Genre Memories and Memory Genres: A Dialogical Analysis of May 8, 1945 Commemorations in the Federal Republic of Germany." *American Sociological Review* 64 (1999b): 381–402.

_____. 2005. *In the House of the Hangman: The Agonies of German Defeat, 1943–1949.* Chicago: University of Chicago Press, 2005.

_____. *The Sins of the Fathers: Governing Memory in the Federal Republic of Germany.* Chicago: University of Chicago Press, forthcoming.

_____. "What Does It Mean to Normalize the Past: Official Memory in German Politics since 1989." *Social Science History* 22 (1998): 547–71.

Olick, Jeffrey K., and Daniel Levy. "Collective Memory and Cultural Constraint: Holocaust Myth and Rationality in West German Politics." *American Sociological Review* 62 (1997): 921–36.

Olick, Jeffrey K., and Joyce Robbins. "Social Memory Studies: From 'Collective Memory' to the Historical Sociology of Mnemonic Practices." *Annual Review of Sociology* 24 (1998):105–40.

Ong, Walter. *Orality and Literacy: The Technologizing of the Word.* London: Methuen, 1982.

Ortmeyer, Benjamin. *Argumente gegen das Deutschlandied: Geschichte und Gegenwart eines Lobliedes auf die deutsche Nation (Arguments against the German National Anthem: History and Present of a Hymn of Praise to the German Nation).* Cologne, Germany: Bund-Verlag, 1991.

Ortner, Sherry, ed. *The Fate of "Culture": Geertz and Beyond.* Berkeley: University of California Press, 1999.

Osiel, Mark. *Mass Atrocity, Collective Memory, and the Law.* New Brunswick, NJ: Transaction Publishers, 2000.

Pelinka, Anton. "Tabus in der Politik: Zur politischen Funktion von Tabuisierung und Enttabuisierung" ("Taboos in Politics: On the Political Function of Tabooization and Detabooization"). Pp. 21–28 in *Tabu und Geschichte: Zur Kultur des kollektiven Erinnerns*, edited by P. Bettelheim and R. Streibel. Vienna: Picus Verlag, 1994.

Pennebaker, J. W., D. Paez, and B. Rimé, eds. *Collective Memory of Political Events: Social Psychological Perspectives*. Mahwah, NJ: Erlbaum Associates, 1997.

Perrow, Charles. "A Society of Organizations." *Theory and Society* 20 (1991): 725–62.

Perry, Michael J. *The Idea of Human Rights: Four Inquiries*. New York: Oxford University Press, 1998.

Pillemer, David B. *Momentous Events, Vivid Memories: How Unforgettable Moments Help Us Understand the Meaning of Our Lives*. Cambridge, MA: Harvard University Press, 1998.

Powell, Walter W., and Paul J. DiMaggio, eds. *The New Institutionalism in Organizational Analysis*. Chicago: University of Chicago Press, 1991.

Proust, Marcel. *A la recherche du temps perdu*. 3 vols. Paris: Gallimard, 1961.

Rabinbach, Anson. "The Jewish Question in the German Question." *New German Critique* 44 (Spring–Summer 1988): 159–92.

Ranulf, Svend. *Moral Indignation and Middle Class Psychology*. New York: Schocken Books, 1964.

Rappaport, Joanne. *The Politics of Memory: Native Historical Interpretation in the Columbian Andes*. Cambridge, UK: Cambridge University Press, 1990.

Reichel, Peter. *Politik mit der Erinnerung: Gedächtnisorte im Streit um die nationalsozialistische Vergangenheit* (*Politics with Memory: Places of Memory in the Controversy about the National Socialist Past*). Munich: Carl Hanser, 1995.

Renan, Ernest. "Qu'est-ce qu'une nation?" Pp. 887–906 in *Oeuvres Complètes*, vol.1. Paris: Calmann-Levy, 1947–61.

Richter, Melvin. *The History of Political and Social Concepts: A Critical Introduction*. New York: Oxford University Press, 1995.

Ricoeur, Paul. *The Just*. Chicago: University of Chicago Press, 2001.

_____. *Memory, History, Forgetting*. Chicago: University of Chicago Press, 2004.

Richter, Melvin. *The History of Political and Social Concepts: A Critical Introduction*. New York: Oxford University Press, 1995.

Robertson, Geoffrey. *Crimes against Humanity: The Struggle for Global Justice*. New York: New Press, 2000.

Rosenberg, Bernard, and David Manning White. *Mass Culture: The Popular Arts in America*. New York: Free Press, 1957.

Rosenberg, Tina. *The Haunted Landscape: Facing Europe's Ghosts after Communism*. New York: Random House, 1995.

Rosenzweig, Roy, and David Thelen. *The Presence of the Past: Popular Uses of History in American Life*. New York: Columbia University Press, 1998.

Rotberg, Robert I., and Dennis F. Thompson. *Truth v. Justice: The Morality of Truth Commissions*. Princeton, NJ: Princeton University Press, 2000.

Samuel, Raphael. *Theaters of Memory: Past and Present in Contemporary Culture*. London: Verso 1996.

Sandage, Scott. "A Marble House Divided: The Lincoln Memorial, the Civil Rights Movement, and the Politics of Memory, 1939–1963." *Journal of American History* 80 (1993):135–67.

Savage, Kirk. "The Politics of Memory: Black Emancipation and the Civil War Monument." Pp. 127–49 in *Commemorations,* edited by J. Gillis. Princeton, NJ: Princeton University Press, 1994.

Schachter, Daniel L. *Searching for Memory: The Brain, the Mind, and the Past.* New York: Basic Books, 1996.

Schäffner, Wolfgang. "Event, Series, Trauma: The Probabilistic Revolution of the Mind in the Late Nineteenth and Early Twentieth Centuries." Pp. 81–91 in *Traumatic Pasts: History, Psychiatry, and Trauma in the Modern Age, 1870–1930,* edited by Mark S. Micale and Paul Lerner. Cambridge, UK: Cambridge University Press, 2001.

Scheler, Max. *Ressentiment.* Milwaukee: Marquette University Press, 1998.

Schieder, Theodor. "The Role of Historical Consciousness in Political Action." *History and Theory* 17 (1978): 105–13.

Schirmer, Dietmar. "Strukturen und Mechanismen einer deformierten Wahrnehmung. Der 8. Mai und das Projekt 'Vergangenheitsbewältigung'" ("Structures and Mechanisms of a Deformed Perception: The 8th of May and the Project 'Mastering the Past'"). Pp. 190–208 in *Politische Psychologie Heute,* edited by H. Loenig. Opladen, Germany: Klett, 1988.

Schivelbusch, Wolfgang. *The Railway Journey: The Industrialization of Time and Space in the 19th Century.* Berkeley: University of California Press, 1986.

Schluchter, Wolfgang. *Paradoxes of Modernity: Culture and Conduct in the Theory of Max Weber.* Stanford: Stanford University Press, 1996.

Schoeps, Julius H., ed. *Ein Volk von Mördern?: Die Dokumentation zur Goldhagen-Kontroverse um die Rolle der Deutschen im Holocaust* (*A Nation of Murderers: The Documentation of the Goldhagen Controversy Concerning the Role of the Germans in the Holocaust*). Hamburg: Hoffman and Campe, 1996.

Schudson, Michael. "The Politics of Narrative Form: The Emergence of News Conventions in Print and Television." *Daedalus* 111, no. 4 (1982): 97–112.

———. "The Present in the Past versus the Past in the Present." *Communication* 11 (1989):105–14.

———. *Watergate in American Memory: How We Remember, Forget, and Reconstruct the Past.* New York: Basic Books, 1992.

Schuman, Howard, Robert F. Belli, and Katherine Bischoping. "The Generational Basis of Historical Knowledge." Pp. 47–77 in *Collective Memory of Political Events: Social Psychological Perspectives,* edited by J. W. Pennebaker, D. Paez, and B. Rimé. Mahwah, NJ: Lawrence Erlbaum Associates, 1997.

Schuman, Howard, and Amy Corning. "Collective Knowledge: The Soviet Era from the Great Purge to Glasnost." *American Journal of Sociology* 105 (2000): 913–56.

Schuman, Howard, and Cheryl Rieger. "Historical Analogies, Generational Effects, and Attitudes toward War." *American Sociological Review* 57 (1992): 315–26.

Schuman, Howard, and Jacqueline Scott. "Generations and Collective Memory." *American Sociological Review* 54 (1989): 359–81.

Schwan, Gesine. *Politik und Schuld. Die zerstörerische Macht des Schweigens.* Frankfurt: Fischer, 1997.

Schwartz, Barry. "Memory as a Cultural System: Abraham Lincoln in World War II." *American Sociological Review* 61 (1996): 908–27.

_____. "Social Change and Collective Memory: The Democratization of George Washington." *American Sociological Review* 56 (1991): 221–36.

_____. "The Social Context of Commemoration: A Study in Collective Memory." *Social Forces* 61 (1982):374–402.

Schwartz, Barry, Yael Zerubavel, and Bernice M. Barnett. "The Recovery of Masada: A Study in Collective Memory." *Sociological Quarterly* 27 (1986): 147–164.

Schweigler, Gebhard. *National Consciousness in Divided Germany*. Beverly Hills: Sage, 1975.

Segev, Tom. *The Seventh Million: The Israelis and the Holocaust*. New York: Hill and Wang, 1993.

Seifert, Jürgen. "Die Verfassumg" ("The Constitution"). Pp. 40–70 in *Die Geschichte der Bundesrepublik Deutschland, Band 1*, edited by W. Benz. Frankfurt: Fischer, 1989.

Sewell, William. "Three Temporalities: Toward an Eventful Sociology." Pp. 245–280 in *The Historical Turn in the Human Sciences*, edited by Terence J. McDonald. Ann Arbor: University of Michigan Press, 1996.

Shils, Edward. *Tradition*. Chicago: University of Chicago Press, 1981.

Shriver, Donald W. *An Ethic for Enemies: Forgiveness in Politics*. New York: Oxford University Press, 1995.

Simmel, Georg. 1959. "The Ruin." in *Georg Simmel, 1858–1918*, edited by Kurt Wolff. Columbus: Ohio State University Press, 1959.

Smith, Anthony D. *The Ethnic Origins of Nations*. Oxford: Blackwell, 1986.

Somers, Margaret R. "What's Political or Cultural about Political Culture and the Public Sphere? Toward an Historical Sociology of Concept Formation." *Sociological Theory* 13 (1995): 113–44.

Steiner, Franz. *Taboo*. New York: Philosophical Press, 1956.

Steiner, Henry J., and Philip Alston. *International Human Rights in Context: Law, Politics, Morals*. New York: Oxford University Press, 1996.

Sturkin, Marita. *Tangled Memories: The Vietnam War, The AIDS Epidemic, and the Politics of Remembering*. Berkeley: University of California Press, 1997.

Tavuchis, Nichola. *Mea Culpa: A Sociology of Apology and Reconciliation*. Stanford: Stanford University Press, 1991.

Tawney, R. H. *Commonplace Book*. Edited by J. M. Winter. Cambridge, UK: Cambridge University Press, 1972.

Teitel, Ruti. *Transitional Justice*. New York: Oxford University Press, 2000.

Terdiman, Richard. *Present Past: Modernity and the Memory Crisis*. Ithaca, NY: Cornell University Press, 1993.

Thelen, David. "Introduction: Memory and American History." Pp. vii–xix in *Memory and American History*, edited by David Thelen. Bloomington: Indiana University Press, 1989.

Thompson, John B. *The Media and Modernity: A Social Theory of the Media*. Stanford: Stanford University Press, 1995.

Tilly, Charles. *Big Structures, Large Processes, Huge Comparisons*. New York: Russell Sage, 1984.

Torpey, John. *Making Whole What Has Been Smashed: On Reparations Politics*. Cambridge, MA: Harvard University Press, 2006.

Trouillot, Michel-Rolph. Abortive rituals: Historical apologies in the global era. *Interventions* 2, no. 2 (2000): 171–86.

———. *Silencing the Past: Power and the Production of History*. Boston: Beacon, 1995.

Vinitzky-Seroussi, Vered. *After Pomp and Circumstance: High School Reunion as an Autobiographical Occasion*. Chicago: University of Chicago Press, 1998.

Vromen, Suzanne. "The Ambiguity of Nostalgia." *YIVO Annual* 21: 69-86.

Wagner-Pacifici, Robin. "Memories in the Making: The Shape of Things that Went." *Qualitative Sociology* 19 (1996): 301–22.

Wagner-Pacifici, Robin, and Barry Schwartz. "The Vietnam Veterans Memorial: Commemorating a Difficult Past." *American Journal of Sociology* 97 (1991): 376–420.

Wallerstein, Immanuel, and Etienne Balibar. *Race, Nation, Class: Ambiguous Identities*. London: Verso, 1992.

Weber, Eugen. *Peasants into Frenchmen: The Modernization of Rural France, 1870-1914*. London: Chatto and Windus, 1979.

Weber, Jürgen, and Peter Steinbach, eds. *Vergangenheitsbewältigung durch Strafverfahren? NS-Prozesse in der Bundesrepublik Deutschland* (*Mastering the Past through Criminal Proceedings? Nazi Trials in the Federal Republic of Germany*). Munich: Olzog, 1984.

Weber, Max. "Politics as a Vocation." In *From Max Weber: Essays in Sociology*, edited and translated by H. H. Gerth and C. Wright Mills. New York: Oxford University Press, 1946a.

———. "Science as a Vocation." In *From Max Weber: Essays in Sociology*, edited and translated by H. H. Gerth and C. Wright Mills. New York: Oxford University Press, 1946b.

———. *The Sociology of Religion*. Boston: Beacon, 1963.

White, Harrison. *Identity and Control: A Structural Theory of Social Action*. Princeton, NJ: Princeton University Press, 1992.

White, Hayden. *Metahistory: The Historical Imagination in Nineteenth-Century Europe*. Baltimore: Johns Hopkins University Press, 1973.

Wolffsohn, Michael. *Ewige Schuld? 40 jahre Deutsch-Jüdisch-Israelische Beziehungen* (*Perpetual Guilt? Forty Years of German–Jewish–Israeli Relations*). Munich: Piper, 1988.

Wood, Nancy. "Memory's Remains: Les lieux de mémoire." *History and Memory* 6 (1994): 123–50.

Wuthnow, Robert, and Marsha Witten. "New Directions in the Study of Culture." *Annual Review of Sociology* 14 (1988): 49–67.

Yates, Frances A. *The Art of Memory*. Chicago: University of Chicago Press, 1966.

Yerushalmi, Yosef. *Zakhor: Jewish History and Jewish Memory*. Seattle: University of Washington Press, 1982.

Zamponi, Simonetta. "Of Storytellers and Master Narratives: Modernity, Memory, and History in Fascist Italy." *Social Science History* 22, no. 4 (1988): 415–44.

Zelizer, Barbie. *Covering the Body: The Kennedy Assassination, the Media, and the Shaping of Collective Memory*. Chicago: University of Chicago Press, 1995a.

———. "Reading the Past against the Grain: The Shape of Memory Studies." *Critical Studies in Mass Communication* 12 (1995b): 214–39.

Zerubavel, Eviatar. *Hidden Rhythms: Schedules and Calendars in Social Life.* Berkeley: University of California Press, 1981.

_____. "Social Memories: Steps to a Sociology of the Past." *Qualitative Sociology* 19 (1996): 283–300.

Zerubavel, Yael. *Recovered Roots: Collective Memory and the Making of Israeli National Tradition.* Chicago: University of Chicago Press, 1994.

Zielinski, Siegfried. "History as Entertainment and Provocation: The TV Series 'Holocaust in West Germany.'" In *Germans and Jews Since the Holocaust: The Changing Situation in West Germany,* edited by Anson Rabinbach and Jack Zipes. New York: Holmes and Meier, 1986: 258-283.

Zolberg, Vera. "Contested Remembrance: The Hiroshima Exhibit Controversy." *Theory and Society* 27 (1998): 565–90.

Zonabend, Francis. *The Enduring Memory: Time and History in a French Village.* Chicago: University of Chicago Press, 1995.

Index